The
Norfolk Broads
A landscape history

MANCHESTER
UNIVERSITY PRESS

The
Norfolk Broads
A landscape history

Tom Williamson

Manchester University Press

Manchester and New York

distributed exclusively in the USA by St. Martin's Press

Published by Manchester University Press
Oxford Road, Manchester M13 9NR, UK
and Room 400, 175 Fifth Avenue, New York, NY 10010, USA

Distributed exclusively in the USA by
St. Martin's Press, Inc., 175 Fifth Avenue, New York,
NY 10010, USA

Distributed exclusively in Canada by
UBC Press, University of British Columbia, 6344 Memorial Road,
Vancouver, BC, Canada V6T 1Z2

British Library Cataloguing-in-Publication Data
A catalogue record for this book is available from the British Library

Library of Congress Cataloging-in-Publication Data
Williamson, Tom.
    The Norfolk broads : a landscape history / Tom Williamson.
        p.   cm.
    Includes index.
    ISBN 0-7190-4800-1. — ISBN 0-7190-4801-X (pbk.)
    1. Broads, The (England)—Historical geography.   2. Norfolk
(England)—Historical geography.   3. Landscape—England—Broads,
The—History.   4. Land use—England—Broads. The—History.
5. Landscape—England—Norfolk—History.   6. Land use—England—
Norfolk—History.   I. Title.
    DA670.B695W55   1997
    914.26′17—dc21   96–51935

ISBN 0 7190 4800 1 *hardback*
     0 7190 4801 X *paperback*

First published 1997

01 00 99 98 97   10 9 8 7 6 5 4 3 2 1

Typeset in Hong Kong
by Graphicraft Typesetters Ltd

Printed in Great Britain
by Alden Press, Oxford

Contents

Acknowledgements

This book could never have been written without the help and encouragement of students and colleagues at the Centre of East Anglian Studies of the University of East Anglia. My greatest debts are to Kate Skipper, who carried out a vast amount of documentary research; and to Jo Parmenter, who taught me so much about the ecology of the Broadland fens. Much of Kate Skipper's work was generously funded by the Broads Authority. Other past and present students of the Centre of East Anglian Studies who provided advice, information and assistance include: Ian Atherton, Nick Avery, Keith Bacon, Sarah Birtles, John Dean, Pat Field, Roger Sweet and Tim Pestle. Two groups of undergraduate students on the Landscape Archaeology Field Course surveyed St Benet's Abbey, and Bill Milligan of the Castle Museum identified the pottery. Special thanks go to Phillip Judge, who drew the diagrams and maps, and to Michael Brandon Jones, who printed my photographs, and made them look much better than they would otherwise have been.

Various members of Norfolk Landscape Archaeology were, as ever, helpful in innumerable ways: particularly Edwin Rose, Derek Edwards and Andrew Rogerson. The staff of Norfolk Record Office, and of the various Suffolk Record Offices, provided invaluable assistance. Thanks also to the following for help, information, or advice: Rob Andrews, John Buxton, Gerry Barnes, Ian Atherton, Clive Doarks, Declan Keiley, Eric Edwards, Richard Starling, Robert Lang, M. D. Wright, Peter Edrich, Frank and Julie Futter, Michael Seago and Peter Allard.

I owe a special debt to three writers whose work on Broadland has provided me with so much information and inspiration: Bob Malster, Barbara Cornford and above all Martin George. This small volume constitutes, in effect, an historical postscript to the latter's monumental work on the *Land Use, Ecology and Conservation of Broadland*.

Thanks, finally, to my children, Matthew and Jessica, for helping with fieldwork; and to my mother, Jean Williamson, who introduced me to the beauties of Broadland on childhood holidays long ago.

1

The landscapes of Broadland

Introduction

This book is about the landscapes of the region known as 'Broadland', or 'The Norfolk Broads': a seemingly timeless world of marshes, fens, rivers and lakes which lies in East Anglia, between the town of Yarmouth and the city of Norwich. The majority of this area, as the second of these names suggests, lies within the county of Norfolk, although parts lie in Suffolk. Three large rivers, which collectively drain much of East Anglia, meet here and provide the basic structure to the landscape: the Waveney, the Yare and the Bure. Lesser rivers – although with an important impact upon the local landscape nevertheless – drain into these: the Ant, the Chet and the Thurne (Figure 1). Most people in England have heard of 'the Broads', and many have visited them. The 200 kilometres or more of navigable waterway, combined with the beauty and variety of the scenery, have together ensured that over the last century or so the area has developed as a major tourist centre. The region also has a place in the national psyche for *cultural* reasons. The marshes, drainage mills and rivers have been the subject of numerous paintings, most notably those of the Norwich School – Cotman, Crome, Bright, Stannard and the rest – which flourished in the area in the early nineteenth century. But above all, Broadland has an immense ecological importance. To botanists, zoologists and others the area is famous as the most important surviving wetland habitat in lowland England, rich in a wide diversity of wildlife.

Yet in spite of its significance for nature conservation, this is emphatically *not* a purely natural landscape. Even the wildest areas of fen bear the marks of past human activity. Indeed, the habitats so prized by natural scientists were, as we shall see, largely created by specific forms of management which were not intended to encourage wildlife diversity, but rather to supply raw materials and sustenance for man. In many cases, these traditional management practices have declined in the course of the past century, with grave effects upon the environment. But the 'natural' landscape is also threatened by a range of other factors, and especially by modern intensive agriculture, which has led to the deep drainage and ploughing of some areas of ancient marshland. The needs of nature conservation are also sometimes at odds with those of the holiday industry, so

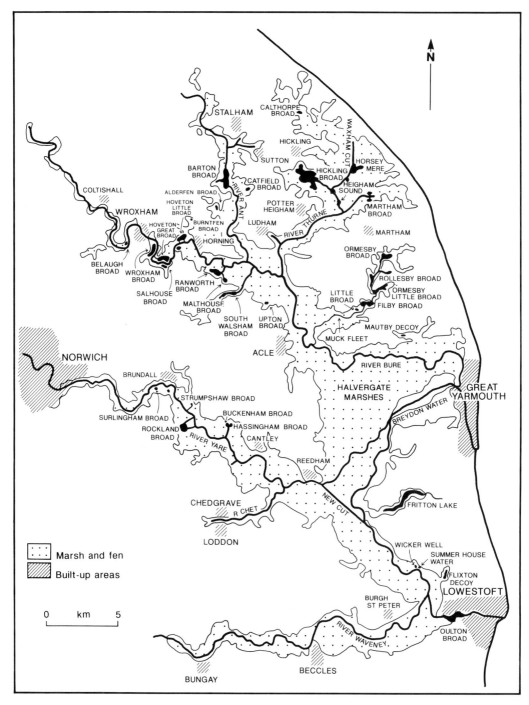

Figure 1   The Norfolk Broads – principal features.

important to the local economy. Created and maintained by human activity, the Broadland landscape is – and to some extent probably always has been – an arena for conflict between different interest groups.

And different people, with different interests and concerns, see a landscape in profoundly different ways. The holidaymaker, cruising at a leisurely pace down the Bure or the Ant, might see in the extensive beds of reed or sedge a romantic wilderness, far removed from the mundane stress of city life. To the botanist and ornithologist, in contrast, these are habitats, vital for the survival of a range of rare plants, and above all for the bittern which, with its strange booming cry, is almost an ornithological icon of Broadland. To the commercial reed or sedge-cutter, on the other hand – and many such areas are still managed for a profit, to provide thatching materials – the beds are, in effect, agricultural fields in which a valuable crop is grown. In this case, the different perceptions of, and demands made upon, the landscape can coexist quite happily. But this is not always so. The areas of drained marshland which occupy a considerable percentage of Broadland might be valued by the walker for their striking panoramas of open grass under an endless sky. But the botanist would concentrate instead on the dykes between the portions of marsh, rich in rare or uncommon plants like water soldier and water parsnip. Certain farmers, in contrast, might focus upon the richness of the soil beneath the turf, and – given the right incentives – would drain the land more effectively by deepening the dykes, thus destroying much of the vegetation there, and turn the greensward to ploughsoil.

There are thus many Broadland landscapes, depending on the interests and concerns of the observer: and also, more mundanely, on their vantage point – on when, and from where, observers view the landscape. To see the Broads from a boat in late autumn or winter, when the waterways are largely empty of other craft, is a rather different experience from cruising there in summer, when the traffic on the river Bure, in particular, must remind some visitors of their daily journey to work on the M25. Either experience is fundamentally different from that enjoyed from a car. Only the marshes in the east of the region are fully exposed to the motorist's view, as he or she hurtles along the ruler-straight section of the A47 known, universally, as the 'Acle Straight'. The wilder landscapes of fen and broad in the upper reaches of the rivers, in the west of the region, are glimpsed only occasionally from the road: to the dedicated motorist, this landscape might as well not exist. The walker, too, often has difficulty gaining access to this part of Broadland. Conversely, the more tamed marshlands in the east of the region can be enjoyed, perhaps, better on foot than by boat or car, for public footpaths penetrate deeper into the Halvergate marshes than either road or navigable river.

Broadland's three landscapes

In spite of this diversity of experience, for many purposes (and certainly for the purposes of this short volume) the landscapes of Broadland may be divided into two – a simple dichotomy already hinted at – although the precise boundary between them may be open to debate (Figure 2). The first is the landscape of level open marshland, criss-crossed by water-filled dykes and dotted with old drainage mills, which occupies a huge triangle of *c*.5,500 hectares immediately to the west of Great Yarmouth (Plate 1). Open, hedgeless, and largely treeless, with field gates standing strangely prominent above the level marsh, this is traditionally a landscape of pasture although limited areas have now been put to the plough. This great flat expanse is crossed by the rivers Bure (or 'North River'), Yare (or 'Norwich River') and Waveney, the last two joining at the south-western end of Breydon Water, a vast, 877-hectare area of tidal mudflats which occupies the centre of the marshes. In fact, the whole area was once a tidal estuary, as William Marshall recognised as early as 1787 when he provided the first detailed description of the landscape here:

> The MARSHES were a new world to me – They form a vast level, containing many thousand acres, of a black and somewhat moory soil; formed, perhaps, originally of sea mud; it being highly probable that the whole level has once been an estuary of the German Ocean.[1]

This was a landscape very much in the news in the 1980s, when the accelerating pace of arable conversion led to a well-publicised campaign of 'direct action' by Friends of the Earth and others, a struggle which culminated in the establishment of Broadland as the country's first Environmentally Sensitive Area (ESA), in which farmers are paid to follow 'traditional' agricultural practices, favourable to wildlife and landscape conservation.[2] The controversy put the name of the 'Halvergate Marshes' into all the newspapers: but while the whole area is often referred to in this way, such usage is strictly speaking incorrect, for the parish of Halvergate embraces only one part, albeit the largest, of the marsh. The rest is divided among numerous other parishes, some mainly situated on the adjacent 'upland' but others located several kilometres away: a complex and unusual pattern, which is of some significance in elucidating the area's early history. 'Halvergate marshes' is nevertheless a term with wide currency, and will often be employed in the pages that follow.

In technical terms the marshes are an area of 'secondary wetland': that is, they are embanked but only minimally drained, and thus distinct from primary – unembanked – wetland, or tertiary – intensively drained polderland.[3] They are not an area of salt marshes (although sporadically described as such) for only in exceptional conditions of flood or drought is the water in the marsh dykes saline. Nevertheless, they are always in need of drainage, lying as they do at or just below sea level, and having three large tidal rivers, and a number of smaller streams, flowing across them. They are kept dry through a network of dykes and drains, some curving or serpentine, some ruler-straight, which form a complex, irregular pattern. These watercourses require constant maintenance, for areas covered with water for any length of time during the winter months give a poor yield during the summer grazing season. Traditionally, the dykes were cleared of vegetation – 'cromed' – every year. 'Bottom finding' or 'bottomfying' occurred

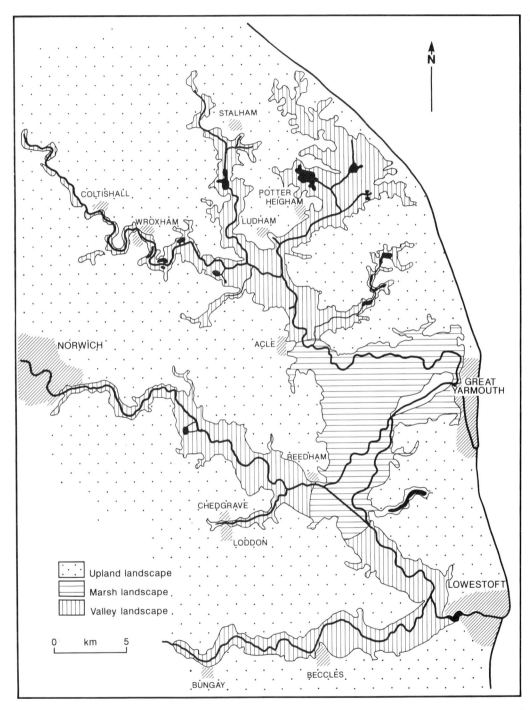

STALHAM

COLTISHALL

POTTER
HEIGHAM

WROXHAM   LUDHAM

NORWICH   ACLE

GREAT
YARMOUTH

REEDHAM

CHEDGRAVE

LODDON

Upland landscape

Marsh landscape

Valley landscape

0   km   5

LOWESTOFT

BUNGAY   BECCLES

The Norfolk Broads – principal landscape regions, as used in this book.   Figure 2

Plate 1   Halvergate: the ruins of the drainage windmills accentuate the flat and open character of
                 the drained marshland landscape.

less frequently. This was a more complex operation, involving the damming off of sections of dyke and the removal of accumulated sediment to a depth of a metre or more.[4]

While the dykes were, and are, essential for drainage, they have always been more than mere drains. They also operate as fences, dividing one area of marsh from another and thus serving to keep stock in. Traditional practice was to put animals out to graze in the spring after the 'freeboard' or water level in the dykes had been set to a height of about 2 ft (0.6 metres). This not only prevented the animals from straying: it also provided them with drinking water. In the autumn, when the animals were taken off, the level of water was allowed to fall, preparatory to the dykes receiving increased winter run-off from the adjacent uplands.

With a few exceptions, the various portions of the marsh are not – and have not been within the last two or three centuries – drained solely by the natural flow of water. As in the Fenlands of Cambridgeshire and Lincolnshire, pumps are used. These were originally driven by wind power, later by steam or internal combustion engines, today by electricity. Drainage windmills first appeared on the marshes around the end of the seventeenth century although, as we shall see, most surviving examples are of nineteenth-century date. The various minor dykes led into a Mill Dyke or Main Drain which brought the water to the mill, which was located beside one of the principal watercourses (usually one of the three rivers). It was then lifted some 1.5–2 metres over the 'walls', the low earth flood banks bordering these watercourses, which are largely (although not usually entirely) man-made earthworks, thrown up above the level of high tide. Materials for the 'wall' were quarried from a 'soke dyke' or 'sock dyke' immediately behind it, although additional material was generally derived from dredging the adjacent watercourse. The walls do not usually lie immediately adjacent to the water course, but a little way back, providing a 'washland' to hold excess water in times of flood: these areas were, and indeed still are, referred to as 'ronds' or 'rands'. The water was initially thrown by the mills into a dammed-up receptacle separated from the watercourse: a sluice gate, fixed in a brick archway in the wall, was opened at the fall of the tide to let out the accumulated water. At the head of the drain there was usually a valve gate, to prevent the water from flowing backwards when the mill stopped working.[5] As already noted, during the course of this century the role of the wind pumps gradually declined, as more 'modern' methods of drainage were gradually adopted, and none is now in use. Many are in a state of decay, although a significant proportion have been, to varying extents, restored by the Norfolk Windmills Trust and the Broads Authority, or by private owners.

In addition to the principal water-filled dykes the surface of the marsh is crossed by numerous shallow winding depressions, relics from the natural watercourses which once flowed across the saltings and mud flats; and also by large numbers of minor 'foot drains', spade-dug channels *c.*0.1–0.3 metres deep which were used to remove water from irregularities or hollows. The process of repeatedly 'bottomfying' the dykes and spreading the material across the adjacent ground surface ensured that over the years the individual areas of marsh acquired a slightly 'saucer-shaped' profile, impeding drainage. These minor drains carry water through this low 'wall' of material deposited on the side of the dykes.

The marshes were traditionally divided into areas called 'levels', usually separated from each other by low earth banks. It is sometimes said that these were 'the area originally drained by one windpump', and to some extent this is true, although these divisions generally predate the building of the mills, and not all levels ever actually possessed a mill of their own. Levels usually bear the name of the parish to which they belong, or that of some prominent past landowner, although some have archaic names going back many centuries. The mills were looked after by 'marshmen', who were also responsible for the care of the stock grazing on the marsh – stock which was usually owned by farmers living on the neighbouring uplands – and for the maintenance of the drainage works. Some of the isolated marsh houses in which they lived, often located far from the upland, still survive, although few are now used for their original purpose.

This, in brief, is the landscape of the drained marshland within the great Halvergate 'triangle'. The second landscape of Broadland, that of the river valleys draining into this, is rather different. It is more diverse and, to most people, perhaps more attractive. Here – above Reedham on the Yare, Acle Bridge on the

Plate 2   The landscape of the valleys: the River Ant, north of Barton Broad, surrounded by fen and
                 alder carr (Derek Edwards, Norfolk Landscape Archaeology).

Bure, St Olaves on the Waveney, and in the valleys of the Chet, Thurne and Ant
– some areas of drained marshland can be found, again with drainage windmills
in various states of dereliction. But such areas are less extensive than on
Halvergate, do not normally feature isolated marsh houses, and are invariably
contained within parishes situated on the adjacent upland: we do not find here
the complex, splintered pattern of parochial organisation characteristic of the
Halvergate area. Moreover, in contrast to the rather meandering pattern of dykes
encountered within the latter, here the divisions of the marsh often have a more
rectilinear, and on occasions grid-like, quality. In addition to the drained marshes,
however – and especially in the valleys of the Ant and the Bure – there are many
much wilder areas. Undrained fens with extensive beds of reed and sedge occur,
together with tangled wet woods or 'carr' of alder and willow: landscapes which,
at first sight, appear almost as a primeval wilderness, untouched by human hand
(Plate 2).

  It is within these wilder areas that the 'broads' themselves are to be found
– the picturesque lakes from which the region takes its name. These vary

considerably in size, from huge areas of water such as Hickling (*c*.140 hectares) or Barton (*c*.77 hectares) to diminutive pools. Indeed, it is in part the difficulty of deciding how many of the latter should be classed as 'broads' which explains why estimates of their number advanced by different authorities vary from as few as forty to as many as fifty. In part, however, such disagreements also stem from an uncertainty over how to treat those cases where conjoined but separately named areas of water have been created out of single bodies in comparatively recent times, by the construction of river or rail bridges, by the encroachment of reed swamp and the accumulation of peat and silt. Such natural processes have thus created the two broads at Ranworth – Ranworth Broad, and Malthouse Broad – from a single body of water since the mid-nineteenth century. They have also led to the complete disappearance of some broads in comparatively recent times: Honing Broad, Carleton Broad, Sutton Broad and others have thus vanished in the course of the last two centuries.[6] The surviving broads are richly, endlessly varied in form and appearance. Some are found in the valleys of the principal rivers, usually standing a little back from the river itself. Others, however, occupy minor tributary valleys, usually those feeding into the lower reaches of the principal watercourses. Some are directly connected to the main river system, some are not. Some are navigable, some are not: indeed, almost all are privately owned, and only thirteen have unrestricted year-round access to pleasure craft.[7]

To these two landscapes of Broadland – that of the Halvergate 'triangle', and that of the valleys – we need to add a third, although we shall examine it only briefly. This is the landscape of the surrounding 'uplands'. To those coming from the more elevated parts of England this might seem rather an odd term to use for terrain which seldom rises above 40 metres OD and is generally well below 30. It is upland only in relative terms, *terra firma*, dry ground above the low-lying fens and marshes. This agricultural landscape frequently impinges upon a visitor's experience. Not only does it often form a backdrop to the view from a boat, but the villages where the tourist moors at night are, strictly speaking, part of the upland, for they are built on the hard surface of dry land rather than on the damp and uncertain soils of the lower grounds. Yet there is a much more important reason why some consideration needs to be given to this higher land. The marshes and fens never constituted self-contained economies, or housed communities with their own particular histories. They were always dependent lands, exploited from, and with, the surrounding uplands. And thus the character of the latter – the way they were farmed, the density of their population – has had, in all periods, a determining effect upon the landscape of the wetlands.

Today, those who leave the lush scenery of the lower ground and make the short climb out of the valleys often experience a sense of disappointment. This is one of the most intensively farmed areas of England, and one which has – in consequence – suffered a considerable amount of environmental degradation. It is a landscape of wide arable fields, and in many places there are few hedges and fewer trees. There are, it is true, some more attractive areas, in the higher reaches of the Ant, Bure and Waveney especially. But this is not, for the most part, a

particularly appealing landscape. Yet landscapes do not need to be attractive to
be interesting, and the quintessential features of the upland scenery are both
intriguing in their own right, and pointers to those aspects of its past development which most affected the lower grounds.

The natural background

Men created the landscapes of Broadland: but they did so within a range of
constraints dictated by nature. Some of these constraints were constant, over
thousands of years. Others changed over time, and local populations responded
to the resulting challenges and opportunities. The critical factors were, and to a
large extent still are, the character of the region's soils and geology; its climate;
and the relative levels of land and water, the latter of particular importance in
this low-lying landscape.

Climate and its effects we can deal with immediately. Over the last two millennia, the period which saw the development in their present form of Broadland's
landscapes, the region's climate has undergone a number of changes, but in all
periods was relatively Continental in character, with cold dry winters and warm
dry summers. These features, combined with relatively deep and fertile soils,
have long ensured that the upland economy has been geared to arable farming.
Indeed, in some periods – most notably in the years around 1800 – the general
economic circumstances encouraged some extension of cultivation even on to
the damp fens and marshes of the lower grounds.

The character of the region's *soils*, in contrast, is more complex, and to under-
stand it we need to consider matters geological, and look back across a much
longer span of time. Underlying the whole of the Broads area (indeed, underlying
the whole of East Anglia) is a thick deposit of Cretaceous chalk. This, however, is
almost everywhere deeply buried, and only exposed in a few places in the west
of the region, in the valley of the Bure around Wroxham and Coltishall, and in
the valley of the Yare around Whittlingham: exposures which, as we shall see,
were of considerable economic significance in the past. Elsewhere it is more recent deposits which form Broadland's 'solid geology': the so-called 'Norwich Crag',
varied deposits (in places up to 40 metres deep) composed of shelly sands laid
down in tidal marshes, estuarine channels and intertidal flats some 300,000 to
two million years ago.[8] Yet these, too, are almost everywhere buried beneath still
later deposits, laid down during the Ice Ages, and it is from these that the region's soils are principally derived.[9] The first, or Anglian, glaciation deposited the
brown sandy clay known as the Norwich Brickearth. During subsequent phases
sands and gravels were laid down by streams of meltwater running out from the
ice fronts. In some places, as in Lothingland to the south of Yarmouth, the
Brickearth is completely obscured by these materials, and sands and gravels form
the principal surface deposit. Elsewhere, and especially in the north of Broadland,
the sands and gravels occur on the higher ground but Brickearth is exposed
on the lower. In these northern areas, however, such deposits are sporadically

covered by material laid down by an even later glaciation, a chalky boulder clay known as the Lowestoft Till. This material completely blankets wide areas of central Norfolk and north Suffolk, and forms the main surface deposit along the southern edge of Broadland.[10]

During the last glaciation permafrost conditions led to extreme weathering of the ground surface, and the resultant particles were blown by strong winds to be redeposited as *loess* or coverloam. This is the principal parent material of the upland soils across the central and northern parts of Broadland, especially on the 'island' of Flegg – the area of upland lying between the marshes of the river Thurne, and those of the Halvergate 'triangle'.[11] It is of considerable importance, for it gives rise to extremely fertile soils. As the agriculturalist Arthur Young put it in 1804:

> One of the most interesting circumstances in the husbandry of Norfolk is the soils of Flegg hundred; and much in Blofield and Walsham hundreds is of the same quality; it is sandy loam, from two to three feet deep, and much of it as good at bottom as on the surface; of so happy a texture that almost any season suits it . . . so fertile a soil I have rarely seen of so pale a colour.[12]

Of course, not all the upland soils are as good as this. The boulder clay deposits in the south of the region are rather less fertile and considerably less tractable in nature. Even in the central and northern areas the deposits of coverloam are of variable thickness and in places are completely absent, so that soils are formed from the underlying materials and derive their principal characteristics from them. Where, especially on the higher ground, outwash sands and gravels form the main parent material, areas of acid heathland often existed in the medieval and post-medieval periods, although most of these were enclosed and ploughed in the late eighteenth or early nineteenth centuries. Nevertheless, *loess* predominates across much of the upland and the consequent fertility of the soils has had a profound effect on the development of the local landscape.

The character of the soils on the lower grounds – in the marshes and fens – is very different, and intimately related to the variations in relative land/sea levels which have occurred in comparatively recent times. This is a complex and diffi-cult topic which we need only touch upon here.[13] In early post-glacial times sea levels were considerably lower than today, due to the fact that much of the world's water was still locked up in the ice caps. The valley floors were as much as 30 metres below their present level, and the rivers much faster-moving than now. They discharged into an open estuary occupying the whole of what is now the Halvergate 'triangle', the relict 'cliffs' – short but steep slopes – of which can still be seen in many places on its margins, often now picked out as a line of wood-land allowed to generate (usually in comparatively recent times) on ground which is relatively hard to plough. A subsidiary estuary – separated by the higher ground of the 'island' of Flegg – occupied what is now the headwaters of the river Thurne, in the low-lying land between Winterton and Waxham.

Sea levels rose steadily during the Mesolithic period, so that the rivers draining the region grew more sluggish. This allowed areas of fen to develop on the valley floors which, as plants died, led in time to the build-up of deposits of peat – the so-called 'Lower Peat'. As sea levels continued to rise, however, tidal conditions penetrated further inland. Layers of sand, silt and clay were deposited not only within the Halvergate estuary, but also further upriver, blanketing the peat deposits in the middle reaches of the valleys.

From around BC 3000 the effects of tidal penetration were reduced, probably as the result of the build-up of a substantial spit of sand and gravel across the mouth of the estuary which diverted the course of the river Yare southwards. The formation of peat – which had continued uninterrupted in the upper reaches of the valleys – now resumed in the middle reaches, and even to some extent within the Halvergate 'triangle' itself. These deposits are generally referred to as the Middle Peat, and in places in the valleys, where the fen vegetation was dominated by alder woodland, as the Brushwood Peat.

Some time around BC 1500, during the Bronze Age, there were further changes. The shingle spit across the mouth of the embayment was first breached, allowing increased tidal penetration; and then, probably during the later Iron Age, disintegrated completely, thus creating an open estuary once more. The fen communities disappeared, and both here and for some distance upriver the peat deposits were overlain by a further deposit of clay, the Upper Clay. In Roman times the Halvergate 'triangle' thus consisted of a vast area of open water, tidal mud flats and saltings. Since then the sea has receded once more, but the fluctuations in land/sea levels just described have established the basic pattern of soils in the lower grounds. In the higher reaches of the valleys fen conditions have generally persisted, without interruption, for millennia. Here the valley floors are dominated by various kinds of peat. In the middle reaches of the valleys, acid peats, clays and sands occur in complex, intercalated layers, especially towards the margins of the valleys. In the lower reaches of the rivers, in contrast – that is, in the valleys of the Bure below Ant Mouth, in that of the Waveney below Barnby, and of the Yare below Buckenham – and within the Halvergate 'triangle' itself – estuarine conditions have generally predominated, and any phases of peat formation have either been eroded, or deeply buried beneath crudely laminated silts and clays. These, because they contain *Foraminifera* and shell fragments, are generally of a neutral or alkaline nature: the peats are, with some notable exceptions, generally acidic (Figure 3).[14]

The final silting of the Halvergate estuary was brought about during Anglo-Saxon times by further changes in land/sea levels and by the accumulation, once again, of a spit of sand and shingle across the mouth of the open embayment: the spit on which the town of Yarmouth had, by later Saxon times, already become established.[15] There is still some debate about precisely how quickly the area became sufficiently dry to be exploited as grazing land by local communities. Indeed, there is considerable doubt more generally about the detailed fluctuations in water levels during the historic period, although universal agreement that from early medieval times relative water levels rose again. To a large extent uncertainty over the precise nature of these matters is due to the fact that the relative height of land and sea – a function of complex geological factors – was

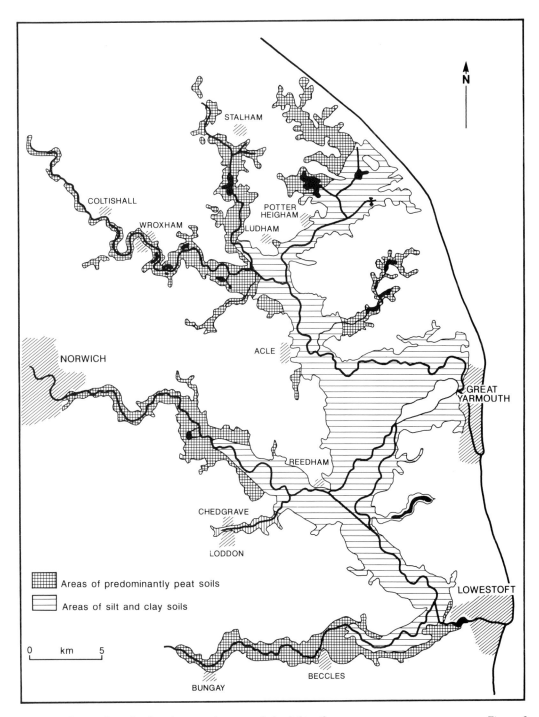

The Norfolk Broads – the distribution of peat and clay/silt soils.   Figure 3

only one factor effecting the levels of water flowing through the fens and marshes, and thus the likelihood of inundation. Water levels were also determined by the extent to which the principal rivers were dredged, for the benefit of navigation (something which seems to have increased the range of tidal flow considerably in the course of nineteenth century): and also by the configuration of the main river outfalls to the sea, for when these were most constricted, the extent of tidal penetration inland was correspondingly less.

The character and configuration of the river outfalls have indeed changed on a number of occasions during historic times. The Waveney, as already noted, now joins the Yare near the southern end of Breydon Water, and this river is in turn joined by the Bure at Breydon's eastern end. The latter river, however, seems originally to have discharged into the North Sea directly, to the north of Yarmouth, through an outlet variously known as Cockle Water or Grubb's Haven.[16] This was blocked, and the river diverted southwards to discharge into the Yare – almost certainly by human agency – in early medieval times, and perhaps at the same time the outfall of the Yare was moved northwards, from a point south of Corton to near Hopton. This was one of several alterations made to the Yare outfall in medieval and early post-medieval times, in order to provide a viable channel for navigation through the ever-changing Yarmouth sand spit.

At certain times in the past some of the water flowing through Broadland had another outfall to the sea. As already noted, the low-lying land around the headwaters of the Thurne originally formed an open estuary (the 'island' of Flegg was at such times literally an island) but this, like the main Halvergate embayment, was gradually closed by an accumulation of sand and shingle at some unknown point in the past. It continued to function as an outfall, however, for in early historic times the river Thurne flowed, at least in part, northwards, along the line of the minor watercourse now known as the Hundred Stream. This outfall must have been extremely constricted for much of the period of its existence, however, given the fact that extensive deposits of peat occur in this area at no great distance from the modern coastline, suggesting that it cannot have been subjected, for a very long time, to significant influxes of salt water. However, the narrow strip of dunes which separates the level marshes here from the sea has, on a number of occasions, been breached when exceptionally high tides and severe storms coincide. It is this which has led to some of the most serious floods in Broadland, most recently in 1938. On a number of occasions, as in 1608, 1770, or 1791, the inflow of water here was so great that not only the valley of the Thurne, but also that of the Bure and even the marshes in the Halvergate 'triangle' were inundated. The floods in the latter year, which resulted from a severe storm which tore nine 'breaches' in the dunes between Horsey and Waxham, are particularly well documented.[17] One wherryman described how he had been 'prevented from navigating the North River [the Bure] for a fortnight' because the banks were invisible, 'the tops of the reeds being his only guide'.[18] The breaches remained open, allowing repeated flooding, until 1806, when the dunes were repaired under the direction of William Smith, an engineer later famous as a geologist.[19]

Not all serious floods in Broadland's history have been the consequence of the sea breaking through the dunes between Waxham and Winterton. Many have been caused by increased volumes of water flowing off the surrounding uplands following a period of heavy rain or a sharp thaw; by sea 'surges', when strong winds in the North Sea funnel water southwards, raising sea levels along the coast and preventing the outflow of water at Yarmouth Haven; or by some combination of these events. Such floods have occurred at fairly regular intervals throughout medieval and post-medieval times, the most serious examples this century being in 1912 and 1953, when enormous damage was caused to the area.

The sea still threatens to break in and inundate the fens and marshes. Indeed, if, as predicted, 'global warming' leads to a steady rise in sea levels the threat can only get worse. And in many other ways, Broadland is a fragile landscape, vulnerable to the complex pressures of agriculture and tourism. Caught uneasily between land and sea, created by man as well as by nature, an understanding of the region's history is essential for its future conservation. In the pages that follow, some attempt will be made to tell this fascinating story.

2

The uplands and islands

The Broadland fens and marshes are nowhere so extensive that the traveller loses sight of the 'upland'. Even in the middle of the Halvergate marshes the higher ground can be seen, low on the horizon, often picked out by lines of woodland growing on the relict 'cliffs' of the former estuary. Some of this higher ground once comprised islands: Flegg covering some 78 sq km, between the Bure and the Thurne; and Lothingland, around 83 sq km, between the towns of Yarmouth and Lowestoft, bounded on the west by the river Waveney and the east by the North Sea. There were smaller islands, too. The village of Horsey, for example, takes its name from the 'Horse Island' which, to judge from the present configuration of soils and topography, covered 1 sq km or so in the marshes, once an estuary, around the headwaters of the Thurne. Finally, there are a number of quite tiny patches of rising ground which once formed islands in fen or saltings: such as Reedham Hills in the valley of the Ant near Irstead, or Cow Holme beside the river Bure.

The earliest landscapes

As our main concern is with how the landscape of Broadland gained its present appearance, we need not dwell at length on the remote prehistory of the uplands and islands. The fens, marshes and mud flats must have teemed with wildlife in prehistoric times, and the adjoining areas of dry land were doubtless frequented by communities of Mesolithic hunters. These, however, did not construct the kinds of monument able to survive to the present: and subsequent prehistoric societies have contributed little to the modern landscape. Most of the land here has been under the plough for centuries, and only a scattering of upstanding features from the Neolithic period and the Bronze Age survives. Significantly almost all are in areas which, because of their status as common land, have remained unploughed to the present day. All are 'ritual' – that is, ceremonial or religious – structures: the Neolithic long barrow and associated Bronze Age round barrows on Broome Heath, or the round barrows on Belton Heath. Nevertheless, stray finds of pottery and stone tools, and the large numbers of ploughed-out monuments (especially round barrows) revealed by aerial photography, leave little doubt that on the lighter soils of the area, at least, settlement was fairly extensive by the end of the Bronze Age.

As elsewhere in East Anglia, settlement seems to have intensified from BC *c.*750, during the Iron Age, although once again little survives in the way of obvious upstanding monuments. It is, however, possible that later prehistory has made a more subtle contribution to the local landscape. Although over much of Broadland the basic pattern of field boundaries is of comparatively recent origin, in the south – on the heavy clay soils – it is older: the result of the piecemeal enclosure of blocks of open-field strips which themselves apparently developed from a much earlier pattern of enclosed fields. In places the earliest boundaries here take the form of a characteristic brickwork-like grid – a so-called 'co-axial' pattern. This is most noticeable in the area between the rivers Chet and the Waveney, around Hales, Loddon and Heckingham. This pattern is apparently earlier than the medieval parish boundaries, which are clearly imposed upon it, or the various features characteristic of the medieval landscape, such as the medieval deer park of *Loddon iuxta Hales*, which obscure it.[20] Elsewhere in East Anglia, such organised field systems seem to be of late Iron Age date – that around Scole and Dickleburgh in south Norfolk, for example, is clearly slighted by the Roman *Pye Road*. Whether these Broadland examples are of similar antiquity is unclear, but certainly possible.[21]

We know much about the local countryside of the Roman period, when Broadland formed part of the *Civitas Icenorum*, a territory administered from the walled town of *Venta*, at Caistor St Edmunds to the south of Norwich. The pottery in use at this time is remarkably durable in the ploughsoil. It was also purchased (and broken) in substantial quantities by the local inhabitants. As a result, settlements of Roman date are easily discovered – as noticeable spreads of debris – during archaeological surveys. In the south of Broadland, on the claylands between the rivers Chet and Waveney, Roman settlements were very thick on the ground, to judge from the survey work carried out in the parishes of Hales, Loddon and Heckingham by Alan Davison. Fifteen major concentrations of debris were recovered within an area of 20 sq km, and one of these – an almost continuous spread of pottery and building material extending for over 1 km along Transport Lane in Loddon – clearly represents a hamlet consisting of several farms. Settlements could even be found on the higher ground, on the more intractable clay soils away from the principal valleys, although here they were fewer in number and much of this difficult land was probably occupied by woodland and pasture.[22] It is true that not all the settlements in the area were occupied at the same time, but most seem to have been in existence around the end of the second century. In the north of Broadland, on the more fertile and tractable *loess* soils of Flegg and the neighbouring areas, less research has been carried out, but the density of settlement may have been even greater. A survey of Witton near North Walsham recovered no less than eight small farmsteads of Roman date within an area of just 2 sq km.[23]

The landscape of Roman Norfolk did not only consist of farms and fields. There were also larger settlements. The site of the 'small town' of Brampton lies beside the Bure to the south of Aylsham. It was a sizeable settlement of timber-framed houses and workshops which included at least one public building – a stone-built bath house. On the western side of the settlement there was a large pottery-production centre, consisting of at least 200 kilns.[24] A similar, though rather smaller, nucleated settlement existed at Ditchingham close to the river Waveney, while at Caister-by-Yarmouth – on the northern shore of the great Halvergate estuary – a sizeable port developed, perhaps for the transshipment of cargoes from sea-going boats to shallower-drafted river craft.

This prosperous Roman landscape became increasingly vulnerable to attack from overseas raiders during the third and fourth centuries, a period of economic decline and political instability across northern and western Europe. The attackers – barbarians from north Germany, Schleswig-Holstein and the Low Countries – sailed across the North Sea and then along the principal rivers, far into the interior. The Roman authorities responded to this threat by defending the main centres of population (the settlement at Brampton was apparently surrounded with a defensive ditch at this time) and by gradually constructing a string of forts along the southern and eastern coasts of Britain – the so called Saxon Shore Forts.[25] The great Broadland estuary must have been a particularly inviting entry point for raiders, giving access to all the main rivers draining the eastern portion of the *Civitas Icenorum*. One of these forts may have been erected in the early third century beside the existing port at Caister. This has left no visible traces: but it was replaced later in the century by a more imposing and up-to-date edifice which does survive, as one of the most striking archaeological monuments in Broadland: Burgh Castle, probably called *Gariannonum* by its builders (after *Gariannos*, the Celtic name for the river Yare) (Plate 3).[26] Its northern and eastern walls still stand to a height of 4 metres, as does much of the southern wall. The western wall has, however, long since tumbled down into the adjacent marshes. The walls stand to their original height, although their base lies at least 1 metre beneath the modern ground surface. They are constructed of a core of mortar and rubble, faced with alternating layers of split flints and tile (the lower levels of this facing have been subsequently robbed in most places for use in buildings elsewhere). The fort displays all the most up-to-date features of military technology in the third century. In particular, it is equipped with circular bastions, placed on the corners and at intervals along the walls. In the top of each is a hole, about 0.6 metres in diameter: this was once thought to have held the base of a piece of artillery, the massive cross-bow called the *ballista*, but most archaeologists now agree that its purpose was to hold a post supporting a timber superstructure and roof. Some archaeologists have recently questioned whether 'Saxon Shore Forts' really were built to control Germanic raiding, pointing out that they were erected *before* this became a serious problem. They may instead have been fortified entrepôts, where the imperial government controlled the import and export of commodities. Whatever its original purpose, the ruins of Burgh Castle remain impressive, looking out across the level marshes.

The ruins of Burgh Castle, the Roman Saxon Shore fort.   Plate 3

The Anglo-Saxon landscape

There is no space here to discuss in detail the end of Roman rule in East Anglia. It is sufficient to say that in the fourth and fifth centuries the economy gradually collapsed, and political disintegration soon followed, as barbarian raiding gave way to permanent settlement. Some of the names of the tribal groups which replaced the *Civitas Icenorum* live on in the names of Broadland's medieval administrative units. In the north of the region, the *Hæppingas* ('the people of Haep') gave their name to Happing hundred; in the south, the *Lodningas* ('the people of the *Ludne*', an earlier name for the river Chet) to Loddon hundred; and the *Cnaveringas* ('Cnava's people') to Clavering hundred.[27] Signs of demographic contraction and economic regression abound. In the Hales/Loddon/Heckingham area the fifteen Romano-British sites were replaced by only four early Saxon ones, and the heavier soils seem to have been abandoned as sites for settlement, although they doubtless continued to be used for grazing.[28] At Witton the eight Romano-British farmsteads were replaced by only four Anglo-Saxon ones, not all of which were occupied at the same time. Excavation here revealed that both the quantity, and the quality, of the occupants' material culture were low: as elsewhere in England, the pottery was locally produced, poorly fired, and made without the use of a wheel.[29]

During Middle Saxon times – roughly, the period between the mid-seventh and the late ninth centuries – the local population probably increased once again, and more complex forms of social and economic organisation developed. The Broads area became part of the Anglo-Saxon kingdom of East Anglia, which was roughly coterminous with the modern counties of Norfolk and Suffolk. It is possible that the uplands here were more densely wooded than most parts of Norfolk at this time, in spite of the excellence of much of the local soil. Certainly, many place-names in the area seem to refer to woodland: Acle for example was the *ac leah*, 'the oak wood'; Fishley, 'the wood of the fisherman'; while both East Ruston and Sco Ruston incorporate the term *hris tun*, 'the settlement among the brushwood'. It is possible that, remote from the main centres of power in East Anglia, and exposed to the threat of continued sea-borne raiding, the district was relatively sparsely settled, principally used for grazing. The importance of the latter in the local economy is again suggested by place-names: Horsey was the 'the horse island'; Woodbastwick and Bastwick both incorporate the element *wic*, 'a grazing farm, ranch'; while the names of Winterton and Somerton – the winter settlement and the summer settlement respectively – suggest the practice of transhumance, the seasonal movement of livestock to distant pastures.[30] Extensive areas of seasonal grazing must have been opening up in the form of low-lying fens and marshes as the estuaries here began to silt up. The role of Broadland as an area specialising in grazing and the exploitation of woodland – complementing the arable specialisms of other parts of the East Anglian kingdom – is also perhaps indicated by a particularly noticeable feature of the area at the end of the Saxon period. Domesday book shows that a very large proportion of the population here was classed not as bondmen – as villeins, sokemen or bordars – but as free men, *liberi homines*. Such individuals were very thick on the ground both in Flegg, and on the uplands bordering the south of Broadland, and the power of manorial lords in these areas was correspondingly circumscribed. There are many views on the nature, and significance, of such men: but one interpretation is that they were the descendants of Middle Saxon peasants whose main role had been that of herdsmen or shepherds, and whose obligations to king and nobles were thus less servile or onerous than those of arable producers. Certainly, the character of the other areas of Norfolk in which, by the time of Domesday, such men were most noticeably concentrated – the edge of the wet peat fens in the west of Norfolk, and the damp, heavy clay soils in the centre of the county – seems to support such an interpretation.[31]

Elsewhere in Norfolk and Suffolk free men were more thinly spread, although they were almost everywhere a more prominent feature than in other areas of England. Like other distinctive aspects of East Anglia's social and tenurial structure, they are often interpreted as a consequence of the settlement here, during the ninth and tenth centuries, of immigrants from Scandinavia. While, in reality, the origins of Norfolk and Suffolk's medieval idiosyncrasies are much more complex than this, a Viking elite clearly did come to dominate the East Anglian kingdom around 869 when, according to the *Anglo-Saxon Chronicle*, 'The host went from Cirencester into East Anglia, and occupied that land, and shared it out.'[32]

In restricted areas there also appears to have been large-scale peasant immigration from Scandinavia. One of these was Broadland. Viking place names – especially those featuring the suffix -*by*, 'farm, settlement' – are densely clustered on the island of Flegg (a name itself derived from a Scandinavian word meaning reeds), widespread in Lothingland, and scattered more thinly along the upland margins of the Yare and the Waveney (Figure 4).[33] Numerous minor names also attest a Danish presence: Lound Farm in Sea Palling derives its name, like the parish of Lound in Lothing, from the Old Scandinavian term *lundr*, 'a grove'.

Precisely why Danish settlement should have been so strongly concentrated in this area is unclear. Perhaps, in spite of its generally fertile soils, it still remained a fairly sparsely settled area as late as the ninth century. The name Stokesby has, as prefix to its Scandinavian ending, the Old English word *Stoc*, probably in the sense of 'outlying, temporarily occupied pasture land'.[34] More probably, Flegg and Lothing, being well-defined territories cut off on all or most sides by marshes and rivers, were easily grabbed and defended by immigrant bands, or could be conveniently ceded to them by treaty.

Whatever the nature (and extent) of Viking settlement in the area, there is no doubt that by the time of the Domesday survey in 1086 the upland parts of Broadland were no longer a sparsely-settled landscape of woodland and pasture. They were now – together with the neighbouring clayland areas to the south and west – one of the most densely settled and intensively farmed regions in the whole of England. This was a consequence of favourable climate and soils, but also perhaps of the general economic sophistication of the region, lying on the fringes of the North Sea, a major highway for trade in this period. Norwich was, by 1066, the second largest city in England; Yarmouth was already a large and flourishing fishing port; and urban vitality stimulated the rural economy. Dense population, and comparative weakness of lordship, were to be the key factors moulding the development of the local landscape throughout the medieval period.[35]

The Middle Ages

One probable consequence of these circumstances is the region's pattern of settlement. Over much of East Anglia, but especially in the eastern and southern parts of Norfolk and in north-eastern Suffolk, churches often do not stand in the middle of nucleated villages but instead lie marginal to, or even completely isolated from, the main foci of settlement in a parish. The farms and cottages lie, for the most part, quite widely scattered: maps surveyed before *c.*1800 reveal that most were originally strung around the periphery of areas of common land, although – thanks to the subsequent enclosure of these areas – this is no longer immediately apparent. In Broadland, such areas sometimes took the form of tracts of moor or heath in the 'uplands'. More usually, they were valley-floor marshes and fens. In the latter case, the houses were sometimes placed close to the edge of the flood-plain; more usually, they were located a short distance away, a strip

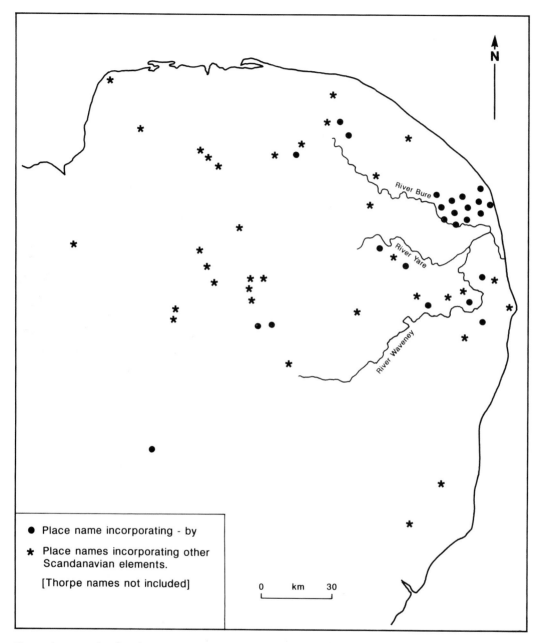

Figure 4   The distribution of major Scandinavian place-names in East Anglia. Note the marked
                concentration in the vicinity of Broadland.

Farms and cottages clustered around the margins of Burgh Common (now technically a 'Poor Allotment'). Before the age of Parliamentary enclosure, this form of settlement was ubiquitous in Broadland, and over much of Norfolk.

Plate 4

of 'dry' common separating them from the 'wet' common below. Such an arrangement can still be seen in one of the few places where a common has (partially) escaped enclosure, at Fleggburgh (Plate 4).

Precisely *why* this distinctive pattern of settlement developed is unclear: but *when*, and to some extent *how*, has now been revealed by archaeological surveys.[36] In later Saxon times the parish churches were not isolated. They normally had nucleated settlements – small villages – clustered around them. Starting shortly before the Norman Conquest, and continuing into the twelfth century, these old sites were abandoned and farms drifted off to relocate beside areas of common grazing. Almost certainly, this development was a consequence of social and economic factors. As population increased, more and more land fell to the plough and reserves of grazing dwindled. In the absence of strong local landowners, it was difficult to regulate the use of what remained. The local farmers moved to the edge of the residual pockets of common waste, in order to stake a clear claim to their use.

The region's dense population, and complex social structure, are manifested in another way: in the small size of parishes, and thus in the large number of parish churches. Indeed, the upland areas of Broadland have one of the highest densities of parish churches in Britain. Many of these (although not the present structures)

Plate 5   Repps parish church. Like many in Broadland, this has a round tower and stands a little
                 away from the main cluster of houses in the village.

were already in existence by the time of Domesday: their proliferation reflects not
only the comparative wealth of this fertile region, and the need to house large
congregations, but also perhaps the confused tenurial structure of the locality.
Families of freemen may have been keen to endow churches in order to establish
their status: church-building was the mark of the lord, rather than the peasant.

Many of the region's early churches have distinctive round towers, a peculiar-
ity of East Anglia (Plate 5). In Norfolk 123 still survive; a further 11 are in ruins
and 10 have disappeared completely. The equivalent figures for Suffolk are 38, 3
and 2. In Essex there are six examples, in Cambridgeshire two: but in the whole
of the rest of Britain there are only eight.[37] Such structures are strongly concentrated in the Broadland area (Figure 5). Most were built in the hundred years
between 1050 and 1150, but archaeologists are divided over their significance.
Many believe that they simply reflect the absence of good-quality freestone in
East Anglia. Flint, which occurs both in the superficial glacial deposits and in the
underlying chalk, could be used for the main bulk of the building, but limestone
had to be brought in from the Midlands, or from northern France, for the open-
ings and corners. This was expensive: and many church builders may have
decided that they could economise, by making the tower circular.[38] Although
this explanation is, in many ways, convincing, it has a number of problems – not

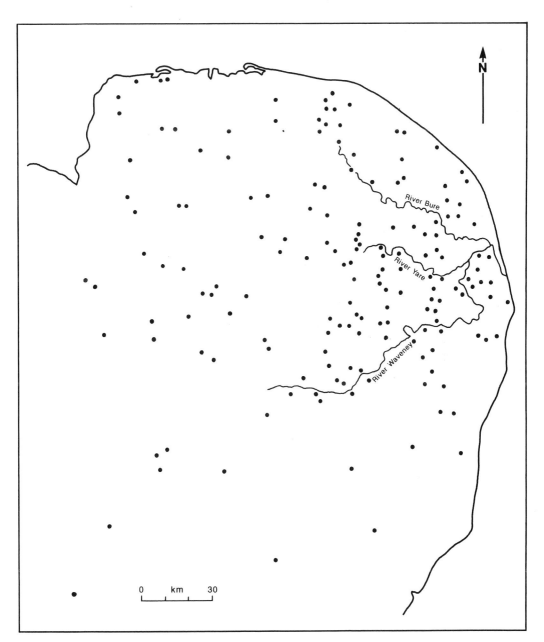

The distribution of round-towered churches in East Anglia. Figure 5

least the fact that it *is* possible to build square towers without freestone, and this
was sometimes done. Cultural factors may also therefore have been important,
and Stephen Heywood has drawn attention to the existence of similar structures,
built at around the same time, in northern Germany and southern Sweden.[39]
The fashion for round towers may well have come from here – an indication of
the strength of contacts across the North Sea at this time – although its enthu-
siastic adoption in East Anglia may well have been stimulated by the paucity of
freestone. Either way, these distinctive towers remain a striking feature of the
local landscape.

In the Middle Ages most of the farm land in the uplands lay in 'open fields'.
That is, the holdings of each farmer lay, not in discrete hedged closes, but in
narrow unhedged strips which were mixed with those of others: a pattern largely
resulting from rapid population growth in early medieval times, and the repeated
division of holdings between co-heirs.[40] East Anglian open fields were not, however, like those familiar from the school textbooks, which were only really characteristic of the Midland counties of England.[41] In these the peasants' strips were
usually scattered evenly across two or three great 'fields' in each township, one
of which lay fallow each year, and the crop to be grown in each bundle
of strips (or *furlong*) was decided by the community. Indeed, in a multiplicity of
ways the actions of the individual farmers in such 'regular' open-field systems
were controlled by communal decisions. In East Anglia, in contrast, medieval
agricultural systems were much more flexible and individualistic: seldom were
the strips widely scattered across two or three great fields, but were instead more
closely clustered in the vicinity of the peasant's homestead, and individual farmers
often had more freedom of choice about what they grew, and when.[42] In the west
of Norfolk, such freedoms were somewhat limited by the institution of the 'fold
course' – the right of the manorial lord to graze sheep across the tenants' land
for much of the year. In Broadland, however – where the power of manorial lords
was more circumscribed – fold courses were rare and tenants enjoyed almost
complete freedom over how they organised their cropping, and rights of grazing
over others' land were often limited to the period after the harvest. As a result of
all this, by the thirteenth century a highly innovative system of agriculture had
developed here, in which fodder crops had replaced bare fallows and manures
were assiduously applied.[43] It was this agrarian flexibility, combined with the
natural fertility of the soil and a climate well suited to cereal growing, which
ensured that the region was able to support a very dense population, although
individual farmers often eked out a meagre existence on tiny holdings, sometimes comprising less than two hectares.

The region's population declined in the fourteenth century, following the Black
Death and associated disasters, and this led to many changes in social and economic organisation. The number of farms decreased, and individual holdings
grew larger, as a prosperous 'middle class' of yeoman farmers gradually emerged.
At the same time, an important textile industry developed, based in particular in
the Waveney valley, and in the area around North Walsham and Aylsham in the
upper valleys of the Ant and the Bure.[44] Late medieval wealth is reflected in the

St Benet's Abbey – the gatehouse.   Plate 6

comprehensive rebuilding of some local churches, and especially in the erection of soaring towers in the fashionable Perpendicular style – like that at Ranworth, which dominates the fens and marshes of the Bure valley for many miles. Although this was a landscape dominated, more than most in England, by a prosperous peasantry, large landowners have nevertheless also left some mark: most notably, in the striking castle at Caister, built by Sir John Fastolfe in 1432–35 and one of the most impressive pieces of fifteenth-century military architecture in England, with its tall brick tower, equipped with gun ports.

St Benet's Abbey

The most striking archaeological site in Broadland – other than Burgh Castle – is unquestionably St Benet's, or St Benedict's, Abbey. Visitors see the strange sight of its gatehouse, with a drainage windmill built somewhat incongruously within it, as they sail down the Bure between Horning and Acle. It is a feature immortalised in countless paintings, sketches and photographs (Plate 6). Observant travellers also notice that, to the east of this curious structure, the ground rises in a low hill, surmounted by the fragmentary ruins of the abbey church. The hill was once an island of dry ground in the damp marshes, called Cow

Holme, and its fifteen hectares are peppered with numerous other remains of the monastic community. It is worth pausing for a while to consider this site in more detail, partly because it is such an icon of Broadland, but also because the history of much of the region was, for several hundred years, closely bound up with that of the monastery.[45]

The early history of the community is shrouded in mystery. In medieval times it was claimed that the monastery was founded by Cnut in 1019 or 1020, and that soon afterwards twelve monks were sent from the abbey to help establish a new monastery at *Bedricsworth*, now Bury St Edmunds in west Suffolk. As Antonia Gransden has argued, however, the Cnut foundation charter is probably a medieval forgery, and the story of the abbey's involvement in the genesis of Bury a thirteenth-century invention. Both houses were probably colonised from Ramsey in Cambridgeshire in the early eleventh century although in both cases this may have represented the reorganisation, on stricter Benedictine lines, of communities which were already in existence.[46] There may be some truth in other medieval traditions, that the St Benet's community was originally established as early as 800 by a hermit, Suneman; destroyed by Viking raids; and re-established by one Wulfric, with seven followers, in the late tenth century. A Middle Saxon origin for the community would not be implausible. The site, an island in relatively damp ground, would be a typical one for an early monastery, and before it was levelled in recent times a substantial linear earthwork cut off the southern end of the peninsula of upland lying immediately to the west of the 'island'. Marshes and early monasteries often go together: Anglo-Saxon monks wanted solitude, and kings and nobles were happy to grant them marginal land which they could then set about improving. Other marshland areas of southern Britain had their great monastic houses in Anglo-Saxon time: Ely and Ramsey in the Cambridgeshire Fenlands, Glastonbury in the Somerset Levels. In Broadland, Dark Age monasteries probably existed at Burgh Castle (founded by the Irish monk Fursa as early as 630); and perhaps at Reedham and Loddon.[47] Hickling – where an Augustinian priory was founded in 1185 – may also have had an earlier history, for it is sited, like St Benet's, on a former island in the marshes.[48] Nevertheless, situation alone cannot prove an early date, for as we shall see the extent to which the lower ground here would, in fact, have comprised damp marshland in Middle Saxon times is questionable. Moreover, when rising water levels did produce wetter conditions, in post-Conquest times, the marshes and fens continued to attract monastic houses: the Premonstratensian Abbey at Langley was established in the late twelfth century, and in the thirteenth further Augustinian houses appeared at St Olaves and Acle.

By the time of Domesday St Benet's Abbey already had extensive possessions in north-east Norfolk. The twelfth-century register records a more extensive patrimony, the result of numerous grants by both wealthy knights and local free men. The buildings on Cow Holme grew steadily in size and sophistication, and in the middle of the twelfth century Abbot Daniel built a hospital at the end of the causeway leading across the marshes to Horning. This was rebuilt in the fifteenth century and still survives, although much altered and converted to a barn.

The archaeological remains on Cow Holme are impressive. The gatehouse –
facing the causeway from Horning – was built in the fourteenth century and
bears a striking similarity to St Ethelberht's gate at Norwich Cathedral, erected
in 1316. Its outer face is now encased inside the eighteenth-century windmill
tower. It has panels of 'flushwork' – that is, knapped flint surrounded by freestone,
a local speciality – and is decorated with two carved figures in the spandrels. The
gate was probably built following the receipt of a license to crenellate in 1327,
after which a wall was erected all around the site, extending to the north beyond

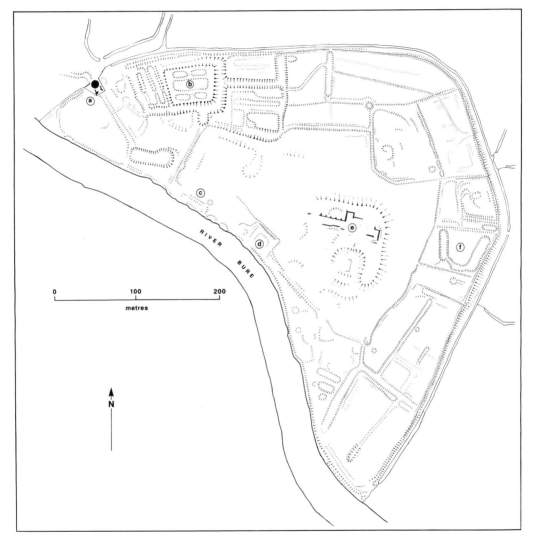

St Benet's Abbey (TG 383156) – principal surviving features. (a) the gatehouse; (b) main
fishpond complex; (c) sites of barns and storehouses; (d) abbot's lodgings (later the Chequers
public house); (e) the abbey church; (f) fishponds.

Figure 6

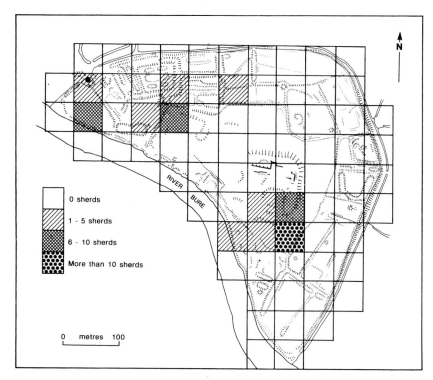

(a)

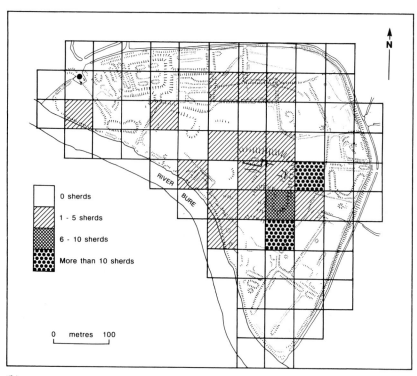

(b)

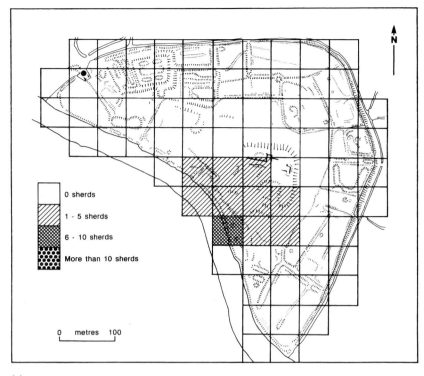

0 sherds

1 - 5 sherds

6 - 10 sherds

More than 10 sherds

0   metres   100

(c)

St Benet's Abbey – distribution of pottery recovered from surface disturbances and mole hills. (a) early medieval pottery; (b) late medieval/transitional pottery; (c) post-medieval pottery.

Figure 7

the rising ground of the 'island' out onto the levels of the marsh. Its remains – also faced, flamboyantly, with knapped flint – can be traced all along this northern side. The remains of the church, on the highest point of the island, are somewhat scanty, but indicate a building of some pretensions – 100 metres long and up to 30 wide, without aisles but flanked on both sides by chapels. It was, apparently, extensively rebuilt in the late fourteenth or early fifteenth century.

Other evidence for the buildings and facilities of the abbey is less immediately obvious. It is provided by earthworks, parch marks, and subtle variations in the vegetation of the grass sward (Figure 6). Amorphous and confused undulations to the south of the church mark the site of the cloister and refectory, and probably the infirmary. Rather clearer is the pronounced ditch which divides the island proper from the lower ground within the walls. This is probably an earlier boundary of the monastic precinct, but it survived as late as 1700, when a map shows it as a hedge containing closely-spaced trees.[49] Levelled areas, fragments of masonry and parch marks show that a range of buildings existed along the side of the river. These included a barn, a chapel, the abbot's lodgings and a store yard. The most striking earthworks are perhaps the elaborate series of fish ponds immediately to the east of the gatehouse. These were stews, or *servatoria*, used to keep fish which had been caught in the local waterways prior to consumption or sale. Other fish ponds existed to the east of the island. Although dry in the summer, the ponds still fill with water in the winter: some have been deliberately slighted in comparatively recent times, presumably to prevent waterlogging and thus improve the quality of the grass. Even when dry in the summer months the vegetation they contain differs significantly from that of the surrounding sward, with hard rush, water crowfoot, water starwort and tufted forget-me-know. In a similar way, the line of buried walls on the site is marked by a distinct vegetation including English stonecrop, creeping cinquefoil, and yellow oat grass. As so often, even the minutiae of human activities and remains can structure the details of the 'natural' environment.

The abbey has not been excavated, and – as it is entirely under grass – cannot be fieldwalked. However, moles happily inhabit the site and a survey of the contents of molehills carried out in the summers of 1993 and 1994 recovered over 250 fragments of pottery, as well as much other material – building rubble, bones and oysters. The distribution of this material (Figure 7) suggests that the main areas of medieval occupation – or at least, the main areas of rubbish disposal – were to the south and east of the church: locations sheltered by the higher ground from the full force of the northern winds.

The abbey ceased to exist when Henry VIII suppressed all English monasteries in 1539. Uniquely, it was not technically 'dissolved', the Crown instead combining the abbacy with the Bishopric of Norwich (Ludham Hall, on the upland to the north, became the bishop's country seat, and he remains abbot to this day). The last monk departed in 1545, and by 1594 a survey described how the church and other buildings had been 'utterly ruinated and wasted' before 1585; most of the buildings had, in fact, been pulled down by Bishop Parkhurst (1560–1575). The survey noted that:

> Onelye there remayneth a howse of fiftie foote long & xxtie foote wide by estimacon Wherein one Edmund Dye fisherman now dwelleth . . . Item there is an old barne in decaye; and there standeth a gate house uncovered . . .[50]

Other features of the abbey continued to function, to judge from a lease of 1617, by which 'Edmund Dey of Horning ffisherman' was granted 'the house called the ffishing house together with all the ffish pondes and holdes to the same belonging scituate and being within the late dissolved monastery of St Bennettes'.[51] Post-medieval occupation on Cow Holme was, to judge from the distribution of surface finds of pottery and coal, more concentrated than that of the medieval period (Figure 7c). The 'ffishing house' – probably the former abbot's lodgings – is shown on the map of 1700, along with various outbuildings, and by the nineteenth century it was being used as a public house, the Chequers. By this time the abbey was already a tourist attraction – there are numerous nineteenth-century graffiti on the gatehouse. G. C. Davies visited the site in the 1880s. The Chequers was now a private house but he described its 'arched doorways, and strong walls . . . whose cool recesses speak of ancient days'. It was badly damaged by fire soon afterwards and its remains subsequently demolished.[52]

After the Middle Ages

In the post-medieval period the uplands continued, in many ways, to develop along lines already established in the Middle Ages. In particular, high land prices – the consequence of the remarkable fertility of much of the local soil – ensured that large landed estates never became characteristic features of the region. This was especially true of the central and northern parts of Broadland. Some absentee landowners did, it is true, acquire land here: like the Evans-Lombe family, who resided at Great Melton to the west of Norwich, who had extensive holdings in Repps and Eccles. But for the most part smaller owneroccupiers seem to have fared better here than in most parts of early modern England, and this is not a landscape which exhibits many of the trappings of gentility. There are relatively few great mansions in the area, although Langley Hall, with its extensive grounds designed by Lancelot 'Capability' Brown, and Somerleyton and Woodbastwick, with their fine parks and picturesque 'model' estate villages, make a significant impact. For the most part, however, the buildings of the region attest the prosperity of the local gentry, and prosperous yeomen, in the sixteenth, seventeenth and early eighteenth centuries. The earliest vernacular buildings are timber-framed, but most of these were subsequently encased in brick; and this material (sometimes combined with flint) became the standard building material from *c*.1600. Some of the larger seventeenth-century houses were given distinctive shaped gables. Farms and cottages were originally thatched with reed from the local marshes, and this material continued to be used for some new buildings until the end of the eighteenth century. From *c*.1680, however, distinctive pantiles were increasingly employed, often replacing earlier roofs of thatch. They were introduced into Broadland from the Low Countries, yet another sign of the region's close links with the lands across the North Sea.

Particularly striking as a feature of the landscape are the many large barns, built of brick and thatched with reed, of seventeenth- or eighteenth-century date (some are earlier, like the huge, cathedral-like structure at Waxham, built in 1581). These proclaim the fact that arable agriculture continued to be the mainstay of the upland economy, with barley the principal crop. Increasingly, however, in the course of the seventeenth and eighteenth centuries, farmers were also involved in fattening bullocks. These were grazed on grass 'leys' – temporary pastures in the arable fields – and on the neighbouring marshes during the summer; and fattened on turnips in yards over the winter, in order to produce rich manure for the arable fields. In the course of the late eighteenth and early nineteenth centuries ranges of cattle sheds were added to (often much earlier) barns, to enclose the required stall yard. The resultant arrangement can still be seen on many upland farms.[53] It is noteworthy that the cultivation of the turnip – the crucial crop in the development of 'improved' methods of farming in the seventeenth and eighteenth centuries – seems to have been adopted earlier here than almost anywhere in England. As in the Middle Ages, Broadland was at the cutting edge of agricultural innovation, and in the eighteenth century cereal yields here were among the highest in England.[54]

Although keen in many ways to experiment with new husbandry techniques, upland landowners – especially those in the central and northern parts of the region – seem to have had less interest in one key feature of eighteenth-century 'improvement' – the enclosure of open fields. Much 'piecemeal' enclosure took place, especially on the heavier clay soils to the south: that is, landowners collected, through sale or exchange, groups of contingent strips, which they then surrounded with a hedge. And in a few small parishes, such as Ashby, total enclosure was achieved at an early date because a single individual had managed to obtain a near-monopoly of ownership.[55] But most parishes still lay largely open at the end of the eighteenth century, when open fields and commons were removed by parliamentary Acts.[56] Thus the arable land of Winterton consisted almost entirely of open fields when it was enclosed in 1811: the pre-enclosure survey records 295 numbered parcels, of which 278 were open-field strips.[57] In some parishes, extensive areas of strips survived well into the nineteenth century: as late as 1838 it was reported of Ormesby that 'there is a considerable quantity of open field and many of the enclosures have more owners than one'.[58] In Runham, where half the arable land still lay in open fields as late as 1805, the 'particulars' compiled by the enclosure commissioners reveal that the unenclosed strips were still overwhelmingly small: 87.6 per cent were of less than two acres, and 62.8 per cent less than one.[59] This is slightly unusual, however. In most parishes, while the extent of *enclosure* was limited, the piecemeal *consolidation* of holdings – in order to create larger though still unhedged plots – was widespread. For the parish of Repps, for example, we can compare a Field Book of 1578 with a 'Book of Reference' made to accompany a lost map in *c*.1753. The former lists 1,207 strips in 71 furlongs, averaging around 17 per furlong; the latter gives 530 strips in 90 furlongs, an average of 6 per furlong. In other words average strip size more than doubled in the intervening period. Nevertheless, very few *closes* are listed in the survey, and when the parish was enclosed in 1809 more than half the arable land still lay open.[60]

In other regions of East Anglia in which the enclosure of open fields came late, it was usually because the principal landowner was also the lord of the manor and, enjoying fold course rights over the unhedged strips of other proprietors, had little incentive to enclose. In Broadland, as we have seen, fold courses were rare and resistance to enclosure here seems to have been the consequence of rather different factors. Firstly, because the land was so fertile, it could command extremely high rents even in an unenclosed state: Arthur Young in the early nineteenth century quoted average annual rentals for Flegg of 25s. to 27s. per acre, but noted that some land could fetch as much as 42s. – well over twice the average for East Anglia.[61] Natural advantages of soil and climate were compounded by the character of local agrarian organisation. Not only was the fold course absent, but so too were almost all other forms of communal organisation and control, so that farmers in the open fields were free to grow what they wanted, how they wanted. There was thus little incentive to enclose.[62]

It was only at the beginning of the nineteenth century, at the height of the Napoleonic Wars, when grain prices were extraordinarily high and landowners

particularly optimistic about the future of farming, that enclosure became a tempt-
ing option. And even then the real interest of landowners was probably in enclosing and ploughing the upland heaths, and improving the common fens and
marshes of the lowlands. The enclosure of the open arable which these parliamentary Acts also brought about was probably of secondary importance. Either
way, although some older hedges exist in Broadland, especially on the clay soils
in the south of the region, the overwhelming 'feel' of the landscape is of relatively
recent planned enclosure. This is largely a landscape of rectangular fields surrounded by straight hawthorn hedges.

In some ways, however, any discussion of the upland fieldscape is rather point-
less, for this is an area which has seen, over the past three of four decades, an
awesome amount of hedgerow loss. In some places, especially in the north and
east of the region, 'fields' as this term is commonly understood have ceased to
exist: they have been replaced by boundless prairies. Yet this, of course, is merely
another manifestation of the extreme fertility of the soil. Hedges serve no practical function in the landscape of modern arable agribusiness. They get in the
way of large machinery, and take up valuable land which would be better employed in growing yet more cereal crops. The fertility of the upland soils, the key
feature in the region's history, thus continues to have a determining effect upon
the appearance of the landscape.

As in the Middle Ages, so too in the post-medieval centuries, not everything in
Broadland was rural. Textile production continued to be of importance in many
places well into the eighteenth century, while agriculture itself spawned a number
of local industries, including milling, malting and lime burning. Prosperous
market towns – Beccles, Bungay, North Walsham and Aylsham – provided goods
and services for their rural hinterlands. Norwich and Yarmouth continued to be
urban centres of some importance, the former only losing its place as second city
in the kingdom in the course of the eighteenth century. Broadland's rivers, as
we shall see, were vital arteries of transport, and past industrial and commercial
activity have left a profound mark on this seemingly 'rural' landscape.

3

The landscape of the marshes

It is sometimes assumed that the landscape of the Halvergate 'triangle' – the great, flat expanse of drained marshland lying to the west of Yarmouth – is a comparatively modern creation: and that before the eighteenth century the area comprised a vast, poorly drained tract of common fen (Figure 8 and Plate 7). In part this view is derived from the earliest detailed description we have of the marshes, that penned by William Marshall in 1787. He described how:

> Until about twenty years ago this valuable tract lay principally under water: except in a dry summer. But during that space of time a number of windmills have been erected, which throw water into the main drains, formed for this purpose. By this means the principal parts of the marsh are freed from surface water early in the spring; so that cattle may be turned into them by the beginning of May, and are kept free long enough to permit them, in general, to remain there until Christmas.[63]

There is no doubt, however, that the impression so conveyed is misleading: various earlier commentators make it clear that the marshes were already productive and valuable at the start of the eighteenth century. In 1722, for example, Daniel Defoe was able to describe the marshes in glowing terms:

> In this vast tract of meadows are fed a prodigious number of black cattle, which are said to be fed up for the fattest beef, though not the largest in England; and the quantity is so great, as they not only supply the city of Norwich, the town of Yarmouth, and the county adjacent, but send great quantities of them weekly in all the winter season to London.[64]

And a century earlier things were much the same, to judge from the preamble to the parliamentary act which established the Sea Breach Commission following the terrible floods of 1608/9. This states that the disaster – caused by the sea breaking through the dunes north of Winterton – had affected

> The greatest parte of the marshes and Lower Groundes within the Townes and Parishes hereinafter mentioned (the same conteyning many Thousand Acres) upon which

The Halvergate Marshes, showing the location of places mentioned in the text.

Figure 8

Plate 7   View near the margins of the Halvergate Marsh.

> a great part of the Wealth of the said Counties doth depend, being grounde of them-
> selves very ritch, and without wch the Uplande, specially of the Countie of Norff,
> being of themselves for the most Parte vy dry and barren, cannot be so well husbanded
> or ymployed.[65]

This is not to deny that *some* areas of poorly drained common land existed in the
area in the early modern period, much of which survived until enclosure in
the early nineteenth century (Figure 9). But these tended to occupy restricted
pockets of land around the outer rim of the marsh, close to the upland. Thus
Marshall in 1787 described the lamentable state of the marsh near Halvergate
village:

> At the foot of the swell, the Marshes commence. For nearly the first mile, we rode to
> our horses knees in water. This watery part is *common* to Halvergate, and there are
> two reasons for it being overflowed: It is no person's business to drain it; and, what
> is remarkable, it lies lower than the middle of the Marshes; which, it seems, is the
> highest, and the best, land.[66]

And many subsequent commentators have drawn attention to the differences
between the areas in the centre of the marsh, and those closer to the upland.
As Mosby, writing in 1938, put it: 'in general the further the marsh is situated
from the "land" the greater its grazing value'.[67] This was largely because minor

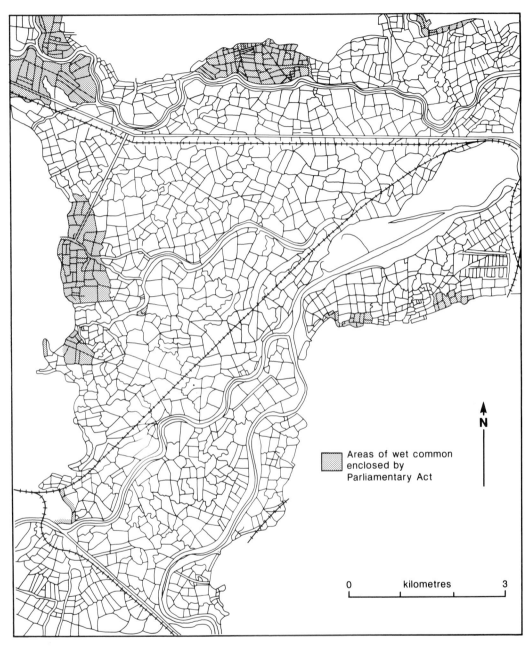

The distribution of parliamentary enclosure within the Halvergate 'triangle'.　　　　Figure 9

watercourses flowing off the higher ground, pour a steady stream of water into the peaty areas on the periphery of the marsh, areas which are anyway comparatively difficult to drain because of their distance from the principal rivers.

A variety of documents shows that the bulk of the marsh was, in fact, owned as private property in the early modern period. Under the terms of the 1609 Act, the Sea Breach Commission established a jury which was required to assess the extent of inundation resulting from the great flood. It was asked to list the names of all the owners of lands in danger from future flooding and 'the content of acres subject to Inundacon and the trewe yerely vallewe of them by the acre as now they are undrowned'.[68] The replies given confirm that most of the land in the marshes was already held in severalty, although the figures are estimates and bear only a vague relationship to the real areas of the lands concerned. Documents drawn up in 1702 and 1715, listing the owners of the marsh and the value of their land in order to assess the level of contribution expected towards the maintenance of the sea walls, present more accurate figures.[69] These show that Halvergate, for example, had only 100 acres of common marsh; Stokesby 180; Wickhampton 150; and Caister 130. No common land at all was listed for the detached sections of South Walsham parish, for Herringby, or for Mautby; the areas of common land thus recorded in these documents are almost the same as those enclosed in the relevant parishes by parliamentary acts in the early nineteenth century. Moreover, although the precise acreages given differ somewhat from those recorded in the document of 1616, in those parishes for which the comparison can be made the relative *proportion* of common to several land recorded in each period is much the same. In other words, in many parishes the extent of common land on the marshes in 1616 was probably little different from what it was to be at the time of the Enclosure Acts nearly 200 years later. True, the rectilinear pattern of dykes in places on the fringe of the marsh – as in Tunstall – suggests that some other areas were enclosed from common land at a relatively late date. But for the most part the landscape of the Halvergate 'triangle' has a more ancient and more complex origin. Far from being a marginal wilderness before the eighteenth century, the Halvergate Marshes were already being intensively exploited, and to some extent settled, by later Saxon times.[70]

The medieval landscape

As described in Chapter 1, the open estuary which occupied the area during the Roman period – a vast tract of open water and intertidal mud flats – became steadily drier during Middle Saxon times. In part this was the result of changes in relative land/sea levels; in part it was the consequence of the build-up of a sand and gravel spit across the mouth of the open embayment, which impeded the daily influx of tidal waters and thus increased the rate of silting. The area of mud flats increased steadily, culminating in the establishment of tracts of salt marsh.

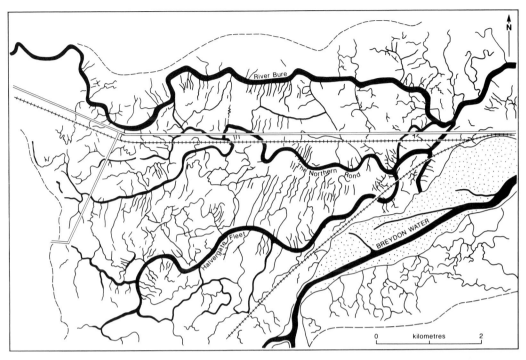

The pattern of relict salt marsh channels in the northern part of the Halvergate 'triangle' (after Coles and Funnel 1981, but with additions from more recent aerial photographs).   Figure 10

These earliest phases in the history of Halvergate, as an untamed world of mud flats and saltings, is still inscribed upon the landscape. The surface of the marsh is covered by a complex pattern of relict watercourses, dry depressions a metre or so wide and *c.*0.3 metres deep, most clearly revealed from the air. These evidently represent several stages in the development of the marsh. Three main types are visible (Figure 10). Firstly, there are close-packed sub-parallel channels, similar to those which exist today on intertidal mud flats in Breydon Water and elsewhere. Secondly, there are more widely spaced, meandering channels, similar to the branching, serpentine creeks which can be seen in modern salt marshes. Some of these have been incorporated into the modern pattern of drainage. Lastly, there are a number of much larger watercourses, sometimes revealed by aerial photographs as broad bands of discoloration in the marsh grass. Again, these have often been preserved in the modern landscape by the line of dykes, although only in one case as a more prominent feature – the Halvergate Fleet. This is now a relatively minor watercourse which runs through the centre of the marsh, but it is flanked by wide 'ronds' and substantial embankments (Plate 8). As we shall see, other features of this type survived into the eighteenth or nineteenth centuries, before being destroyed, their walls levelled and their ronds incorporated into the adjacent areas of marsh.

Plate 8   The old road to Yarmouth, running along the low 'wall' on the northern edge of the
                 Halvergate Fleet. To the left, the former 'rond' of this ancient watercourse; beyond, the
                 southern wall can just be seen.

By the tenth century relative land/sea levels were more than 1.5 metres below
those of today, allowing grazing during much of the year.[71] Not surprisingly,
some of the names traditionally given to portions of the marsh are of Scandinavian
or Old English origin. Names featuring the Scandinavian element *holmr* – 'island'
or 'stream side meadow' – are fairly common.[72] Although this term continued to
be employed well into the Middle Ages its combination with other early elements
suggests that some, at least, of these names are of pre-Conquest origin. The first
element of Skeetholme, for example – the detached section of Acle parish near
Great Yarmouth – is probably the Scandinavian *skitr*, 'dung'; that of Fuelholme in
Postwick Detached the Old English *Fule*, 'wild bird'. Early maps and documents
reveal a number of potentially early names. The name 'Seals' in Tunstall parish
for example probably comes from the Scandinavian *selja*, 'willow'; the name of
Stergott Marsh in Postwick Detached derives from the Scandinavian *storr*, 'sedge,
bent grass', and Old English *gota*, 'a watercourse, a stream'; while that of
Candlecourt Marsh, in the detached portion of Cantley parish, possibly incorpor-
ates the Old English term *cort*, 'a short piece of ground, a piece of land cut off'
– probably in the latter sense, indicating the fact that it was physically separate
from the main body of the parish. None of this place-name evidence is conclusive,

but it does suggest that, by the twelfth century, the marshes were being exploited on a sufficient scale for them to be divided into discrete areas, each separately named (Figure 11).

A more convincing indication of the extent of early exploitation is provided by the configuration of parish boundaries (Figure 12). It is probable that, in a densely settled county like Norfolk, most of these were fixed by *c*.1100, and certainly by *c*.1150. As already described, the marshes within the Halvergate 'triangle' are divided between a number of parishes. Some areas lay within extensions of parishes which were principally located on the immediately adjacent uplands; some comprised detached blocks of such parishes; while some constituted detached portions of parishes which do not lie on the marsh edge at all, but (like Raveningham, or Stockton) are located several kilometres away. Such a pattern indicates that, by the eleventh or twelfth centuries, the marshes were already a valuable resource, eagerly acquired by various Saxon lords through royal grant or purchase. For parishes seem generally to have developed out of private estates, as their owners built and endowed local churches: any substantial property out on the marsh would not have had enough permanent residents to gain a church of its own, and would therefore simply have been attached to the parish created out of the nearest estate belonging to the same owner.

The Domesday Book of 1086 provides some important clues about the nature of landuse on the marshes. It lists large numbers of sheep on many of the manors bordering the Halvergate 'triangle'. These probably provide some indication of the extent of demesne pastures, for the survey records only the herds and flocks of the manorial lord, not the stock of his tenants. Acle had 120 sheep, Stokesby 180, Cantley 400, and Halvergate – the parish later to possess the largest tract of land on the marsh – no less than 960. Some manors situated in vills lying well back from the marsh edge also had substantial flocks, such as Toft Monks. Significantly, these were generally places which were later to possess detached parochial areas out on the marsh. Domesday does not systematically record demesne pasture or marsh, but there are occasional references. Thus one of the manors in Haddiscoe had 100 sheep; on the others, no sheep are recorded but there was said to be pasture for 80, 50 and 40 respectively. Wheatacre had pasture for 200 sheep, Herringby for 100. Heckingham actually had a 'marsh for 60 sheep', presumably to be identified with the detached portion of this parish within the Halvergate 'triangle'. Substantial demesne holdings continued to be a feature of the marshes throughout the Middle Ages. St Benet's Abbey had extensive properties in the detached sections of South Walsham and Postwick parishes in the twelfth century; Norwich Cathedral Priory held 200 acres in Fowlholme (or Fouldholme) and Skeetholme, around what is now Scaregap Farm near Yarmouth, in one of the three detached portions of Acle parish.[73]

Although they were clearly a valuable resource by later Saxon times, we should not assume that the marshes already had a landscape like that of today. In particular, they were crossed by a number of tidal creeks: for as well as sheep and pasture, Domesday records a number of salt pans in the area, especially on the island of Flegg.[74] Some of these were presumably situated close to the coast – the

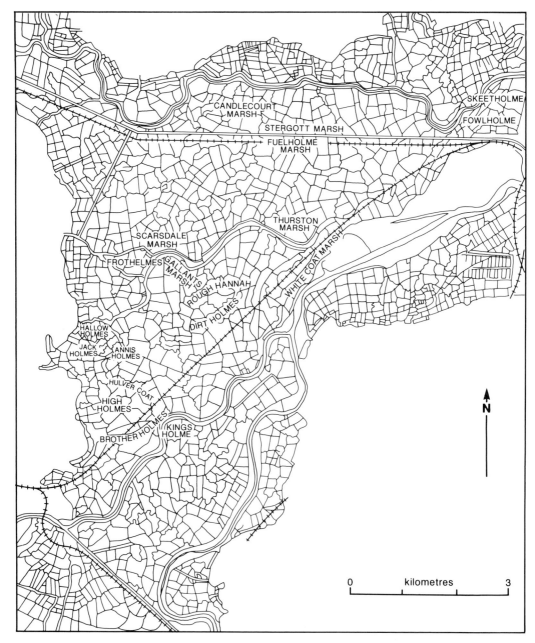

Figure 11   Some early place-names in the Halvergate 'triangle'. 'Holme' and 'helm' names come
              from the Scandinavian term *holmr*, meaning an island or an area of stream-side meadow.
              Names featuring 'coat' refer to sheep cotes, and thus presumably date back to the time
              when sheep were the main animals kept on the marsh. 'Gallants' probably comes from
              Old English *galla*, 'barren, wet land'. The other names are discussed in the text.

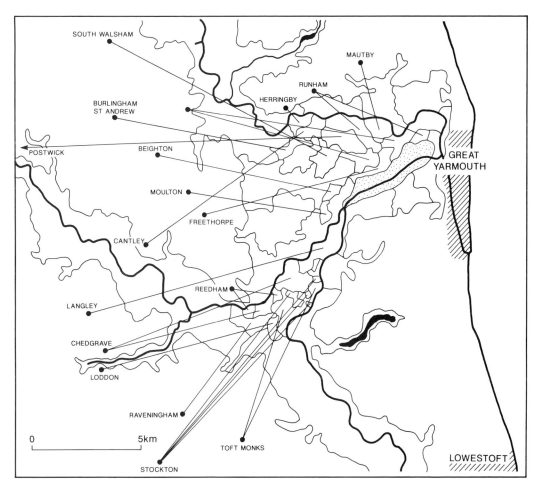

The complex pattern of parochial organisation within the Halvergate 'triangle'. Some areas of marsh lay within parishes principally located on the adjacent upland, but others formed detached portions of parishes situated several kilometres away. The map shows the detached parochial blocks, and the location of the settlements to which they were attached.

Figure 12

vill with the largest number was Caister, with no less than 39 – but others were probably located on tidal creeks. In fact, there are considerable problems with Domesday's account of salt pans. Some vills with large numbers – such as Rollesby – cannot possibly have had direct access to tidal water by this time. Although the present parish of Rollesby does contain areas of low-lying ground which comprise a continuation of the main body of the Halvergate Marshes, these are occupied by areas of relatively recent peat which cannot have formed in saline conditions. Like other high-value resources listed by Domesday, salt pans may often have been located some way away from the parish which now bears the name of the vill under which they are listed, and thus a detailed analysis of their location is meaningless. Nevertheless, when combined with the evidence of slightly later documents, Domesday can sometimes provide an indication of the extent of tidal penetration. Domesday records that, included in St Benet's holding in South Walsham, there were two salt houses; and in the 1140s, when the abbey leased its demesne lands in South Walsham, the property included a marsh with 300 sheep and salt pans.[75] This marsh, which later became the detached section of South Walsham parish in the heart of the 'triangle', had no river frontage and any salt pans here must have made use of tidal water flowing up what is now the Halvergate Fleet, which forms its southern boundary. Perhaps the pans which Domesday lists in Halvergate and Tunstall were similarly located beside this lost watercourse.

Yet although tidal creeks still flowed far inland, the high value of the marshes in the twelfth and thirteenth centuries suggests that they were more than mere saltings, used only as rough grazing and regularly flooded by high tides during much of the year. Presumably relative water levels were so low that the areas between the creeks comprised 'upper salt marsh', with a fairly well-developed sward, only periodically inundated. According to the cartulary of St Benet's Abbey, in 1147 Phillip Basset granted to the abbey the marsh of Fuelholme (in what is now the detached section of Postwick parish) together with 300 sheep, salt pans and all things pertaining to it for a rent of five marks a year – a substantial sum. Around 1180 the same marsh was granted to one Geoffrey, son of Master Nicholas, again with salt pans and unspecified numbers of 'sheep'. The fact that sheep were granted as part of the property strongly implies that they were a permanent fixture there, present for the majority of the year.[76] Certainly, by the start of the thirteenth century the flock of sheep belonging to the Norwich Cathedral Priory at Fowlholme seem to have stayed on the marsh all the year round, except for ten weeks after harvest when it was fed and folded on the stubbles at Martham.[77] Medieval landowners grazed vast numbers of sheep on the marshes. The abbot of St Benet's had over 1,500 in 1343. In some cases, they were penned up in folds at night and their dung carefully collected and taken by boat to the 'upland', where it was spread on the arable fields to enhance fertility: the practice is recorded on the Earl of Norfolk's demesne marshes in Acle, Halvergate and South Walsham, where 1,800 sheep were being grazed in 1278.[78]

The exploitation of this valuable grazing, as well as the production of salt, necessitated the establishment of farms and cottages, and a number of medieval settlements are now known from the heart of the marsh. Most take the form of low mounds, whose character is revealed when they are put to the plough: spreads of pottery sherds and other debris are left in the ploughsoil. Only one such mound has, to date, been excavated, that standing next to the Acle New Road, near Ashtree Farm. When dug in 1948 it was found to contain pottery ranging in date from the eleventh century to the thirteenth. There was a layer of slag, from wood fires, preserved beneath the mound, and eleventh-century pottery was found below this, well over a metre below modern sea level. The excavator tentatively identified the site as a saltern, although it could just as easily have been a marsh farm.[79]

Another interesting case is Six Mile House in Halvergate parish, which stands just over 4 km to the west. The house – in part of eighteenth-century date, but much rebuilt in the nineteenth – stands on a low mound which has been incorporated into the southern 'wall' of the river Bure. Trenches dug for sewers and cables, together with probing, revealed that the mound stands some 1.5 metres above waterlogged deposits and is between 40 and 60 metres in diameter. All over its surface crudely made, clamp-fired bricks were found, probably of medieval date. To the west of the house a trench dug to take a cable exposed a rough pavement constructed of the same bricks. A pit dug at the north-eastern angle of the house revealed quantities of unglazed grey pottery, probably of twelfth- or early thirteenth-century date, associated with layers of soot. Beneath the centre of the house a thick layer of burnt red earth was encountered, associated with layers of charcoal, suggesting that salt-making may have occurred on the site. But, at the same level as the pottery, large quantities of sheep bones were also discovered. In all probability, this early medieval establishment was engaged both in salt production and in sheep ranching.[80]

The true extent of early settlement within the marsh is difficult to ascertain for two main reasons. One is that many medieval sites, like that at Six Mile House, probably lie hidden beneath existing marsh farms. Another is that most of the marsh remains under grass, so that it cannot be systematically fieldwalked. It might be thought that the pattern of early settlement could be reconstructed by locating upstanding mounds surviving in the unploughed areas of marsh, but some of these have been levelled in the past even when land has remained under pasture. Conversely, where low mounds *do* survive it is often unclear whether they mark the sites of settlements, or whether they have some other explanation, such as refuges for cattle: in a number of cases, careful examination of the ploughsoil in places where mounds have been levelled following conversion to arable has revealed no sign of occupation debris. Nevertheless, by systematically fieldwalking sample areas, scrutinising available archaeological records, and carefully examining the gardens of surviving marsh farms, it is possible to obtain some impression of the extent of medieval settlement.[81] Figure 13 shows the distribution of known medieval sites in the northern part of the Halvergate Marshes. In addition to the Ashtree Farm mound and Six Mile House, careful examination of the site of Lockgate Farm (now demolished) recovered medieval pottery, including sherds of late Saxon Thetford Ware. Within the 6 sq km systematically fieldwalked, two medieval sites were located, both again beginning in later Saxon times, possibly as early as the ninth century (both produced substantial amounts of Thetford Ware). These sites also produced large quantities of oyster shells and animal bones – principally from sheep. In addition, medieval pottery was recovered from the garden of one occupied marsh farm within the fieldwalked areas, and from the site of another, demolished in relatively recent times. Although more survey work clearly needs to be done, the available evidence is enough to show that the lonely marsh farms are not, as has sometimes been claimed, the consequence of seventeenth- and eighteenth-century reclamation. Men and women have lived on Halvergate for a thousand years.

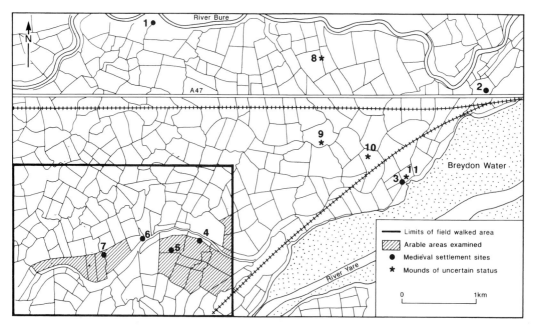

Figure 13   Medieval settlement in the northern part of the Halvergate 'triangle'. Evidence for medieval
                 occupation recovered by archaeological excavation, or from observation of trenching,
                 etc.: (1) Halvergate Six Mile House; (2) Ash Tree Farm mound. Evidence for medieval
                 occupation recovered from disturbed ground at the sites of existing, or recently demolished,
                 marsh farms: (3), (4), (6). Evidence for medieval settlement discovered by fieldwalking:
                 (5), (7). Sites of levelled mounds which, when investigated, produced no evidence of
                 occupation: (8), (9), (10), (11).

The post-medieval landscape

There was a gradual rise in relative water levels during the medieval period, the
effects of which were compounded in the late thirteenth and fourteenth centuries
by an increased incidence of storms and sea surges, associated with a general
climatic deterioration affecting the whole of Western Europe. Low-lying marshes
both in eastern England, and elsewhere, suffered from increased levels of flooding
and damage to embankments and sluices.[82] Particularly serious were the Broadland floods of 1287, the effects of which were described in some detail by John
of Oxnead.[83] There is, however, no indication that all this led to any interruption
in the exploitation or settlement of the Halvergate Marshes. On the contrary, a
scatter of surviving leases shows that they continued to be valuable property:
such as an agreement of 1323, relating to 'Hilmersh', in the detached portion of
Moulton parish;[84] or the various fifteenth-century leases for 'Swetmans Mersh'
in Thurlton, Newcote in Raveningham, and 'Banyardys', lying partly in both
parishes.[85] Sheep were still being grazed here on a regular basis, rather than
being drifted sporadically across increasingly waterlogged tidal saltings, for there
are references to permanent sheepcotes. Thus when the Abbot of St Benet's leased

Chambers Marsh in Runham to William Paston in 1494 the latter agreed, among other things, to leave at the end of the term the 'cotes belonging to the said marsh . . . sufficiently repaired'.[86] Some medieval farm sites seem to have been abandoned – those discovered by fieldwalking referred to above produced only small quantities of late and post-medieval pottery, suggesting sporadic use rather than regular or permanent occupation. But where – as at Six Mile House – a modern farmstead occupies a medieval site, it is difficult to believe that settlement has not been continuous. Certainly, documentary evidence makes it clear that isolated marsh farms were a normal part of the late medieval landscape. A Norwich Cathedral Dean and Chapter lease from the 1550s for example, concerning the estate in Fowlholme and Skeetholme, refers to the tenants' obligation to 'Maynteyn repare and kepe the reparacion off the howses which be buylded in and upon the premysses in good and sufficient reparacion'.[87]

Although no medieval buildings survive on the marsh, a number of early post-medieval ones do. On Haddiscoe island, for example, Raven Hall (in Langley Detached) is a picturesque thatched building which is probably of early seventeenth-century date, while Seven Mile House in Chedgrave Detached, beside the river Waveney, is unlikely to have been constructed after *c*.1650. Similarly, the western portion of the lost Lockgate Farm near Breydon North Wall was, to judge from surviving photographs, of early seventeenth-century origin.

It is true that Manship, writing in 1619, implies that large areas of the Broadland marshes had been under water in the previous century, for he asserts that the dredging and realignment of the entrance to Yarmouth Haven in 1560 had led to the reclamation of thousands of acres previously subject to regular flooding, rendering them 'useful and valuable' for livestock grazing.[88] Yet the surviving documentary evidence clearly indicates that his account is misleading, and there is certainly no indication in the description of the 'very ritche' marshes in the preamble to the 1609 Sea Breach Commission Act, quoted above, that Halvergate was in need of reclamation from *permanent* inundation.

Nevertheless, much greater attention must now have been paid to flood-defence work. Of course, even in early medieval times, when relative sea level was between one and two metres lower than today, the marshes had been vulnerable to flooding – which explains, of course, why medieval farms were built on low mounds. Even then many areas must have been protected by embankments, and care taken to keep drainage dykes open. But as water levels steadily rose these activities must have been of increasing importance. Barbara Cornford has noted a number of references to the construction of ditches and banks in the account rolls of various Flegg manors in the late thirteenth and fourteenth centuries.[89] A terrier of land in the parish of Horning, dating from the reign of Edward IV, similarly makes a number of references to 'new dykes'.[90] Banks were raised beside the principal watercourses – streams like the Pickerell Holme draining off the upland, major tidal creeks like the Halvergate Fleet, and the principal rivers. Often they were set a little back from the watercourse itself, partly to provide a wide rond which could act as a reservoir to hold water in times of flood, but partly because banks were often – as we shall see – built on top of natural silt banks or *levees*. Their construction, however, seems to have only just kept pace with the rising water levels. In 1625 Mr Briggs, reader in mathematics at the University of Oxford, reported to the Sea Breach Commissioners that the water in the marshes between Horsey, Norwich and Beccles

> doeth run so slowly that it is impossible by an instrument how long soever to discern the difference of the height or how much water doeth fall in any distance of miles . . . the marshes are everywhere little or nothing higher than the rivers, save that in some places the banks defend them.[91]

The Sea Breach Commission was established, as we have seen, following the disastrous floods of 1608. Its purpose was to survey the breaches in the sea defences and, through levying a rate on those who were affected by the flooding, remedy the problem. Sea Breach Commissions were temporary, *ad hoc* bodies, and further commissions were established as need arose, up until the middle of the eighteenth century. There was then a gap of more than half a century before the Commission of Sewers for eastern England – also often referred to as the Sea Breach Commission – was set up in 1802, to deal with the damage caused to the dunes between Horsey and Waxham by the storms of 1791. This body was reconstituted in 1822, 1832, 1844 and 1855, before being made permanent in 1861, under the terms of the Land Drainage Act. It must be emphasised, however, that none of these bodies was directly involved in the instigation of local flood-defence schemes, nor with programmes of marsh drainage (although they might insist on the better maintenance of local drainage works). Their direct activities were limited to the maintenance of the sea defences between Happisburgh and Winterton. The upkeep of river walls, flood banks and drainage dykes was carried out by individual landowners, or by groups of neighbours acting together.[92]

Late medieval and early modern leases were at pains to stipulate the maintenance of drainage works. Thus when in the 1550s the Dean and Chapter of Norwich Cathedral leased out 'All those marshes and pastures called Fowleholme and Sketeholme . . . with all the ditches and stremys Fleetis and Fysshyng to the same marryshes and pastures belonging', the tenant was responsible for 'drawynge skowryng rearyng and matyng [maintaining] off the diches ffences stremes and Fleets and Bridges'.[93] In 1649 the parliamentary surveyors, reporting on the Dean and Chapter's estate on Fowlholme and Skeetholme, estimated the cost of maintaining the banks at 13*s*. 4*d*. per annum.[94] Throughout the post-medieval period, maintenance of flood banks and payment of flood-defence rates were regular sources of dispute between owners and tenants, and between owners and the Sea Breach Commission. In 1715, for example, John Turner 'insisted that he might have an abatement for his Estate in Halvergate and Freethorpe in regard of the charge he was at in keeping upp the Banks against Long Thurston Marshes' (the bid was unsuccessful).[95]

As banks were raised along the margins of the principal watercourses, sluices had to be constructed at the points where these intersected with the main drainage dykes running across the open marsh. These were 'flap sluices', held shut by the pressure of water when the creek or river into which they discharged filled at high tide, and opening to allow the outflow of water when the tide ebbed. Their construction and maintenance, like that of other flood-defence works, was often a co-operative endeavour. A document of 1675, relating to the marshes in Raveningham, thus describes 'The Severall Marshes with theire Quantities which have theire Drayn through the Sluice Lyinge between Glover Denny gent. and Francis Langley and ought to be Chargeable toward the Renewinge and repayers of the Sayd Sluice'. Fourteen different landowners, with holdings ranging in size from 4 to 65 acres, contributed. The total cost was £4. 2s. 6d., the total amount collected – at 6d. per acre – came to £4. 6s. 6d. leaving 4s. 6d. in hand.[96] A similar document records the payments due from the same area of marsh in 1694.[97] This also includes receipts – marked, rather than signed – for the 11s. 6d. 'in full for ye Damming worke to the Sluice', and for the 'use and carriage of ye Planks and Rafters about ye said Sluice'. Another document in the same collection records 'the names of ye Persons for the Repayr of the Head Damm in Norton Subcors' (i.e., Norton Subcourse). The principal of combining in groups to pay for drainage works was, as we shall see, later to be extended to the construction of drainage mills.

The progressive embanking of the rivers did not mean that there were no further alterations to the configuration of land and water in Halvergate. Careful inspection of early maps indicates that in a number of places particularly wide ronds have been narrowed in comparatively recent times, by raising an embankment nearer the river. Thus an estate map of 1820 shows a field to the west of Mautby Marsh Farm called 'Old Rond', some 120 metres wide, separated from the river Bure by an embankment and a much narrower 'New Rond'. Land could be lost as well as gained, however, and in particular there is good evidence that Breydon Water expanded northwards during post-medieval times. Thus in 1742 'Mr Turner's heirs' successfully appealed to the Sea Breach Commission against the rates charged on 160 acres of land in Halvergate, on the grounds that 'twenty acres parsell thereof are nowe some years since swallowed up by Braydon'.[98]

Saved from inundation, the value of the marshes remained, in general, extremely high. In 1674 Clement Paston mortgaged the 350 acres of Postwick Marsh for £3,000,[99] a phenomenal sum, while in 1672 twenty seven acres of marsh ground and a marsh house in Mautby were rented annually for £15.[100] In the same year in Runham seventy acres of marsh ground were rented for £28 a year, while in Short Rack Marshes (on the south side of the Bure) some let for more than £1. 18s. per acre per annum:[101] sums more than double the average rental for East Anglian arable land in the period.

Nevertheless, there are signs that as relative water levels continued to rise some areas of marsh were suffering from excessive waterlogging. This lowered their value, for they became infested with rushes and other coarse herbage. Thus an undated seventeenth-century document describes marshes in the detached portion of South Walsham: 'There are 18 Acr of Marish ground wch are of late much prejudiced for want of drayning and may be improved & made worth 10s per acre but are now let to diverse persons at per annum – £02 .. 00 .. 00.'[102]

It was this slow increase in waterlogging which eventually led to the widespread construction of drainage mills in the course of the eighteenth century, an improvement which served to maintain the high value of the grazing. By 1804 Arthur Young was able to report that many portions of marsh could be let for 30s. per acre per annum (at a time when average rents for grass land were around 20s.);[103] while Bacon in 1844 described how 300 acres of the marsh had recently been sold for no less than £50 per acre.[104]

The marshes thus continued, throughout the post-medieval period, to be a highly valued resource in a part of England in which good-quality pasture was generally in short supply: and as in the Middle Ages, they were used (and often owned) by people living, in some cases, far from the marsh edge. As William Marshall explained in 1787:

> The inclosures, or 'marshes', run from ten to fifteen to forty or fifty acres each; belong to a variety of owners; and are rented by a still greater number of occupiers; almost every farmer, within fifteen or even twenty miles, having his marsh.[105]

Various documents confirm these complex, and sometimes highly fragmented, patterns of ownership and occupancy. The Minute Book of the Sea Breach Commissioners for 1616, for example, shows that the detached block of Freethorpe parish in the heart of the marsh was held in four units averaging nine acres each, the largest seventeen acres, and the situation next door in the detached section of Postwick parish seems to have been similar. In Halvergate parish itself the marsh was held in nineteen blocks, with an average area of about twenty acres: the largest comprised 100 acres, the next largest 35. The detached portion of South Walsham in the core of the marsh was not described in the document – 'neyther content vallewe or owners sett out' – but it was, significantly, stated to be 'in the occupacon of divers men'. The land towards the edge of the marsh, in contrast, often seems to have been occupied, and to some extent owned, in larger blocks. In Mautby, for example, the 448 acres of marsh were held by only nine tenants; while at Runham the 240 acres of marsh were held by five tenants.[106] The lists of contributors to the costs of sea defences drawn up in 1702 and 1715 show a similar pattern, although they record only the proprietors, and not in any detail the occupiers, of land. The list for Halvergate apparently includes the owners of marsh in the neighbouring detached portions of South Walsham and Acle parishes. Twenty-four separate blocks of property are listed here, ranging from the 300 acres of marsh 'called Skeet Holme and Fowle Holme' (now Scaregap Farm) held by one Mr Fachard and occupied by 'George Wells and others' down to portions of eight or ten acres. The average property had an area of just over 61 acres, but this figure was skewed by the Fachard holding, and also by the property of John Turner (160 acres of Great Thurston Marsh) and Mr King (200 acres of the 'Lord Marsh in his own use'): disregarding these the average holding was around 38 acres. Once again there was a tendency for the peripheral portions of marsh to be owned in larger blocks: in Mautby, for example, all the listed marsh was held by the Earl of Yarmouth, the Caister marshes had a single owner, and all the marshes of Stokesby (except six acres belonging to the 'towne of Yarmouth') were owned by one George England.

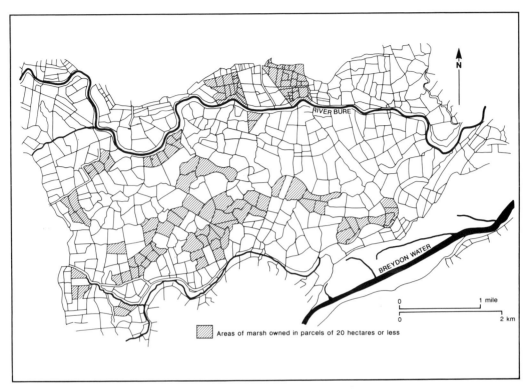

The pattern of land ownership in the northern section of the Halvergate 'triangle', *c*.1840: small landowners (*Source*: tithe award maps).

Figure 14

By *c*.1840, to judge from the Tithe Award maps, both ownership and occupancy in the heart of the marsh were, if anything, even more fragmented (Figures 14 and 15). Tenants generally rented, and landowners often owned, only two or three parcels of marsh. The proprietors, to judge from the evidence both of the Tithe Awards and contemporary Trade Directories, fell into three general categories. The first and smallest consisted, not of private individuals, but of parish churches, for much of the marsh was owned as glebe land: mainly by churches in the City of Norwich, although also by some distant rural parishes, especially in north-eastern Norfolk – places like Sheringham, Tuttington, or Corpusty. Most of this land had been acquired fairly recently, under the provisions of 'Queen Anne's Bounty'. Thus the glebe terrier of St Michael at Plea in Norwich for 1801 records the purchase of 11 acres 3 roods and 3 perches of marsh and 'a certain piece of Rond or coarse Marsh containing five acres one rood and thirteen perches', both part of East Bullen Marsh in the parish of Acle.[107] The second and far larger category of owners comprised small freeholders living in parishes on the periphery of the marsh. The third group was made up of minor gentlemen, most of whom appear to have lived in the immediate neighbourhood.

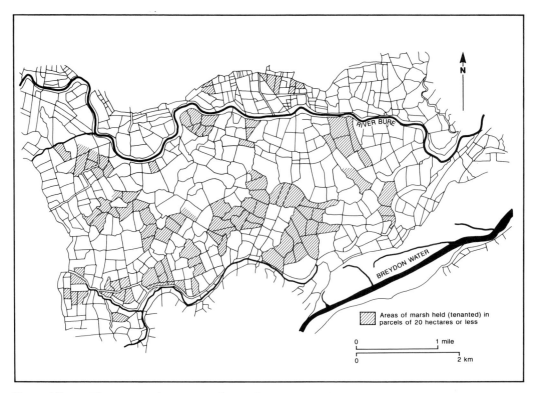

Figure 15   The pattern of tenancy in the northern section of the Halvergate 'triangle', *c.*1840: small
                 occupiers (*Source*: tithe award maps).

By this time, however, there was an even greater tendency for the peripheral
areas of the marsh to be owned in large blocks, partly because when the parliamentary enclosure of the pockets of common land here occurred around 1800
the main beneficiaries were the larger landowners in the parish (Figure 16).
Such consolidated holdings were often owned by individuals who were of some
social standing, and who possessed extensive estates in other parts of Norfolk or
Suffolk: men like Sir Edward Stracey Bart, who owned two large blocks of land
in Tunstall; or Sir Andrew Fountaine, who was Lord of Tunstall Manor, and who
also owned large parts of that parish, but whose seat was at Narford on the
western side of Norfolk. Robert Fellowes, of Shotesham Hall in south Norfolk,
similarly owned most of Mautby Marsh, together with large parts of Halvergate.
Tenancies were also generally more extensive here than out in the core of the
marsh (Figure 17). Some of these compact farms were in the hands of owneroccupiers, some were occupied by tenants of a single owner, some by tenants of
several, but whatever the case the farmer also usually held land on the adjoining
uplands (Figure 18). In contrast, the majority of the small and splintered parcels
out in the core of the marsh were rented by individuals whose names do not
appear in the Tithe Schedules of the marshland parishes. Such people must have

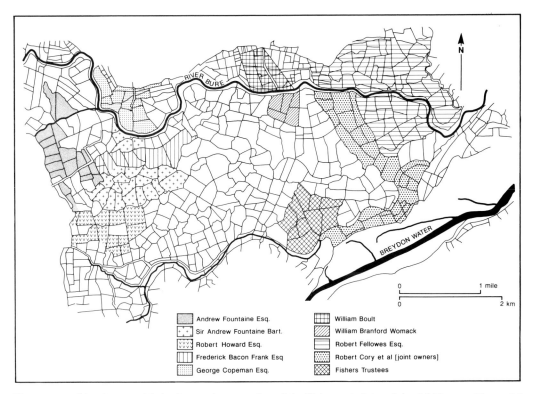

The pattern of land ownership in the northern section of the Halvergate 'triangle', *c.*1840:   Figure 16
large landowners (*Source*: tithe award maps).

lived, and held the main bulk of their land, in parishes located some distance
away from the marsh edge.

The less valuable areas of marsh close to the upland, in other words, were by
the eighteenth and nineteenth centuries exploited as part of integrated arable/
pasture farms, and were perhaps used to some extent for dairying. The splintered
fragments in the distant core, in contrast – where the marsh was of better quality
and more expensive to rent or buy – were used for fattening cattle by farmers
living at a distance, in parishes far from the marsh edge. There was always a
market for good-quality grazing in this predominantly arable county, and ownership or tenancy of a portion of marsh could make a useful contribution to the
farmer's income. Eagerly sought after, the marshes were a useful investment in
an age which lacked secure methods of saving, and an active market and high
land values thus tended to limit the build-up of large, compact estates here. Frag-
mentation of holdings was also, however, encouraged by the practice of partible
inheritance. There are several surviving wills from the seventeenth and eighteenth centuries like that of George Boult (1756), which divided the 'marshes and
ronds' he owned in Acle equally between his two sons, George and William.[108]
This general pattern of splintered ownership has, to some extent, continued into

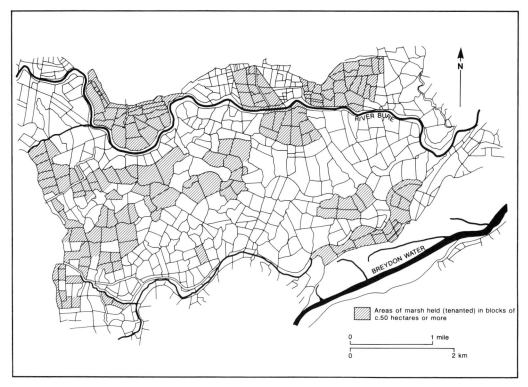

Figure 17   The pattern of tenancy in the northern section of the Halvergate 'triangle', *c*.1840: large
                 occupiers (*Source*: tithe award maps).

modern times, although progressive consolidation has tended to reduce the
number of small isolated units of ownership and occupancy in the core of the
marsh.

The economy of the marsh

In the Middle Ages, as we have seen, sheep were the principal animals grazed on
the marshes, and their bones are prominent among the scatters of debris marking the sites of medieval farms. Even in the Middle Ages, however, other stock
were pastured here. Demesne accounts, such as those from Norwich Cathedral
Priory's Hemsby manor, show that dairy herds were of considerable importance
in the area by the thirteenth century and these animals were almost certainly
grazed on the edge of the marsh. In the thirteenth century the Cathedral manors
of Martham, Scratby and Hemsby sent horses and bullocks to graze with the
sheep on the marsh at Fowlholme, while oxen also seem to have been pastured
in some places.[109] Nevertheless, there is no doubt that in the thirteenth and
fourteenth centuries sheep generally predominated. By the sixteenth century, in

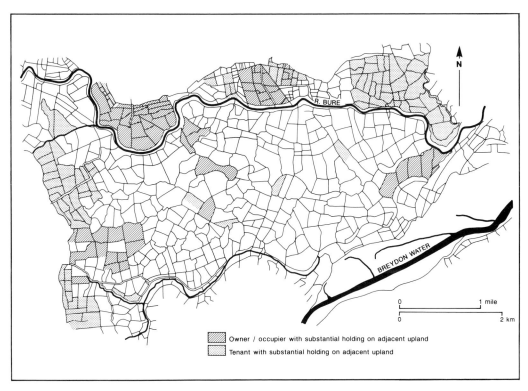

R. BURE

BREYDON WATER

N

0   1 mile

0   2 km

Owner / occupier with substantial holding on adjacent upland

Tenant with substantial holding on adjacent upland

The northern section of the Halvergate 'triangle': types of farming enterprise, *c*.1840 (*Source*: tithe award maps).   Figure 18

contrast – to judge from the evidence of probate inventories – cattle seem to have been the most important stock kept by the farmers living in parishes around the marsh. Typical was Nicholas Bishop of Halvergate, who owned at his death in 1589 16 'neates', 16 yearlings, three steers and a 'bolle'; or John Dymonde who died the following year owning, among other stock, '5 bullockes boughte at Hopton fayre', together with '3 milche neate and a bull'.[110] The change from sheep to cattle does not appear to reflect any great alteration in the environment of the marshes themselves. Rather, it was part of a more general development in the economy of east Norfolk in the fourteenth an fifteenth centuries: manorial accounts generally show a gradual decline in the size of sheep and dairy herds, and an increasing interest in fattening cattle, a trend which culminated in the early modern period. It was, nevertheless, a pattern paralleled in other areas of coastal marsh in England. In the Lincolnshire Fens, and on the Somerset Levels, farmers were also increasingly specialising in cattle fattening and, to a lesser extent, dairying during the fifteenth and sixteenth centuries.[111]

By the early seventeenth century the system which was to be the mainstay of the marsh economy for the next three centuries was already in place. Young cattle, two or three years old, were brought to Norfolk by drovers from the northern and western areas of Britain – especially Skye, Galloway and the Highlands of Scotland, but also to some extent from Ireland – and were sold to farmers at local fairs, such as those at Horsham St Faiths or Harleston. Most of the purchasers were not specialised graziers, but arable farmers: bullock-rearing was an adjunct to cereal production. In the winter the cattle were stalled in yards on the upland farms and fed on turnips; in the summer months they were grazed on the marshes. They were fattened for between a year and eighteen months before being sold in Norwich or London. Defoe in 1722 referred to the 'prodigious number of black cattle', mostly Scots 'runts', on the marsh, which 'Feed so eagerly on the rich pasture of the marshes, that they thrive in an unusual manner, and grow monstrously fat: and the beef is so delicious for taste, that the inhabitants prefer 'em to the English cattle . . .'.[112]

Marshall in 1787 described the stock on the marshes as 'principally young cattle, lean "Scots", and old and young horses. There are, nevertheless, a considerable number of fatting bullocks, and some sheep.' Bacon in 1844 also mentions sheep, but cattle were still unquestionably the most important animals. He describes how locally bred animals, Scots and Irish cattle were all grazed there, the two latter purchased at the Harleston and St Faiths fairs, and at 'other country fairs'.[113]

This predominance of cattle, and especially of stores brought in from Scotland and Ireland, continued into the twentieth century. Mosby in 1938 noted that the proportion of sheep grazed on the marsh was small in proportion to the numbers of horses and cattle. Some dairy cattle were kept, on the periphery of the marsh and by the marshmen dwelling in the interior, but the most important stock were now:

> Irish short-horned cattle . . . bought in the Norwich market and turned out to graze on the marshes. The grass feed is augmented with a small amount of cake. These Irish cattle thrive straight away on the outdoor feeding of the marshes. They make good shape and progress and fetch good prices from the local and London butchers. Scotch Angus (polled) are good stock, but by no means so numerous as the Irish store cattle. English cattle are also grazed here: on the whole they are inferior to the Irish and Scotch, but Devon and Cumberland cattle are quite good.[114]

At the time Mosby was writing, Canadian and Welsh cattle had recently been introduced on to the marsh, although the former were 'rather wild' and had given the marshmen some trouble. These sources all suggest that there was remarkably little change in the economy of Halvergate from the seventeenth to the twentieth century, except that Irish replaced Scots as the principal stock during the nineteenth century. There was also some expansion of dairying here in the 1920s and 1930s. In the 1960s, however, rising transport costs led to a decline in the numbers of Irish shorthorns grazed on the marsh, and their replacement by locally bred Frisian stores.[115] The names given to the various marshes on Tithe Award and other maps clearly reflect the predominance of cattle in the local economy. The name 'Sheeps Marsh' occasionally occurs (the Tunstall Tithe Award records two) but far more common were names like 'Cow Marsh' (as in

Postwick, Acle, Runham, and Stokesby (where there were two)); 'Cow Gate Marsh' (Acle); 'Bullock Marsh' (two in Stokesby); or 'Great Bullock' and 'Little Bullock Marsh' (Postwick).

The earliest comprehensive account of the management of the marshes is that provided by Marshall in 1787. He describes how tenants rented portions of marsh on an annual basis. They turned the stock out onto them in the spring, as soon as they were free from surface water, and kept them there until 'water, or the severity of the weather' obliged them to take them off. Marshall also provides information about the quality of the marsh grazing. This was rather variable: some areas were poached and tussocky, others much better:

> For the individual marshes are far from being level; they being more or less scooped
> out into hollows; where the water lodges a considerable time after the higher parts
> are dry. On these grows a rich luxuriant herbage, composed of the choicest meadow-
> grasses; while on the moister parts grows a long wiry kind of grass, which I think the
> marshmen call 'flat', and which the cattle are very fond of.[116]

The marshes continued to be let annually into the present century: indeed, many portions still are. Eighteenth and nineteenth-century leases often contained stipulations intended to conserve the quality of the grassland. As Marshall says, grazing was usually limited to the summer months – often to the period between 1 May and 24 October – in order to prevent 'poaching' (i.e., the creation of bare muddy patches), and stocking densities were carefully regulated, generally restricted to five sheep, one fat bullock, or two neat stock per acre. In addition, many leases either forbade, or restricted, the cutting of hay, in order to preserve the luxuriance of the herbage. Thus when Mautby New Farm was leased in 1825 the tenant agreed not to 'cut or mow any part of the meadow or marsh land . . . without the consent in writing of the Lessor',[117] while in 1891 the tenant of Scaregap Farm had the option of mowing only certain portions of the marsh, and was not permitted to cut any part twice.[118] Such limitations did not, however, apply to the ronds, which were traditionally cut for reeds and hay.

The splintered pattern of ownership and landholding in the centre of the marsh posed a number of problems in managing livestock. Access could be difficult. The place now known as Runham Swim on the river Bure takes its name from the fact that cows were swum over the river at this point in order to avoid a lengthy walk, as well as the tolls due on the Yarmouth New Road: there was a hard bottom to the river here, which was gravelled every year. Not every area of the marsh was separately served by a public right of way – or at least, there were grounds for doubting the legal status of particular droves – and disputes over access are recorded as early as 1599 concerning the movement of cattle through areas of Halvergate Marsh to Acle 'Estmarsh'.[119] Sometimes leases contained stipulations regarding rights of access. Thus a mid sixteenth-century Norwich Dean and Chapter lease concerning 'all that marsh or pasture called Sketeholm marsh' refers to the tenants' rights of 'egresse and regresse through their marsh called Fowleholme with their cattal at all times convenient'.[120]

Above all, remoteness and the fragmented pattern of landholding explain the vital importance of the marshmen in the local economy. They had long been a familiar feature – the medieval marsh houses known from documentary and archaeological evidence must have had men to live in them – and a 1580 survey of Stergott Marsh, the remote detached portion of Postwick parish, states that the bounds had been given by Thomas Harvey and John Daymes, specifically described as 'bothe marsh men'.[121] But the work and lifestyle of such individuals are first described in detail by Marshall in 1787:

> The stock are under the care of *marshmen*, who live in cottages scattered over the Marshes: – each having his district, or 'level of marshes', to look after. His perquisite is a shilling upon the pound-rent, which is sometimes paid by the landlord but more generally by the tenant.[122]

The marshmen also kept their own cows, which picked about in the ronds during the summer, and which were fed on the mowings from the ronds in winter. They made butter and sold it in Yarmouth. This pattern of existence changed little over the next century and a half. In the 1930s, Mosby described how

> The marshmen are a hardy and independent folk, but there are only about 20 left in the Broadland marshes. Almost every marshman inherits his job, and certain areas have been in the hands of one family for many generations. One marshman may look after as many as 1,000 acres of marshes. During the grazing season he looks after the cattle of a number of different owners, and this keeps him very busy for he counts the cattle every day and sorts them out if need be. On occasion he treats the animals for minor complaints . . . The marshman gets 3s. 6d. per acre for looking after the cattle during the season from April to October, and in the winter he is busy repairing fences and gateways, cutting and 'croming' drains, 'bottomfying', etc. . . . The marshman lives near his work . . . His cottage is often miles away from a town or village.[123]

Surviving accounts kept by Thomas Crisp, marshman for the Beauchamp-Proctor estate on the Hardley Marshes, record in considerable detail the marshman's work of cutting drains, 'slubbing' dykes, repairing the river walls, renewing old sluices and constructing new ones, and tending the drainage mill.[124] But as well as keeping livestock, and carrying out routine maintenance, the marshmen were traditionally involved in exploiting the abundant wildlife of the area – shooting a variety of wildfowl, and fishing:

> When the eels are 'running', he sleeps during the day, and is to be found by the riverside or at some dyke-mouth at night, busy with a sluice-net or sett. In winter, when he drives his cart to the nearest market-town, it is as likely to contain mallard as to be laden with pigs and poultry.[125]

The number of isolated marsh houses declined gradually in the course of the twentieth century (a number, including the Acle Marsh House, had already disappeared during the nineteenth) but the characteristic lifestyle of their inhabitants survived into the 1950s and 1960s. The *Yarmouth Mercury* in 1950 described Lockgate Farm, near Breydon North Wall, as 'One of the most isolated houses in

Norfolk, where . . . life is a hundred years behind the times . . . It has no electricity, modern plumbing or radio, and no newspapers or mail are ever delivered.'[126] The marshman here, Gordon Addison, still kept horses, cows, pigs, chickens, ducks and geese. Following his death in 1967, the house stood empty and vandalised until finally demolished in 1981.[127] Others suffered the same fate, and by 1970 it was reported that 'all but one' of the marsh farms in the Halvergate 'triangle' stood 'empty and derelict'.[128] But this was an exaggeration. Certainly, although a number have, like Lockgate Farm, been demolished in relatively recent years, a dozen or so isolated houses till survive out on the marsh, although few are now used for their original purpose.

Traditionally, then, the Halvergate Marshes had an economy geared to grazing, and in particular to bullock-fattening. The essential nature of this economy seems to have been maintained, with little change, from the early seventeenth century into the twentieth. However, there is some evidence to suggest that portions of the marsh were, at various times in the past, ploughed as arable. There is no hint of such landuse in the surviving medieval documents; but there are a number of post-medieval references. Thus Armstrong in 1781, noting that the marshes were 'exceedingly profitable' and used to feed sheep and cattle, added that they 'sometimes, when ploughed, afford greater crops of corn than any other land'.[129] In 1803 a marshman reported that marshes near Yarmouth had been so much damaged by salt-water flooding in the 1780s 'that they have not since been ploughed', and that other pieces of marshland 'in this part of the district were also cultivated prior to the great Flood which was occasioned by overflowing of the Sea at Horsey'.[130] The Enclosure Award for Runham in 1802 refers to a boundary in the detached section of the parish 'taking in about an acre of an arable marsh' near Southtown in Yarmouth.[131] Landlords generally tried to prohibit ploughing. A valuation of the Dean and Chapter's lands on Fowlholme and Skeetholme Marshes in 1790 noted:

> These marshes lye in thirty nine pieces every one of which I viewed separately some of them I found sown & Query? can Lessee breake them up without consent of the Lessors they ought to be Covenanted against it under a penalty of five Pounds an Acre for every Acre yearly so converted into Tilth.[132]

A lease for New Farm Mautby in 1825 stipulated that the lessee was not to 'plough or otherwise break up any of the pasture or marsh ground'.[133] In 1833, however, a letter to Robert Fellowes, also concerning land in Mautby, noted:

> It was my intention, provided you had no objection, to break twelve or fifteen Acres of the meadows, as I have a great many Marshes, and I also know by ploughing them a few years and laying them down again with good Grass Seeds it will greatly improve them.

The temptation to plough was obviously greatest at times when grain prices were particularly high, and it is probable that the period of the Napoleonic Wars (1793–1815) saw the greatest extent of arable conversion. In a number of places on the marsh, faint traces of ploughing are preserved in the turf and it is probable that most date to this period, although arable landuse continued sporadically into the nineteenth century. A few areas of arable land, generally towards the periphery of the marsh, appear on the Tithe Award maps of *c.*1840. Bacon in 1844 reported that several sections of the marsh were under the plough, and suggested that since the commutation of the tithes, the area of arable was gradually being extended: previously, the higher tithe charge imposed on arable had discouraged conversion. He nevertheless believed that their value as grazing grounds was such that 'the largest portion will in all probability never be touched by the plough'.[134] Arable farming indeed remained a minor aspect of the economy throughout the rest of the century, and the great agricultural depression which set in from the late 1870s saw an end to ploughing. Mosby in the 1930s noted how

> Up to about 50 years ago quite a number of the marshes grew crops of mangolds, wheat and oats, but, with the exception of a few areas in the immediate neighbourhood of Yarmouth and Horsey there is no arable land now.[135]

Only in the very different circumstances of the 1970s and 1980s were large areas of the marsh deep-drained, and converted to arable: with disastrous consequences for both landscape and wildlife.

Reading the marshland landscape

At first sight the landscape of Halvergate has a simple and somewhat repetitive quality: one water-filled dyke, one area of close-cropped marsh, looks much the same as another. But from the air, or on a map, the complex variety in the pattern of dykes soon becomes apparent: a variety born of the long history of land use and settlement on the marsh.

The recent history of the dyke network can be examined using a range of post-medieval maps. Almost the whole of the Halvergate area is shown on the Tithe Award maps produced in the late 1830s/1840s. The pattern of dykes which these depict is, in general terms, very similar to that which still exists in the non-arable areas of the marsh today. But there are a number of places where the pattern has subsequently been modified. Figures 19 and 20 show the extent of such changes in the northern part of the Halvergate 'triangle' in the period up to *c.*1970. Alterations were most extensive in the south-western corner of Halvergate parish, in parts of Thurston Level in the same parish, and in the area of Freethorpe Detached near the North Wall of Breydon Water. Most occurred between *c.*1840 and *c.*1880, when the First Edition 6 inch OS maps were surveyed. These modifications involved both the creation of new dykes and the realignment of old ones. In addition, in a few places, dykes were filled in or silted up, presumably rendered redundant by improvements in, or alterations to, the system of drainage.

There are a small number of detailed maps showing parts of these same marshes which pre-date the Tithe surveys of *c.*1840.[136] All show a pattern of dykes which

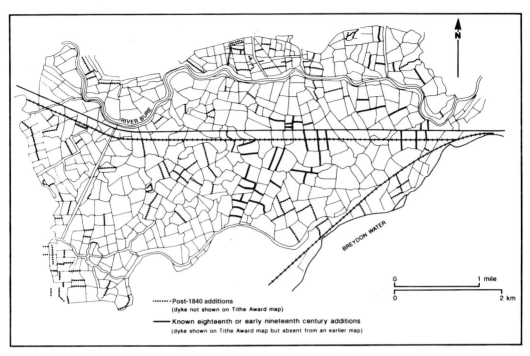

The northern section of the Halvergate 'triangle': known additions to the pattern of marsh   Figure 19
dykes up to *c*.1970 (*Source*: tithe award maps, estate maps).

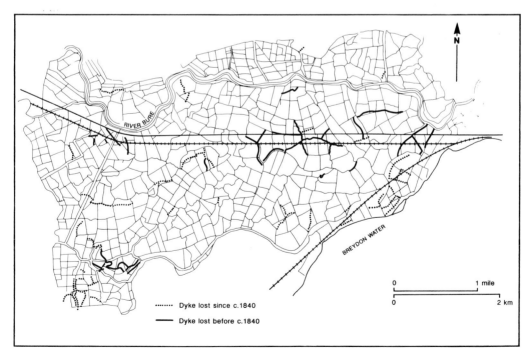

The northern section of the Halvergate 'triangle': known losses from the pattern of marsh   Figure 20
dykes (*Source*: tithe award maps, estate maps).

is generally similar to that depicted on the latter, although again there are a number of differences in detail (Figures 19 and 20). In other words, with the exception of those peripheral areas of the marsh enclosed by parliamentary Act in the late eighteenth and early nineteenth centuries, the dyke pattern on Halvergate has developed gradually over time, with numerous piecemeal additions and alterations.

Such changes are sporadically referred to in letters and documents relating to the management of estates on the marsh. In 1825, for example, Robert Fellowes of Shotesham was informed by his agent:

> I have taken . . . view of your Halvergate Estate and I find every thing is in good order and going on in a proper manner except some small drains is wanted to be cut in the different Marshes, this will be of great use to take the water from the marshes.

While in 1876 the tenant of the Dean and Chapter lands at Scaregap Farm informed his landlords that he was '. . . improving the main drain and others . . . filling in Old Drains now quite dry . . . made dry by my engine'.[137]

Bearing in mind this pattern of gradual, piecemeal change, it is useful to categorise the marsh dykes on the basis of their particular form. Some cannot be placed in any clear category, but most fall into three or four distinct groups. Firstly, there are a small number of long, continuous dykes which cross the marsh in straight lines or smooth curves. These terminate at drainage mills standing beside major watercourses, and were clearly dug when these were first erected on the marsh from the late seventeenth century. Good examples of such 'mill drains' can be seen leading across Halvergate Marsh towards Mutton's Mill, near Manor Farm; or running across Reedham Marshes to the complex of mills near Seven Mile House.

In the second category there are a large number of very straight dykes, their rigidly geometric quality proclaiming a comparatively recent origin (Plate 9). These are particularly noticeable on the fringes of the marsh, where they usually result from the parliamentary enclosure of former areas of common which, as we have seen, were clustered here in pockets of wet and peaty soils. They are, however, also more generally scattered across the interior of the marsh. Indeed, the majority of marsh dykes probably fall into this category (Figure 21). All those seventeenth- and eighteenth-century additions to the dyke network revealed by the map evidence just described take this form. There can be little doubt that most of the undated examples are similarly of late medieval or post-medieval date, improvements made to the original pattern of drainage.

The latter was clearly based on a third category of marsh dyke – serpentine, curvilinear watercourses which originated as natural channels draining across the marshes before any form of embanking had taken place (Plate 10 and Figure 22). These are survivors from the rather denser pattern of natural watercourses which, as already noted, now exists only as a network of shallow indentations in the marsh turf. Some of these lost watercourses lie close to, and seem to form more sinuous and earlier versions of, dykes of the 'linear' type just discussed.

Typical linear dyke, Halvergate Marshes.   Plate 9

These, in other words, are often the result of tidying up and straightening elements of the natural drainage system.

The 'survivors' from the original pattern have a number of interesting characteristics. The majority form parish boundaries, or the boundaries of individual 'levels'. These, presumably, being the boundaries of embanked areas (and often important boundaries in their own right), were less easily altered than those dykes lying *within* such areas. The latter could be modified and straightened over the centuries in order to improve drainage: the 'boundary' dykes, in contrast, could not be adjusted so easily and thus retained their original, irregular, form.

Of particular interest are those curvilinear dykes which mark the courses of the larger creeks and channels which once ebbed and flowed across the salt marsh. Only one of these has survived as a recognisable feature of the landscape. As already noted, the Halvergate Fleet is today only a minor watercourse, but it runs between broad ronds separated by embankments from the surrounding marshes. The 'wall' on its northern side is followed by a track, the Fleet road, which before the construction of the 'Acle Straight' turnpike in the 1830s formed the main routeway across the marshes to Yarmouth. The Fleet Dyke and its flanking ronds cross the marsh in a number of bold, broad curves, in a manner reminiscent of the principal rivers in the area. Today, it turns abruptly southwards at TG 476071, flowing into Breydon Water through Breydon Sluice.

Figure 21   The distribution of linear dykes in the Halvergate 'triangle'.

Typical curvilinear dyke, Halvergate Marshes.   Plate 10

To the west of this point, it forms the parish boundary between Reedham Detached and Beighton Detached: to the east the long, boldly sinuous parish boundary between Freethorpe Detached and Halvergate, and Freethorpe Detached and Acle Detched, seems to continue the line, running roughly parallel to the edge of Breydon Water. This was also the route taken by the old Yarmouth road. There seems little doubt that the road and parish boundary together preserve the old course of the Fleet, before it was diverted southwards at some unknown date.

Marshall in 1787 described how

> The Marshes, taken collectively, are, though nearly *level*, not perfectly *smooth*; being furrowed into inequalities by swamps; which, in their natural state, seem to have been the main drains of the mud-banks. These swamps, or 'reed-ronds', in some places of considerable width, are now the main drains to the Marshes; from the grassy drier parts of which they are detached by banks of soil; which at once serve the purposes of roads, fences and embankments.

The phrase 'in some places of considerable width' suggests that other broad ronds, former creeks like the Halvergate Fleet, still existed at this time. A map of a property in the detached portion of South Walsham parish, made in 1768, shows one example (Figure 23).[138] The property was bounded to the south by the wall and

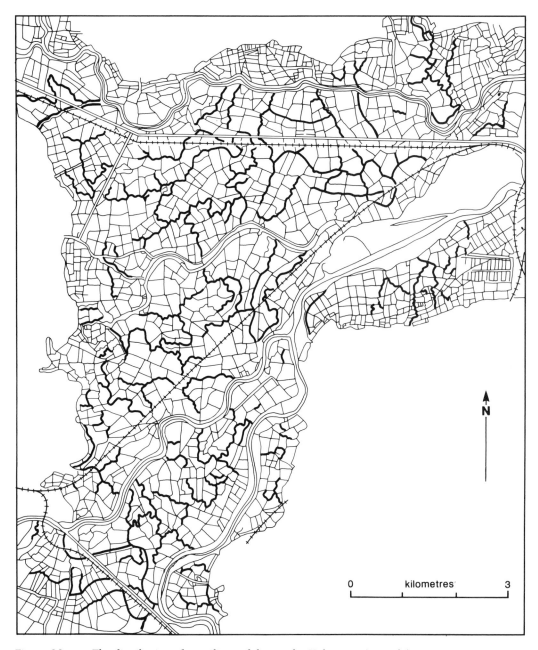

Figure 22   The distribution of curvilinear dykes in the Halvergate 'triangle'.

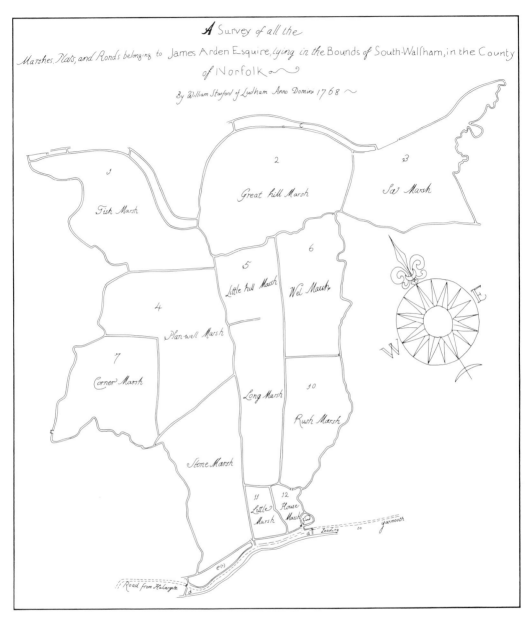

A Survey of all the
Marshes, Flats, and Ronds belonging to James Arden Esquire, lying in the Bounds of South-Walsham, in the County
of Norfolk
By William Stowford of Ludham Anno Domini 1768

Estate map showing marshland in the detached section of South Walsham parish, 1768.   Figure 23
The south of the property is bounded by the Halvergate Fleet and its ronds. The north is
bounded by another substantial rond, which has since disappeared.

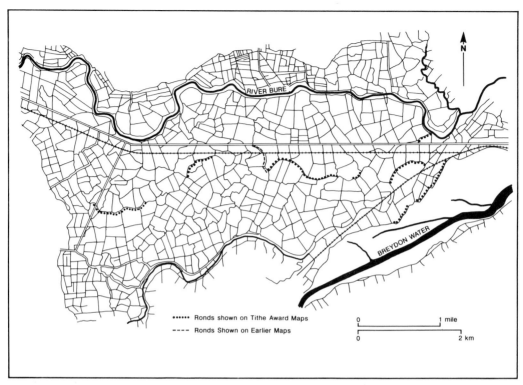

Figure 24   The northern section of the Halvergate 'triangle': lost 'ronds'.

rond of the Halvergate Fleet: and to the north by another rond, which has not survived. There are no maps of similar antiquity showing the adjoining areas, but the distribution of 'rond' names on the Tithe Award maps shows that this was still a recognisable feature of the landscape as late as *c*.1840 (Figure 24). This *Northern Rond*, to coin a name, is now only followed by minor dykes. As in the case of the lost eastern continuation of the Halvergate Fleet, its embankments have been levelled and its ronds amalgamated with the adjoining portions of marsh – although its line, or perhaps more accurately the line of the natural channel from which it developed, can still be followed on aerial photographs. Other similar features – with widely spaced ronds, and substantial embankments – seem to have survived into the eighteenth century in a number of places within the Halvergate 'triangle'.

The 'walls' or embankments which confine the ronds of the Halvergate Fleet, and those of the main rivers flowing across the marsh, are usually interpreted simply as man-made embankments, and so indeed they are in large measure. But a number of distinctive characteristics suggest that they are partly natural. It is noteworthy that the walls were the chosen location for most marsh farms: not only the surviving examples, but many of the lost ones (like Acle Marsh House, beside the lost Northern Rond) were built on them. As we have seen, Six

Mile House in Halvergate parish stands on a medieval mound which has been incorporated into the river wall: the mound, that is, *pre-dates* the embankment, which has been raised around it. These features suggest that the walls originated as banks of firmer, and slightly higher, ground within the level marsh, which were later heightened by man. The ronds which they confine would originally have been tidal, and would have filled and overflowed at high tide. The heavier particles of silt and stone suspended in the water would not have been carried far from the channel, but would instead have been deposited as *levées*, strips of ground slightly firmer than the surrounding sediments. When water levels fell during Saxon times the drying out of the marsh would have made these stand slightly higher than the adjacent ground: obvious sites for habitations, and – at a later date – obvious bases on which to raise embankments.

Halvergate thus has a long history. Like all landscapes it is the product of a complex interplay between man and nature. Some of its history can be reconstructed from old documents and maps: but much can be read from the landscape itself, from the intricate pattern of dyke and drain, rond and wall, road and farm. We can be truly thankful that – so far – the grants and subsidies available through the Environmentally Sensitive Areas scheme has preserved much of this ancient landscape from destruction, so that future generations can continue to enjoy the endless green panoramas under that boundless Norfolk sky.

4

The landscape of the valleys

Introduction

The wide, lonely marshes of the former estuary between Acle and Yarmouth have a striking and distinctive landscape. Yet it is the scenery encountered higher up the rivers that the majority of visitors find most appealing, and which they remember as the 'real' Norfolk Broadland. Here, too, some areas of flat drained marshland can be found. But in addition most of the valleys contain stands of damp, tangled woodland, extensive tracts of undrained fen, and the 'broads' themselves – the lakes from which the region takes it name (Plate 11).

The relative proportions of these various kinds of landscape vary markedly from valley to valley, each of which has, to a large extent, its own distinctive character and history. In the Waveney valley, drained marshland predominates; in the valley of the Ant, in contrast, vast areas of fen and carr occur. One key to this complex variety lies in the diverse range of soils which the valleys contain. In essence, these fall into three broad categories. A minority are similar in general character to those found in the central parts of the Halvergate 'triangle': that is, they are formed in deposits of estuarine silt and clay, and are non-acidic. Such soils occur in the lower reaches of the valleys of the Bure, Waveney and Yare, and throughout much of the valley of the Thurne, including its higher reaches. More significant in creating the distinctive character of the valley landscapes, however, are soils developed in peat or, in places, in a mixture of clay and peat. Such soils are much the same as those which we have noted occurring in small pockets around the edges of the Halvergate 'triangle': but in the upper reaches of the river valleys they are much more widespread and extensive. They dominate the Waveney valley above Burgh St Peter and Oulton dyke, the Yare valley between the confluence with the Chet and Brundall, that of the Bure between St Benet's Abbey and Horning, and almost the whole length of the valleys of the Ant and the Chet. Lastly, and of less significance, are small areas of soils which, while essentially based on peat, are – somewhat unusually – alkaline rather than acid in character, owing to the nature of the ground water percolating through them from springs rising in the adjacent chalk. Such soils occur above Horning in the Bure valley, above Brundall on the Yare, and sporadically

Wroxham Broad from the air (Derek Edwards, Norfolk Landscape Archaeology).   Plate 11

in the Ant valley. The distinction between acid and alkaline peat has a major impact on the natural history of the valley mires, but its effect on landscape history is more muted: the real difference is between the silt/clay deposits, and the peat.

Sailing or cruising along the rivers, this difference is often very marked. Whereas, for the most part, the silts and clays now carry a landscape broadly similar to that of the Halvergate 'triangle' – essentially, one of drained marshland – the areas of peat are often dominated by much damper and wilder scenery. It is here that the wet woodland or 'carr' of alder and willow occurs; that the extensive beds of reed and sedge can be found; and that the 'broads' themselves are located (Plate 12). The contrast between these two kinds of landscape is very clear, for example, passing up the Bure beyond St Benet's. Before the gaunt ruins of the medieval gatehouse are reached, the landscape is open, with wide panoramas in all directions. A little upstream of the abbey, woodland closes in: channels lead off on either side to broads – South Walsham, Ranworth, Decoy, Hoveton – which are themselves surrounded by carr and reed beds.

Plate 12   View across Catfield Fen. This extensive areas of reed and sedge beds is now managed as
                a nature reserve.

Changes to the river system

In spite of its sometimes wild and primeval appearance, the landscape of the
upper valleys is as man-made as that of the Halvergate Marshes. Indeed, even
the courses of the rivers are in several places artificial. This is especially true of
the Ant, the Bure and the Thurne. Some changes occurred in comparatively recent
times, and can be traced on successive maps. Thus the old course of the river Ant
to the south of Wayford Bridge ('A'–'B' on Figure 25) is shown on William Faden's
county map of 1797, but not on the Stalham Enclosure map of 1807.[139] Most
diversions, however, were made in the remote past, and are only revealed by the
configuration of parish or hundred boundaries. These often followed major
watercourses, and where diversions have subsequently been made they now run
along obscure streams and dykes, with the river following a different course tens
or even hundreds of metres away. Thus the line of the boundary between Happing
and Tunstead hundreds clearly shows that the river Ant originally 'by-passed'
Barton Broad, flowing a little to the east ('C'–'D' on Figure 25). Today it runs in
at the northern end of the broad, and out at the southern. Moreover, the line of
the hundred boundary to the south of the broad shows that the river originally
skirted the eastern edge of Catfield Fen, rather than following its present course

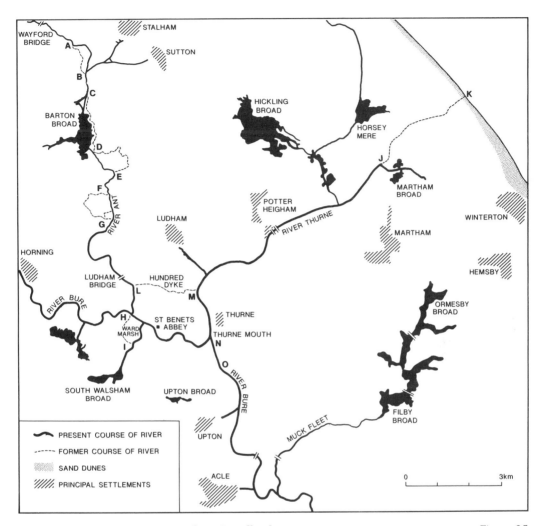

Changes to the river system in northern Broadland.   Figure 25

further to the west, through its centre ('D'–'E' on Figure 25); and that it once flowed to the west, rather than through the middle, of Reedham Marsh ('F'–'G' on Figure 25: there is another early course of the river here, a short loop opposite How Hill which is marked as 'Old River' on the Ludham Enclosure map).[140] Most striking of all, immediately to the east of Ant Mouth a ruler-straight stretch some 500 metres long cuts off the long loop once followed by the Bure around the south of Ward Marsh. It is the old course, rather than the new, which is still followed by the boundary between Walsham and Tunstead hundreds ('H'–'I'). Most of these alterations were probably carried out to improve navigation, although precisely when in the medieval or post-medieval period remains unclear. The last mentioned diversion, at least, had been achieved by the early seventeenth century, and the fact that a document of 1617 appears to refer to this stretch of the Bure not as the river, but as 'Ward Dyke', perhaps suggests that it was not then of any great antiquity.[141]

All these changes are relatively minor, however, compared with those which occurred in early medieval times to the course of the river Thurne, and to the lower reaches of the Ant. Today the Thurne drains southwards: collecting water from the marshes in the Hickling and Horsey area, and from the adjoining uplands of Flegg and Happing, it joins the Bure at Thurne Mouth. In the remote past, however, some at least of its water appears to have flowed *north*, entering the sea between Winterton and Horsey.[142] In prehistoric times it discharged into an open estuary, but at an early date – probably before Romano-British times – its mouth became blocked by the accumulation of a substantial sand spit (as was later to happen with the larger Halvergate estuary). Although an outfall here continued to exist, this was sufficiently constricted for areas of fresh-water fen to survive over extensive areas of the former estuary, at no great distance from the sea. The river's course in early medieval times is preserved by the line of the Hundred Stream ('J'–'K' on Figure 25), so called because it formed the boundary between the hundreds of Happing and West Flegg. Today this no longer has any connection with the sea, and is a very minor watercourse, although still bounded by wide ronds and banks: for at some unknown date in the Middle Ages its outfall was finally extinguished by the ongoing accumulation of sand, and its waters redirected southwards, towards Thurne Mouth.

Some of the water flowing through this northern outfall of the Thurne was derived from the river Ant. To the south of Ludham Bridge this river once flowed in a continuous line eastward to join the Thurne a kilometre above Thurne Dyke ('L'–'M'), rather than – as today – turning somewhat abruptly to the south. The relative modernity of the present course is indicated by the fact that the river here does not form a parish boundary, but rather runs right through the middle of the marshland portion of the parish of Horning. The old course, in contrast – in a direct parallel with the situation at the northern end of the Thurne – survives as a watercourse, again flanked by wide ronds, called the Hundred Dyke. This forms both the parish boundary between Ludham and Horning and the hundredal boundary between Happing and Tunstead (Figure 25).

Were the changes in the courses of the lower Ant and the Thurne connected? It is possible that they were. As the outfall of the Thurne became increasingly blocked by the accumulation of sand at its mouth, flooding would have increased in both the lower and in the higher reaches of the river. By diverting the flow of the Ant southwards, into the Bure, the volume of water flowing down the Thurne would have been considerably reduced. Such a change could well have been effected by the monks of St Benet's Abbey, the site of which lies close to both the new and the old courses of the Ant. The abbey had much to lose from increased flooding in the Thurne valley, having extensive properties in Martham, Waxham, Winterton, Ludham and Thurne, and minor holdings elsewhere. Monastic involvement in large-scale drainage and water-management schemes is attested from other marshland areas in early medieval England. The diversion of the Ant would have been a fairly minor affair, compared with the kinds of scheme carried out by Glastonbury Abbey in the Somerset Levels, or by Ramsey or Ely in the Cambridgeshire Fenlands.

It is just possible that an even more radical change in the natural drainage pattern of this area occurred during medieval times. Before the Thurne's outfall into the sea became blocked it may have taken not only the waters of the Ant, but also those of the *Bure*: that is, the Thurne may at this time have been the lower course of the Bure. One indication of this is the curious configuration of waterways in the vicinity of Thurne mouth. Examined on a map, or indeed on the ground, the Bure here appears to flow *into* the Thurne, in a smooth curve. Its course below Thurne Mouth ('N'–'O' on Figure 25), in contrast, is ruler-straight for 1 km and looks remarkably artificial. The river here passes through a fairly constricted section of valley, containing at least one small 'island' and – to the south – extensive peat deposits. It is perhaps possible, then, that the lower course of what is now the Bure, across the northern edge of Halvergate Marshes, was at this time a tidal creek, into which the Muck Fleet, the stream draining the interior of the 'island' of Flegg, discharged (although in a still earlier period, of course, the Bure may have flowed across the north of Halvergate: there will have been many changes in the course of the rivers). If there *was* a time in the early Middle Ages when Bure and Thurne were one, then the problems caused by the closure of the latter's northern outfall would have been severe indeed: diverting the waters of the Bure along a new straight cut below Thurne Mouth, and thus into an existing channel to the south, would have been an effective way of alleviating flooding. There are, however, a number of serious problems with this suggestion, not least the fact that the ronds bordering the Hundred Stream are of no very great width, much narrower than the modern Bure in its lower reaches. However, as land/sea levels in the early Middle Ages were more than a metre lower than today, the river would have been faster-flowing and its channel correspondingly narrower – especially if, as suggested earlier, the degree of tidal penetration was limited by a constricted outfall. Certainly, the complex history of the northern rivers, and especially that of the Thurne, still needs to be elucidated.

The traditional economy

Whereas the broad expanses of marsh in the Halvergate 'triangle' had for the most part always been held as private property, in the upper valleys the situation was very different. Here the majority of the land – whether on silts and clays, or on peat – remained as common until well into the post-medieval period. In legal terms, common land belonged to the lord of the manor in which it lay, but the local inhabitants enjoyed certain rights over it.[143] They could use it for grazing, and could harvest a range of natural products from it. Normally the exploitation of common land was controlled by a manorial court, and because it was used by groups of people in this way it could not be physically subdivided by hedges and

fences. Common rights were allotted to the inhabitants in various ways in different Broadland parishes, but were always jealously guarded. In some, rights were
attached to particular properties, but in many (especially in Flegg) all parishion-
ers enjoyed their use. In the case of Beccles, the right to turn animals out onto
the common fen was restricted to those who were 'an householder and dweller
within the saide towne that payeth taske to the king', and the number of animals
that could be pastured was related to the amount of 'taske' or tax which the
householder paid.[144]

Many areas of common land – especially those occupying the silt deposits –
were primarily used as grazing marsh. But others – those on the damper peat
– were principally mown, for a variety of products, and grazing was here a subsidiary use. As Marshall explained in 1787:

> The produce and principal use of a fen are totally different from those of a grazing
> marsh. The profits of a fen arise, in general, from Reed and gladdon, cut for thatch,
> for buildings; Sedge and rushes, for litter; and thatch, for hay and corn-ricks, and
> sometimes for buildings; Coarse grass, for fodder, and sometimes for pasturage; – and
> Peat for fuel.[145]

The areas of common land lying on the peat deposits in the valley of the Ant,
in that of the Bure above Ant Mouth, and in the upper reaches of the Yare,
were often composed entirely of such damp fen grounds. But elsewhere parishes
often had both grazing marsh *and* areas of fen. Thus, according to an undated
seventeenth-century document, at Carlton Colville in the Waveney valley the
wet commons were divided into three separate areas: Horde Marshe of fifty acres,
Redefenne of forty acres and Slypp Marsh of ten acres. The first of these the
inhabitants used for 'pasturing there horsebeasts and other cattall all the year';
the other two they 'doe use to mowe in somer and wth in some tyme after
mowinge the grass being growne . . . doe feade wth there cattall'.[146]

Eighteenth- and nineteenth-century agricultural writers regularly bemoaned
the poor management of the commons but – keen advocates of enclosure and
'improvement' – they exaggerated their deficiencies. Far from being waterlogged
quagmires which it was no one's business to drain, local communities often invested considerable amounts of time, trouble and money in their maintenance.
This was particularly the case with the common grazing marshes. These generally contained a number of drainage dykes, were protected from the rivers by low
walls and were separated from adjacent areas of marsh by flood banks or 'dams',
particularly prominent examples of which occurred on parish boundaries. Here
they were often raised on either side of a natural watercourse, a stream draining
off the uplands which had been used to demarcate the boundary between adjacent parishes (good examples are the Worlingham Wall, dividing Worlingham
from Beccles; and the Hundred Stream, separating North Cove from Barnby;
both in the Waveney valley).

Dykes, embankments and other works required constant maintenance. At
Beccles, in 1552 alone, 950 rods of dyke, all belonging to 'the comen fenne',
were 'drawne and skorrede'. Numerous payments were also made for maintaining

the causeways which provided access to it: 'Item payd to Robert Gibson for caryeng of 75 lodes of gravell to Saltfengate and into saltfen causey 18s. 3d.'. The 'dams', walls and principal drainage dykes were reinforced with faggots, many cut from a particular area of the common, Oxholmes, in which large numbers of pollarded willows and alders grew: 'Item for caryeng 16 lodes of wode from Oxholmes in to Saltfen'; 'Item pd to Drightman and little Robert for stowyng and maken of wyllowe faggetts'.[147] In most parishes a rate was levied (often by the surveyors of the highways) to pay for such maintenance works. At Martham in the sixteenth century this was raised specifically for 'casting, carting, or other repairing or drayning of the common'.[148] At Cantley in the early eighteenth century all commoners had to pay 3s. a year for each bullock grazed on the common marsh, 'for the repairs of the Walls, Banks, Sluices, Ditches Drains Gates and Fences of the Said Common'. This custom was changed in 1728 to a more flexible system, by which a committee of five (one of whom was always the rector), chosen by the commoners, would decide each year what works were required, and levy a rate accordingly.[149]

The use of the grazing marshes was carefully regulated. The manorial court (or, in the case of Beccles, the town corporation) set the dates on which animals would be admitted to the marsh, and by which they had to be removed, although these could be altered as circumstances demanded. Thus in the case of the Beccles Salt Fen, animals were usually allowed in on the third day of May, but – presumably because of particularly wet weather – in 1672 opening was delayed for several weeks, and in 1709 it was 'Ordered that Salt Fenn be continued shut until the sixth day of June next enssueing'.[150] Courts also tried to ensure that commoners did not overstock the commons, and attempted to prevent their illegal use by 'foreigners' from neighbouring parishes. In the case of Beccles, all animals put on the common had to be entered in the 'Warning Book'. Non-inhabitants could pasture animals by special licence, but others chose to do so illegally, by getting inhabitants of the town to claim ownership, a procedure known as 'colouring of cattell', and which was considered a very serious offence. The operation of these rules was monitored at the 'drift', where those guilty of transgressions went out of their way to escape detection: in 1671 Andrew Williams was presented at the fen court for 'refusing to have his cattell brought into the drift and for threatening the officer'.[151]

Communal management of the damper fen grounds on the peat soils presented a rather different range of problems, in part because of the diverse range of ways in which they were used. Some areas were grazed on a regular basis, but in most animals were only put on at certain times of the year, after the fens had been mown, for as Marshall suggests, their real value came from the other things they produced. Large areas were cut for 'marsh hay', a mixture of fen grasses and rushes (principally *Juncus subnodulosus* and *Juncus effusus*), which was used for cattle fodder. This was ancient practice: Domesday shows a marked concentration of meadow land in the river valleys of Broadland.[152] Mowing usually occurred on a yearly basis but sometimes at longer intervals. Other areas were cut every other year, or occasionally every third or fourth, for 'litter', which was coarser herbage with a greater preponderance of rushes, which was principally used for cattle bedding: or for rushes alone, much in demand for covering domestic floors, a practice referred to at Beccles in 1544:

> Also yt shalbe lawfulle to all women inh[abit]yng wythyne the seyd towne of Becclys att all tymes mete and convenyent to go into the sayd fen lands ... to shere and gather wythe thyr sykkle ... for the thyr dressyng up of thyr houses.[153]

In addition, soft rush (*Juncus effusus*) and, to a lesser extent, compact rush (*Juncus conglomeratus*) were used to make 'rush lights'. The rushes were carefully pulled by hand, and then piled in heaps until they became 'clung' – that is, had lost their natural stiffness. The outside green skin was then peeled with a knife, to leave the soft white pith: a thin strip of skin on each side, however, was left to provide a measure of rigidity. They were dried in the sun, and tied in bundles of twelve called *whips*, and then formed into larger cone-shaped bundles, around 1.5 metres high and 0.3 metres circumference at the base. In the eighteenth and nineteenth centuries they were sold at the Norwich Rush fair, held at the Artichoke Inn near the Magdalene Gates.[154] Rushes, marsh hay and litter were all harvested from the late summer into the autumn (manorial regulations often stipulated that cutting could not begin 'till the day after Midsummer'). In the Middle Ages it was usually forbidden to sell any of these crops out of the parish, although by the seventeenth century this prohibition was beginning to break down.

The damper areas of the fen were cut for sedge (*Cladium mariscus*) and for reeds (*Phragmites australis*). The latter was a particularly important crop, for reed was the main thatching material over large areas of East Anglia. In contrast to rushes and litter, reeds were always cut in the winter and early spring, beginning in early December and extending through to March or April: it was the dead stems of the plant that were harvested. Thus the regulations for the commons of Ludham, Catfield and Potter Heigham drawn up in 1677 typically ordered that 'no reed be cut upon any of the said commons before the day after St Andrew under penalty of 6sh 8d for every fathom so cut'.[155] Court rolls contain numerous presentments for cutting out of season. The reed cutters used a scythe, and worked the beds either from wide, flat-bottomed marsh boats, or from a plank suspended over the surface of the water, or – where the water was relatively shallow – they waded: an unpleasant experience even when wearing the traditional stout wading boots. The reeds were tied in bunches called 'shooves', which were sold by the fathom: that is, in bundles of shooves with a combined circumference of 6ft (*c.*2 metres). In some areas five shooves went to make a fathom, in others – where the reeds grew taller and thinner – it took six.[156]

Medieval and post-medieval records also make many references to the cutting of sedge, by which they meant not true sedge but *Cladium mariscus*, or saw-sedge. *Cladium* was, and in places still is, principally used for thatching the ridges of roofs – it is extremely pliable when dry – and was usually cut at intervals of three or four years. It was also to some extent used as cattle bedding. Unlike reed, saw-sedge was harvested in the summer, and the two plants were cut from different areas of the fens. This was because the regular cutting for one tended, over time, to suppress the growth of the other, and indeed of other kinds of plant, leading to the emergence of ever purer stands.

There were a number of minor crops. 'Gladdon' – the local name for lesser reed-mace (*Typha angustifolia*) – and yellow flag (*Iris pseudacorus*) were harvested and sold, in post-medieval times at least, for making mats, horse-collars and baskets; the bull-rush (locally known as 'bolder') was also cut for mat-making.[157] All these various fen crops were transported in shallow-draught boats or reed-rafts which were rowed, quanted, or towed to the place where the crop was to be stacked.

As well as being harvested for this diverse range of crops, the low commons were also extensively cut for peat throughout the medieval and post-medieval periods: indeed, it is the extraction of peat which has, perhaps more than anything else, contributed to the present appearance of the landscape. Peat was used as a fuel, and could be extracted either from deep workings, reaching down to the better-quality, denser and more combustible 'brushwood peat' at a depth of three metres or more; or from shallower excavations, half a metre to a metre below the level of the fen surface. The former excavations have now all flooded, to produce – as we shall see in a moment – the distinctive lakes known as the Broads. The shallower cuttings also soon filled with water, producing 'turf ponds' which rapidly terrestrialised: that is, once abandoned, they soon became invaded by reed, saw-sedge and other species, which would then die and form new layers of peat. This more recent peat is, however, generally of a less consolidated nature than the uncut material around it. In places the newer material has not quite filled the ponds so that their boundaries – old baulks of solid peat between adjacent workings – can just be seen as low ridges running through the fen. More dramatically, a severe fire on East Ruston Common a few years ago ignited this less consolidated material, more clearly exposing the layout of old excavations (Figure 26). The date of these particular workings is unknown, although peat continued to be dug here well into the twentieth century. An account of the common made in 1909 describes how the peat blocks or 'hovers', each about 0.1 metres wide, were cut using a heart-shaped spade around 0.2 metres wide and the same deep, with a wooden handle fixed at a slight angle to the shaft. They were then placed in stacks 6 metres by 1 metre, and 2 metres high. A good man, it was said, could cut around twenty hovers in a minute.

Some areas of the valley floors were occupied by damp woodland or 'carr' of alder and willow, and – less commonly – by osier or willow beds. The former were managed by coppicing – that is, by cutting the trees back to the stump every five or ten years in order to produce a regular crop of straight, thin-sectioned 'poles' suitable for firewood, tool-handles and fencing – alder takes a long time to rot. Osier beds were cropped more frequently, the willow used principally for basket-making. Today carr woodland is a prominent feature of the valleys but before the late nineteenth century it was a relatively minor component of the landscape.

Surviving court rolls reveal how difficult it could be to prevent over-exploitation of the commons, and to reconcile their multifarious uses. In the

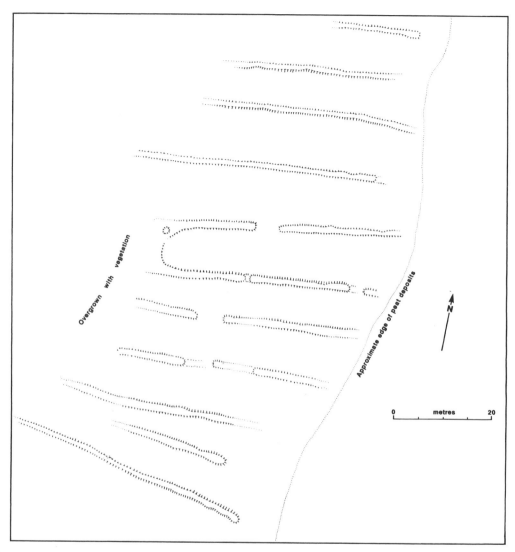

Figure 26   Peat cuttings on East Ruston Common (centred TG 34372830). A fire on the 'common'
               – in reality, a Poor Allotment-ignited much of the more recent, less consolidated peat, thus
               revealing this pattern of old baulks.

Middle Ages there seems to have been a general assumption that no one was to
take more rush, sedge, reed or whatever than was required for their own use, nor
cut any more fodder than would be needed to carry their own livestock through
the winter. As an increasingly commercial society developed in the later Middle
Ages, however, such informal customary regulations began to break down, and
many communities seem to have appointed an officer (often referred to as the
Fen Reeve) to monitor the common's exploitation. In the sixteenth and seventeenth centuries, moreover, there was an increasing tendency for customary

regulations to be committed formally to writing. Unrestrained turf-cutting was a particular problem, for once the surface peat had been stripped away the grazing was destroyed, ponds were produced and the vegetation which eventually grew back was dominated by reed and saw-sedge and was therefore less suitable for either grazing or for hay. Manorial courts thus attempted to limit the scale of extraction, or to restrict it to the damper areas of ground, of less use for grazing and hay-production. At Martham in 1404, for example, two men were accused of taking peat from part of the common which should have been left for hay, and in 1509 an order was made forbidding the extraction of peat from all the commons in the parish, except Cess Heath and parts of South Fen.[158]

As well as conflicts within and between communities over the use of the commons, there were also sporadic disputes between communities and their manorial lords. In 1679 the copyhold tenants of the Bishop of Norwich in Irstead and Neatishead claimed that they had the right to

> Take cut and carry away Fodder Rushes Reed and Sedge growing in any of the said Fenns for their cattle and repairing the said messuages and also Liberty of Fishing in a certain water there called Alder Fenns and in all other the Broads and Waters in Irstead aforesaid as belonging to the said tenants

– as well as rights of 'Common of Pasture of all Commonable Cattle' there. All except the latter right was strenuously denied by the lord of the manor, especially the right to take fish.[159] These rights were still being disputed in 1803, when one man asserted that:

> He had always cut Boulder and Gladding on Irstead Broad for a Right of a Cottage he was owner of at Irstead . . . He used to dry his Boulders on a Hills in the Broad called the rakes . . . He have Fish on the Broad but did not make a practice of it but he have known others do it, frequently, and never known any person interrupted.

(The document adds, by way of explanation, that 'These Rakes are Hills in the Broad that are 2 or 3 feet higher than the surface of the Water where people cut Flags and Rushes'.)[160]

One way of allowing a fair distribution of resources was through 'doling', by which specific areas of the common were allotted to particular individuals. By such an arrangement the fen continued to be treated as common land, open for grazing for part of the year, but the holder of the dole was allowed the exclusive right to extract a range of commodities from it. The land so allotted usually took the form of long, thin strips, similar to the ploughlands in the open fields of the uplands. The practice of doling is recorded as early as the thirteenth century but may have become increasingly important over time. By the end of the medieval period the majority of the wet fens appear to have been 'doled' in this way, and a map of the banks of the Yare, drawn up in 1767, thus shows most of the areas of peat ground divided into narrow strips, allocated to specific individuals.[161] Doles were not only mown. They were also cut for peat. At Upton the area to the north of the Broad, now known as the Doles, is shown on the Enclosure Map of

1802 as 'turf lands', divided into narrow strips, each between one and five acres in extent.[162] Here, the peat seems to have been extracted on an *ad hoc*, small-scale basis, so as not to interfere with the other fen products required by local households. For most of their history, the Broadland fens seem to have been dug for peat in this essentially casual, domestic way. But in two periods much less restrained extraction took place. The first of these occurred in the early Middle Ages and – as is now well known – led to the formation of the lakes or broads which today form the most characteristic feature of the valley landscape.

Broads, fisheries and decoys

The broads were for long something of a geographical mystery. Nowhere else in Britain can such a concentration of areas of open water be found in wide, flat valley plains; and nowhere else do lakes occur which display such distinctive locational characteristics. The broads fall into two categories. Either they are 'by-passed' broads, which stand a little way back from the principal rivers, separated from them by often relatively narrow baulks of peat; or they are 'side-valley' broads, which occur in the middle of the valleys of minor tributaries feeding in to the lower reaches of these rivers. Examples of the latter type include the so-called 'Trinity Broads' – Ormesby, Rollesby, Filby – in the valley of the Muck Fleet, and Fritton Decoy. By-passed broads are particularly concentrated in the upper reaches of the Bure, where Belaugh, Wroxham, Salhouse, Hoveton, Ranworth and Upton Broads are all to be found.[163]

The broads were long thought to be natural features, and geographers and geomorphologists puzzled over their origins. It was only relatively recently that their true character was established, largely as a result of a now-famous research project carried out in the 1960s by Lambert, Jennings, Green, Hutchinson and Smith.[164] This research revealed that far from being the shrunken relics of once continuous areas of water occupying the valley floors, as some geographers had suggested, the broads are separated by areas of solid peat (or peat and clay). Borings and soundings revealed that they are fairly shallow, varying in depth from 1.5–5 metres, averaging 3–4 metres; but that they were originally somewhat deeper, having accumulated much silt and mud since first formed. Significantly, their sides originally consisted of almost vertical walls of peat, except in a few cases, where they extend as far as the rising ground of the valley sides. Here sloping edges of sand or gravel can occur (a feature particularly characteristic of the larger side-valley broads like Fritton). The sheer sides are often now obscured by erosion, and by the growth of marginal vegetation, but clearly testify to an artificial origin: as does the presence within many of the broads of steep-sided islands and narrow, well-defined peninsulas of solid peat, the latter often continuing out into the open water as submerged ridges. Where they have not been destroyed by recent dredging, both islands and ridges generally form parallel lines and, where parish boundaries run (as they often do) through the centre of a broad, they change direction abruptly at them. Sometimes (as in the case of the Stalham–Sutton boundary across Sutton Broad) the parish boundary is itself marked by a prominent submerged ridge.[165]

All these features proclaim the fact that the broads are, in origin, pits dug for the extraction of peat which have subsequently become flooded: an explanation which was, in fact, suggested for Barton Broad by the naturalist Samuel Woodward as early as 1834, and further developed by H. Woodward in the 1880s.[166] The islands and ridges represent baulks left between adjacent workings, in part perhaps as defence against flooding. Where the edges of the excavations are bounded by areas of uncut peat the characteristic vertical faces occur: where the excavators followed the deposits to the edges of the valleys, they extracted the material down to the underlying sands or gravels, leaving the sloping edges. There is documentary evidence for turbaries in Broadland from the twelfth century onwards – mainly from the Register of St Benet's Abbey – and a range of manorial documents from the thirteenth and fourteenth centuries contains numerous further references.

Some of the pits seem to have been dug on manorial demesne land. Most, however, were on commons: the majority occur within areas which were, up until the eighteenth or nineteenth centuries, common fens. Each strip, defined by its solid baulks, probably represents a 'dole' to a particular individual or family (significantly, the broad now known as Summer House Water in the south of Somerleyton parish was still known in the seventeenth century as *Dole Fen*). It has been pointed out that broads often lie on parish boundaries, and the suggestion has been made that this is because 'the peat pits were, whenever possible, located in such a way that people from several adjoining parishes had access to them'.[167] In fact, the relationship is probably a simple function of local administrative topography *before* the pits were dug. Here, as elsewhere in Norfolk, strips of common land could often be found running along parish boundaries, partly because they occupied low-lying land flanking streams and rivers which themselves served as convenient lines along which to establish parochial limits. It is hardly surprising that when peat was extracted from these areas the resultant workings tended to cluster beside such boundaries.

The scale of extraction was truly massive: Smith calculated that around 900 million cubic feet of peat must have been removed before the pits were abandoned and flooded. The extent of the excavations reflects, of course, the character of the surrounding uplands in the early Middle Ages. North east Norfolk was, as already noted, one of the most densely settled regions of England, and Norwich – only a short journey away by river – was the second largest city in the country. The region was also one of the least wooded, and most sparsely-timbered, in England.

In such circumstances large-scale exploitation of such a serviceable source of domestic fuel is hardly surprising. Deep excavation – rather than shallow surface stripping – was encouraged by the fact that the better, more combustible peat occurs at depth: the so-called 'brushwood peat', which has a firmer consistency and burns more slowly, in a manner more akin to coal, than the more fibrous material won from nearer the surface. In many places this better-quality peat was blanketed by the clay deposits laid down by the Romano-British transgression, and the peat diggers therefore chose for their excavations places where this deposit does not occur – in the higher reaches of the valleys, or along their margins – or (as in the middle sections of the Bure and Yare) where the clay layer is of minimal thickness. In such locations the edges of the excavations often came close to the rivers, and the diggers were understandably careful to leave here a strip of uncut peat, like those separating Wroxham or Salhouse Broads from the Bure.

The excavators were thus clearly concerned about the dangers of flooding: but why didn't the pits fill immediately, through the lateral seepage of water through these baulks of peat? In part, perhaps – as Joyce Lambert's team suggested – it was because they were excavated in early medieval times, when water levels were lower by a metre or so than they are today. They were thus below the level of the less compacted surface peat, and lateral seepage of water was therefore limited by the less pervious nature of the compressed peat which occurs at a greater depth. The fact that few of the broads are deeper than 4 metres, however (in spite of the fact that the best peat often lies still deeper), implies that below this level problems caused by seepage from adjacent rivers would have been too severe for extraction to be feasible: and in this context it is noteworthy that the deepest broads are found in the side valleys, away from the larger watercourses and separated from them by extensive areas of impervious clay.

According to Lambert's team, it was the gradual rise in water levels in the course of the medieval period, coupled with the climatic changes of the late thirteenth and early fourteenth centuries, which led to the flooding and abandonment of the workings. Probably the latter was of greater significance than the former: it would only take one major flooding incident, caused by the various storms and surges recorded in this period, to render a pit unworkable. It is, in fact, doubtful whether relatively minor changes in water levels alone would have made much difference to the viability of deep workings. Deep pits excavated in the peat today fill up relatively slowly, and the medieval excavations could probably have been kept dry by regular baling, given sufficient incentive and enough labour. But in addition to the impact of environmental change, there may have been important social and economic reasons why deep excavation was abandoned. The twelfth and thirteenth centuries were a time of chronic overpopulation. This ensured a ready market for fuel, and also relatively low wage levels. As local population levels fell dramatically in the wake of the Black Death, however, the costs of extraction and pit maintenance would have escalated, while the demand for peat – and thus the profits to be made from its extraction – would have declined. In such circumstances, it is hardly surprising that no further deep pits were dug, and those already in operation were abandoned. Extraction continued but on a smaller scale, principally to satisfy domestic needs.

While it seems certain that *most* areas of open water in Broadland were created by medieval peat-digging, not *all* of them were. Heigham Sound was largely, and Horsey Mere and Martham Broad partly, created by the extraction of clay during the Middle Ages, although for what purpose remains unclear. Indeed, before enclosure and drainage in the nineteenth century there were a number of other lakes and pools in the silt marshes around the headwaters of the Thurne which were probably of a similar character: Gages Broad, Wiggs Broad, Hare Park Broad, all of which appear on the 1808 Enclosure Map for Hickling but disappeared soon after;[168] and five substantial pools, shown but not named on William Faden's map of 1797, which lay in the area between East Somerton and Horsey.

Once flooded, the margins of the broads quite rapidly became colonised by reed, saw-sedge and other marginal vegetation. As these plants died, peat began to fill the basins once more. In the case of the shallower broads, this build-up of peat and encroachment of marginal vegetation has led to drastic shrinkage or even complete disappearance in comparatively recent times. Sutton Broad, Carleton Broad, Dilham Broad and Strumpshaw Broad have all dwindled to nothing over the last century or so. Others disappeared in the more distant past, like the lost Honing Broad, shown on a map of *c*.1730,[169] its presence still marked in the local landscape by the great loop made by the road from Honing to East Ruston in order to avoid it. Nevertheless, the depth and width of the broads normally prevented full terrestrialisation, although some shrinkage invariably occurred (Figure 27); and in late and post-medieval times they came to play a number of important roles in the local economy.

The most important was the provision of fish. Freshwater fish were an important part of the diet of people in the pre-industrial age and the rivers and lakes of Broadland teamed with them. The earthworks of St Benet's Abbey include a number of thin rectangular ponds, *servatoria* or 'stews', used to keep fish caught in nearby pools and waterways until eaten or sold. As early as the 1140s there are references to fisheries in the abbey documents, but the flooding of the turbaries in the fourteenth centuries greatly increased their number, and by the sixteenth century Simon Tobye was paying 12*d*. rent for 'three acres of fishing in Barton Brode'.[170] By the sixteenth and seventeenth centuries the broads were often referred to as 'fishings' or 'fisheries'. Thus a survey of 1662 refers to 'one great water or ffishing knowne by the name of Brunn Fenn alias Burnt Fenn', that is, Burntfen Broad.[171] The broads continued to be managed in traditional ways for fish into the nineteenth century: the account books for the Beauchamp-Proctor estate record payments for 'Cutting fish stews . . . at Carleton Broad' as late as 1832.[172]

In the sixteenth and seventeenth centuries fish ponds were often considered objects of beauty by their owners, and were frequently constructed within the gardens of great houses. Conversely, where ponds existed some way away from a country house they might become the focus for a detached area of pleasure grounds. Somerleyton Hall had a fine series of gardens, and a large deer park, when it was surveyed in 1652. But it also had a separate area of gardens some 1.25 km to the south of the hall, well outside the park, arranged around two small broads, one now known (significantly) as Summer House Water.[173] An accompanying survey describes how:

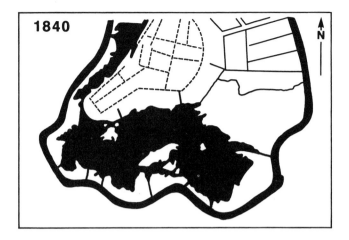

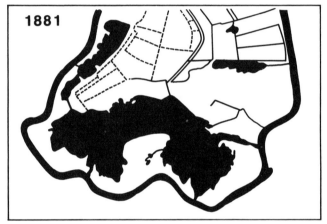

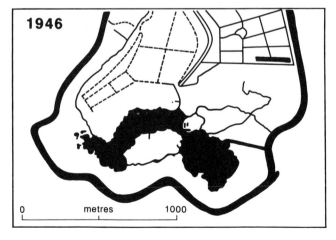

Figure 27   The contraction of Hoveton Great Broad, 1840–1946 (after Lambert, Jennings and Smith 1965).

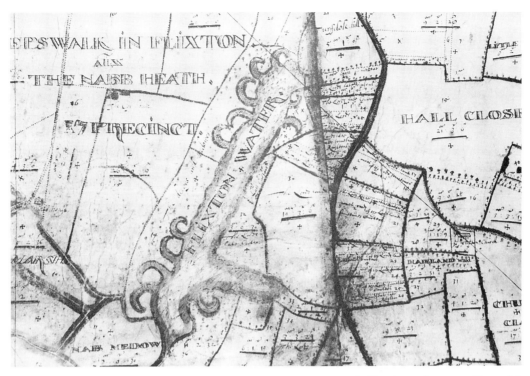

Flixton Decoy, as depicted on an estate map of 1653. This is probably the earliest   Figure 28
representation of a duck decoy in England.

> The Lady Wentworth hath . . . divers fish ponds gardens and walks with a house in
> farm . . . the waters called the Island Pond and the Wall Pond they are outward lying
> being part in Somerleyton part in Blundeston. There is likewise one other great area
> of water that is also a private water of the said Lady Wentworth called Dole Fenn with
> walks and mounts dividing lying part in Somerleyton and part in Blundeston.

The map shows the gardens clearly, complete with islands in the middle of the
broads, on which elaborate fishing lodges stood. Some traces of this elaborate
landscape still survive in the form of earthworks, most notably the substantial
'mount', which is not an entirely artificial feature at all but a relatively minor
alteration of the natural valley contours.

The same map also shows another interesting modification of a broad: it indicates that Flixton had already been converted into a 'decoy' (Figure 28). Decoys
were an ingenious method of catching wildfowl.[174] They consisted of a number
of curving 'pipes' – tapering channels covered by netting supported on a framework of wooden or iron hoops – leading off from an area of open water. These
were typically about 100 metres long, and 20 metres wide at the mouth. Each
pipe terminated in a long bow-net which could be detached from the rest of the
apparatus. Along one side of the pipe a number of screens, made of reeds, were

arranged *en echelon*, behind which the decoy man could conceal himself. Widfowl were usually lured in to the pipe by using a combination of tame decoy ducks and a specially trained dog called a 'piper'. The former would enter the pipe when commanded to do so by a low whistle from the decoy man. At the same time the dog would run around the screens, jumping over the lower boards or 'dog jumps' placed between them. For reasons which have never been fully explained, the wildfowl which had gathered near the mouth of the pipe were attracted towards what must, to them, have looked like an appearing and disappearing dog. This, plus the example set by the tame decoy ducks, induced them to swim up the pipe. As soon as they had entered, the decoy man – who had up to this time remained well hidden – revealed himself. By waving his arms or a handkerchief the birds were scared into flight down the tapering pipe, and into the bow-net, which could then be disconnected from the rest of the structure and the birds despatched.[175]

The wetlands of the east coast teemed with wildfowl in the seventeenth and eighteenth centuries, particularly mallard, pintail, teal and widgeon (or 'smee', as they were traditionally called in Broadland), and the Norfolk Broads was an area with a particularly high concentration of decoys (Figure 29).[176] Not all were like Flixton, constructed around the edges of pre-existing broads. In some places, as at Sutton, they were erected around a purpose-built area of open water.[177] Either way, they were valuable pieces of property, usually leased by their owners to professional operators.

Decoys are sometimes said to have been introduced from Holland after the Glorious Revolution of 1688. In fact, some had been established before the Civil War: and it is probable that the earliest in England were in Broadland. Sir William Wodehouse had, as early as 1620, a 'device for catching DUCKS, known by the foreign name of a koye' at Waxham;[178] those at Acle and Hemsby were probably established at about the same time;[179] while Flixton Decoy was clearly in full operation by 1652, when it was carefully drawn on the Somerleyton estate map. In all, the sites of fifteen decoys are known from the Broadland area, although not all were in operation at the same time (that at Buckenham Broad was already defunct by 1736, when a document referred to it as 'A large fishery . . . wherein lately a decoy was').[180] Their numbers dwindled in the second half of the nineteenth century, partly because of competition from foreign imports, partly because of changes in dietary habits, mainly because their successful operation demanded peace and quiet, and as the century progressed the fens and marshes were increasingly disturbed by recreational shooting, tourists and railways. Nevertheless, Fritton decoy continued to operate into the twentieth century, and in the winter of 1899–1900 no less than 2,721 wildfowl were caught there.[181] It was last worked in the 1950s. Most decoys have left but scant traces in the landscape. Once abandoned, the pipes – and often the open water of the pond itself – rapidly became colonised with vegetation and subsequently filled by peat. However, the decoy generally lives on in the names it has given to neighbouring features in the countryside, such as Decoy Farm, Decoy Plantation, Decoy Wood, Decoy Carr or Decoy Covert.

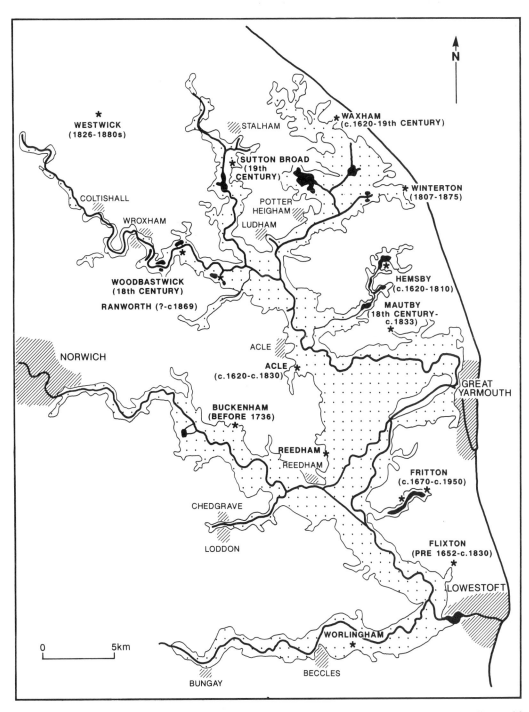

The location of known duck decoys in Broadland.

Figure 29

The progress of enclosure

It is sometimes assumed that the fens and marshes of Broadland's valleys remained as common land until the parliamentary enclosures of the early nineteenth century. In fact, although these did have a profound impact on the landscape, enclosure has a long and complex history in Broadland. Indeed, some of the low-lying land in the valleys was already held as private property in the early Middle Ages. Such areas were mainly (although not exclusively) located in the lower reaches of the principal valleys, in areas of silt soils, so that their landscape forms, in effect, an extension of that of the Halvergate 'triangle'. The marshes around St Benet's, for example, consisted of enclosed demesne land of the abbey from the earliest times. A fine map of the Bishop of Norwich's lands here, surveyed in 1702, shows a landscape of meandering dykes which has largely survived, with some modification of detail, to the present (Figure 30).[182] Similarly, the Somerleyton estate map of 1652 shows that the Somerleyton marshes were already enclosed demesne land, and probably always had been.[183]

Nevertheless, while some enclosed ground existed from the earliest times there is no doubt that its area increased over time. To judge from the available evidence, enclosure occurred fairly gradually during the medieval period, but more rapidly in the course of the sixteenth, seventeenth and eighteenth centuries. Early references thus normally concern relatively small areas of ground, like the half rod of marsh 'some time parcel of the Common Pasture called Clynt Fenn Well' referred to in a terrier for Horning in the reign of Edward IV.[184] In post-medieval times, in contrast, legal agreements drawn up between manorial lords and the principal freeholders in parishes indicate the enclosure of rather larger areas. A number of these survive. One, dating from 1573, describes how the lord of the manor of Clippesby reached an agreement with some of his tenants to fence off part of the common and take it into private ownership.[185] Similarly, in 1614 the lord of the manor of Aldeby and his tenants agreed to enclose 'all such marshes rushe grounds and reede grounds . . . as nowe bee or are reputed to bee or might be used or fedd in common', something finally achieved in 1635, although some common land continued to exist in the parish. The size of the allotments given to each landowner here was in proportion to the commonable rights claimed on the basis of land held on the adjacent 'upland': twenty acres were set aside 'for charitable and good uses to and for ye benefitte of ye said towne only'.[186] Again, in 1676 an agreement was drawn up for the enclosure and division of the Great Marsh, one of the commons in the parish of Langley,[187] and a similar partial enclosure seems to have occurred around this time in the adjacent parish of Hardley, where a document of 1678 refers to twelve acres 'one marsh late parcell of the Common called East Marsh'.[188] Large-scale enclosures could lead to disputes and legal action, if carried out without the general assent of freeholders. In 1589 six yeomen in Ormesby complained to the Court of Exchequer the Sir Edward Clere, lord of the manor, had locked the gate leading to the common called Barrow Lowes and prevented the inhabitants from using the common marshes there as summer pasture, and had taken thirty acres of common land into his own use.[189]

St Benet's Abbey, as shown on a map of 1702.   Figure 30

Alongside such formal enclosures, common rights to the damp fen grounds were constantly being eroded, from medieval times, by the tendency for 'doles' to become treated as full private property. This was particularly a feature of the Yare valley. Here a map of 1767 shows large areas of fen grounds divided into narrow strips with separate owners. Later enclosure acts for parishes like Strumpshaw or Surlingham treated these doles, although unfenced, as already quite free of common rights: the commissioners restricted their attention to undoled areas of fen and the open grazing marshes. In a few places in the course of the post-medieval period consolidation of holdings led to the progressive amalgamation of adjacent doles, and sometimes to the demarcation of the resultant blocks with ditches, thus producing a pattern of long, dyked, roughly parallel strips: as in the Worling-ham Marshes, although here (as elsewhere) the layout has been much simplified since the earliest surviving maps were made. Where enclosure occurred by planned agreement during the post-medieval centuries, in contrast, a roughly rectilinear dyke pattern was usually created, as for example in the Langley Marshes, although occasionally (as at Clippesby) a more irregular layout resulted through the adaptation of an earlier pattern of natural watercourses.

The different Broadland valleys have rather different enclosure histories. Generally speaking, those of the southern rivers – the Chet, Waveney and Yare – experienced a higher degree of early enclosure than those of the northern: it was thus in the valley of the Bure and, in particular, in those of the Thurne and the Ant, that parliamentary enclosure made its greatest impact (Figure 31). In part this was because these valleys contained large areas of peaty soil, less valuable than the silt marshes, less susceptible to improvement, and thus of less interest to landowners until the process of enclosure was facilitated by the adoption of parliamentary Acts in the course of the eighteenth century. In part, however, it reflected the fact that – as already noted – the astonishing fertility of the soils in the central and northern parts of Broadland encouraged the survival of large numbers of small freeholders here. This made it more difficult to gain the general agreement required to enclose areas of common ground until the development of enclosure by parliamentary Acts: for while this method, too, required the assent of a majority of landowners, this was now calculated on the basis of the acres they owned, rather than on the number of individual proprietors assenting to the proposal.

Few Enclosure Acts dealt exclusively with areas of low-lying marsh and fen. Most also enclosed upland heaths and commons, and a high proportion – high, at least, for Norfolk – dealt with residual areas of open-field arable. The earliest Enclosure Act in Broadland – and also incidentally the earliest in Norfolk – was for the marshes at Stokesby in 1720. No further Acts were passed in the area, however, until 1797, when 2,646 acres of commons and open fields were enclosed in the parish of Acle (the actual award was made in 1799). In the following decades they came thick and fast (Figure 32), before tailing off again after 1815, although the Act for enclosing Thorpe Low Common in Thorpe St Andrew was not passed until 1861.[190] This spate of early nineteenth-century enclosure was not unique to Broadland. Rather, it was a pattern shared by other areas of England. Grain prices were abnormally high during the Napoleconic War years, and landowners were in an optimistic frame of mind and willing to invest the sums necessary to bring about enclosure and reclamation of commons and 'waste'. They were also motivated, to some extent, by a desire to control the ever-expanding rural population, to make them more dependent on wages and less on the exploitation of the various natural resources that the commons had to offer.

The effects of Parliamentary enclosure were greatest in the common grazing marshes of the Lower Bure and Thurne valleys. Here new networks of dykes were established across what had formerly been fairly open land (Figure 33). Some earlier watercourses were retained, usually in 'tidied up' form, but most of the pattern was created as the commissioners divided and allotted the commons in carefully surveyed rectilinear blocks, and as this network of straight lines was

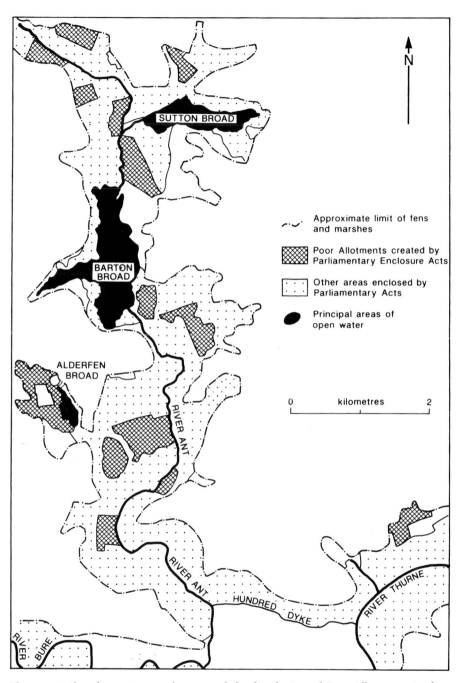

The extent of parliamentary enclosure, and the distribution of Poor Allotments, in the   Figure 31
Ant valley.

Figure 32   The chronology of parliamentary enclosure in Broadland.

replicated in the system of internal dykes cut by individual proprietors. Such
geometric grids of dykes were the watery equivalent of the neat mesh of flimsy
hawthorn hedges which the commissioners established in the adjacent uplands
in the same period, when open fields and 'dry' commons were being enclosed.
Good examples of such regular marshland landscapes can be seen at Upton, to
the north of Upton Broad and the Doles, an area enclosed in 1802 following an
Act of 1799; or in Horning, to either side of Ludham Bridge, enclosed in 1818
following an Act of 1807. It must be emphasised, however, that not all rectilinear
dyke patterns in Broadland resulted from parliamentary enclosure. Some were
created by private land-improvement schemes occurring in the same general
period, like those carried out by the Rising family on the Horsey estate in the
early 1800s.[191]

In addition to the dykes dug around and within individual allotments, there
was usually a main drain, mill dyke, or 'Commissioners' Drain' leading to a mill
which lifted water into a high-level dyke leading to the river or, more usually,
directly into the river itself. Often the Enclosure Act not only stipulated the erection of a new mill but also established a Drainage Commission for its maintenance, and for that of the other drainage works. No less than seventeen such
Commissions were set up between 1800 and 1820, some embracing (like the
awards themselves) a single parish, some two (like Catfield and Sutton, 1808)
and a few several (Winterton and East and West Somerton, 1805). Even when
a mill was not immediately erected, one was often subsequently built, either by
the Commissioners or by individual proprietors. When Haddiscoe and Haddiscoe
Thorpe were enclosed in 1806 a piece of land was awarded to the Drainage

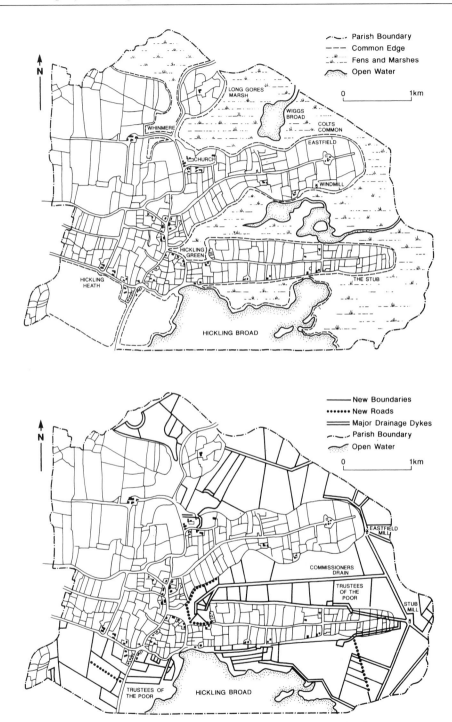

The effects on the landscape of the parliamentary enclosure of Hickling, 1808. Above, the landscape before enclosure; below, the landscape after enclosure.

Figure 33

Commissioners 'as an outfall to the river in case they should find it necessary or expedient to erect a Mill thereon for the better drainage of the said Lands and Grounds'.[192]

Once enclosed, and divided between those landowners who could assert a legal claim to a share, the new lands could be used in a variety of ways. Where commons occupied areas of silt soils, especially in the valley of the Thurne, they had mainly been used as grazing marsh and this continued to be the principal function of the enclosures which succeeded them. But some landowners, spurred on by advocates of 'improvement', were also keen to convert the damper peat fens – the wet meadows, reed and sedge beds, and turf grounds – into good-quality grazing land. This was an age of boundless optimism: those responsible for the enclosure of Hickling, for example, believed that the Broad itself could be completely drained and put to productive use (indeed, much very damp land was reclaimed on its southern side, following the construction of the 'New Bank' here, as stipulated by the Enclosure Act for Potter Heigham in 1801).[193]

A number of areas of peat fen, both newly and more anciently enclosed, were in fact reclaimed in the first half of the nineteenth century. Bacon in 1844 described how peat marshes at Surlingham had been embanked, under-drained, top-dressed, manured, and provided with drainage mills: 'loose peat bog' had thus been turned into valuable pasture grounds.[194] Few such reclamation schemes were entirely successful, however. These areas often continued to suffer from waterlogging (caused in particular by springs or streams flowing off the adjacent upland) so that the quality of the herbage often remained fairly poor, and only just justified the continued expense of maintaining the drainage works. In addition, peat tended to contract (to a much greater extent than silt and clay) when drained, rendering drainage steadily more difficult. So long as agriculture prospered, landowners continued to invest in the protection of such reclaimed land. But in the period after the 1870s a severe agricultural depression set in, and many of the peat marshes were gradually abandoned. This often occurred after some natural disaster had severely damaged the drainage works, so that the owner was simply unable or unwilling to pay for the necessary repairs. Thus Strumpshaw Marsh was abandoned for grazing following the great flood of 1912, which wrecked the windmills and sluices.[195] Today Strumpshaw 'Fen', as it is now known, is a swampy morass of reeds and rushes. A number of the valley fens, in spite of their wild and primeval appearance, have a similar history: they were reclaimed in the nineteenth century and subsequently abandoned. Thus the ruined brick drainage mills in the middle of Catfield Fen, or to the south of Hickling Broad, attest the fact that these wild areas were once drained for grazing land (Plate 13). Nevertheless, a significant proportion of reclaimed fen was maintained, and is used as grazing ground to this day, especially in the Thurne valley.

By and large, however, the peatlands continued to be used in traditional ways even after enclosure: cut for turf, hay, litter, sedge and reed. Not all such areas were allotted to private landowners, for some were set aside as 'Poor Allotments' (Figure 31). Their character varied from parish to parish. Most were used by the poor (generally classified as those owning property worth less than £10 per

Swim Coots Mill, Catfield. The location of this diminutive drainage mill shows that the fen grounds on the southern shore of Hickling broad were once reclaimed for grazing.	Plate 13

annum), in effect, as a smaller area of common land: for grazing, or 'for the purpose of cutting fuel and fodder'. Unlike the old commons, however, the allotments were administered by a committee consisting of the lords of the principal manors in the parish, the vicar or rector, the churchwardens and the overseers of the poor: that is, comprising the wealthy or middle-class residents. The management of the 303-acre 'common' at East Ruston was described in some detail by M. C. H. Bird in 1909. The area was still at this time regularly cut for peat, mown for reeds and fodder, and grazed by livestock, the numbers of which were carefully regulated.[196] Other Poor Allotments were rather different. They were areas of land which were simply rented out, and the income used to purchase coal for the poor, as at Irstead, where the 'Allotment to the Trustees of Irstead Poor' made at the enclosure in 1810 was expressly 'for the purchase of fuel'. In some places, as at Thurne, allotments of the first type were gradually, over time, converted into allotments of the second type.[197] Either way, allotments were a necessary sweetener for the poorer elements of the community. In Stokesby the principal landowner, Major England, was obliged to provide one at his own expense following the enclosure of 1720 because 'The poor inhabitants finding that no allotment was set out for their benefit under the Inclosure Act . . . proceeded in a riotous manner and insisted upon having some allotment given to them.'[198]

Yet while both on private fen grounds, and on Poor Allotments, traditional forms of landuse generally persisted, there were subtle changes. In particular, so far as the evidence goes, the late eighteenth and nineteenth centuries witnessed a considerable increase in the scale of peat-digging after three centuries or more of comparatively small-scale extraction. This renewed activity did not normally involve the kind of deep excavations which had occurred in the medieval period. Instead, the customary post-medieval practice of shallow extraction – from pits less than a metre deep – was perpetuated, but now on a far larger scale, creating very extensive, if shallow, 'turf ponds'. As already noted such areas of water were relatively unstable features in the landscape. They were rapidly colonised by reed, sedge and other vegetation which, gradually decaying, filled them with peat once more. Their former extent is, however, clear on nineteenth-century maps – most notably the First Edition 6 inch Ordnance Survey of the 1880s and 1890s. It can also be revealed by boring into the surface of the fen, for the recent peat which fills the ponds in much looser and less consolidated than that found in adjacent uncut areas.

It is hard to overestimate the extent to which peat has been stripped from the Broadland valleys in such shallow, relatively recent workings. Research on Irstead and Catfield Fens by Wheeler and Giller, for example, suggests that more than half the fen surface has been removed to a depth of 50–80 cm, with a few areas excavated to a greater depth. Here the majority of cuttings appear to have been made in the middle decades of the nineteenth century: no ponds are shown here on the Tithe Award maps of 1840, but by 1880, according to the Ordnance Survey, large rectangular wet compartments dominated much of the fen. Moreover, borings revealed that other areas had been stripped of peat, although the resulting ponds had terrestrialised before the Tithe Award maps were surveyed: excavations which had presumably begun after the enclosure of the fens in 1808, for their boundaries respect the patterns of land division established at this time (Figure 34). The excavations were made both in the areas of the fen allotted to the poor, and in those given to private proprietors.[199]

To judge both from other studies made by Wheeler,[200] and from the extensive surveys carried out more recently by Jo Parmenter,[201] the situation at Irstead and Catfield is fairly typical. Well over half of the surviving areas of open fen in Broadland – possibly as much as three-quarters – appears to have been stripped of peat in the past. Of course, some of this was removed through the kind of casual, domestic exploitation which had continued for centuries on innumerable 'doles'. Overall, however, there is little doubt that the late eighteenth and nineteenth centuries saw a marked escalation in the scale of peat extraction in Broadland. Indeed, such was its extent that in some places areas of water were created which were as extensive as the 'true' broads, although – being much shallower – less permanent features in the landscape. They disappeared as quickly as they had come. Thus by 1839 a very large turf pond had been created in Woodbastwick Fen, known as Broad Waters. On a map of 1773 most of this area was still dry marsh, and by the 1880s it had once again returned to (relatively) dry land (Figure 35).

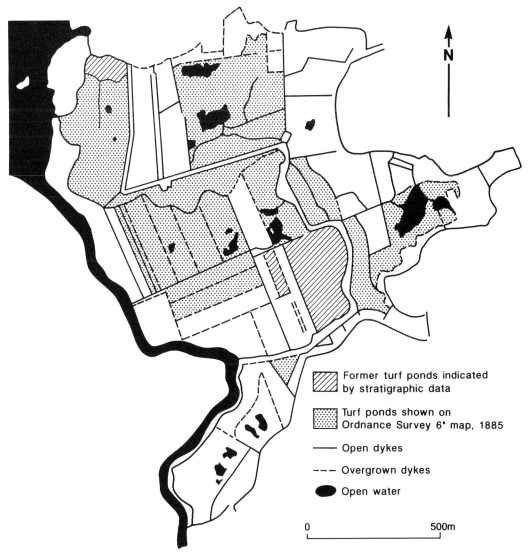

Distribution of nineteenth-century turf ponds in the Catfield and Irstead Fens (after Wheeler and Giller 1986).

Figure 34

Although most peat-digging in the eighteenth and nineteenth centuries took the form of shallow excavations, deeper pits were sporadically excavated. In Catfield Fen, for example, some areas were dug to a depth of 2 metres in order (as in medieval times) to reach the brushwood peat. It is therefore possible that some broads might, in part, be of post-medieval date: that is, existing bodies of water may have been extended by these much later deep workings. Surlingham is a case in point. The 1839 Tithe Award map shows an area of water here much

1773

1839

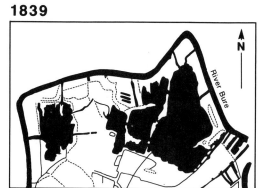

1845

1881

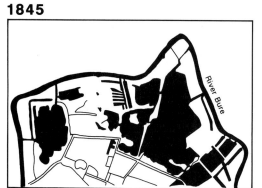

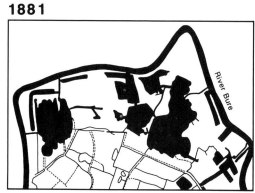

1988

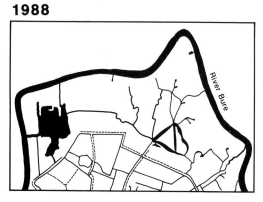

0   metres   1000

Figure 35   The development of Broad Waters, an extensive turf pond in Woodbastwick Fen, 1773–
               1988 (after Lambert, Jennings and Smith 1965, with additions from estate maps and
               aerial photographs).

more extensive than that which exists today, and dissected by a multitude of parallel lines marking the limits of the various doles, which extended out from the adjacent areas of dry land.[202] Subsequent maps show its rapid contraction in the course of the nineteenth century, leaving the rather diminutive pool which had formerly comprised only the eastern quarter of the broad. The Enclosure Map of 1809, however, marks only this area of water clearly as 'Surlingham Broad'.[203] What the Tithe Map shows as the main area of water, to the west, is on this map more ambiguously defined, suggesting that the 'doles' here were at this time only partially and shallowly filled with water; while a map of 1767 showing the banks of the river Yare simply describes this area as the 'Coarse Out Meadows' of Surlingham parish.[204]

An escalation in the rate of peat extraction in the nineteenth century has been recorded from other wetland areas of England, such as the Cambridgeshire Fenland.[205] But why did it occur? As we have seen, in the sixteenth and seventeenth centuries manorial courts had generally tried to limit the scale of peat-digging because of the way it conflicted with other forms of land use. Similarly, within individual 'doles' the extent of extraction had to be limited, so that the other resources required by households would not be impaired. It seems that in the eighteenth and nineteenth centuries all this changed, and communal management of the fen grounds began to break down. The number of small farmers was declining steadily, the number of landless poor increasing. At the same time, the larger farmers began to lose interest in some of the key resources formerly provided by the commons. New agricultural methods were now being adopted on the uplands, and with the arrival of the 'Norfolk four-course rotation', and its variants, cattle could be fed on turnips over the winter, and during the summer grazed on the grass leys which were now a regular feature of the arable fields. The larger farmers therefore had less interest in marsh hay, or rough fen grazing. The poorer members of the community, in contrast, kept few animals. They had more interest in peat, for heating and cooking, than in hay or litter or grazing: and thus the extent of extraction escalated.

All this, however, was doubtless accentuated by enclosure. Traditionally the common fens had been used in a variety of ways, and careful management was necessary in order to prevent conflict and argument. After enclosure, however, areas of *private* fen could be used by their owners in whatever way they chose. In some places, as we have seen, the fens were reclaimed and grazing became the most important form of landuse. Elsewhere, peat-cutting became the favoured mode of exploitation, landowners and tenants finding a ready market among the expanding numbers of the local poor: it was, in Dutt's words, 'a good and cheap substitute for coal in the hearths of the marshmen's cottage homes'.[206]

Man and nature in the Broadland fens

The subsequent terrestrialisation of the turf ponds had an important impact on the landscape and economy of Broadland. Where the pits were cut beside rivers, or went down as far as the underlying estuarine clay, the chemical properties of the water which filled them ensured that the colonising vegetation was generally dominated by reed, a dominance further promoted by the systematic management of such areas as reed beds. As Carrodus put it in 1949, looking back to an earlier age, 'The turf was mainly cut on the water-logged banks of the river, and in its place the graceful reed beds which now fringe the waterside sprang into existence, like a rotational change of crop.'[207] Where the pits were dug towards the margins of the fens, in contrast, over areas of uncut peat, saw-sedge was more likely to dominate the vegetation and, through management, sedge beds to emerge: a pattern especially noticeable in the Ant valley, and in the Thurne valley around Hickling. Indeed, extensive beds of sedge are rarely found growing to any significant extent over uncut peat. Most of the largest commercial sedge beds in Broadland, and many of the principal reed beds, have thus developed over abandoned peat workings. It is in fact doubtful whether there were so many very extensive beds of either plant in Broadland before the development of large-scale shallow peat extraction from the end of the eighteenth century. The presence of former peat cuttings has other effects on the pattern of fen vegetation, however: the distribution of a number of species, including the fen orchid (*Liparis loeselii*), is determined to a significant extent by the presence of former turf ponds.[208]

Peat extraction was not the only kind of 'traditional' landuse to structure the pattern of fen vegetation communities. Everywhere the fens bore – and often still bear – the marks of human management, in spite of their superficially 'natural' appearance. At the most basic level, grazing and mowing kept the fens open and free of scrub, and prevented the progress of a natural succession which would otherwise, in time, have covered them with woodland. Those areas which were regularly mown developed a rich and varied flora, dominated by blunt-flowered rush (*Juncus subnodulosus*) and with little sedge or reed. Regular grazing also tended to suppress the latter plants and encouraged the growth of rush, but it also suppressed the taller and more palatable species such as Greater Tussock Sedge (*Carex paniculata*) and Black Bog Rush (*Schoenus nigricans*), leading to the development of a rich mixture of low-growing species.[209]

Traditional forms of management, however, slowly declined in Broadland during the twentieth century. Dutt in 1903 could still describe a landscape of managed reed beds, of river banks 'almost covered' with reed-stacks in early spring, in which laden reed-craft were 'constantly being rowed or quanted down the dykes' and rafts heavy with marsh hay were still a common sight.[210] Not long after he was writing, however, many of these practices began to be abandoned: the First World War marked something of a watershed. The decline continued during the inter-war years, and accelerated rapidly in the post-war period. But it did not affect all 'traditional' practices to the same extent. Peat-cutting disappeared entirely, as did grazing, and by the middle of the century mowing for hay and litter had effectively come to an end. Reed and sedge beds, in contrast, were only partly abandoned: the market for thatching materials remained buoyant and many beds are still managed commercially, although today they are cut with power cutters (based on those designed for harvesting rice in the Far East) rather than by hand.

One result of this general decline in management is that the various communities of fen vegetation have gradually become less distinct. Nevertheless, as Parmenter has recently demonstrated, it is remarkable how long signs of past management persist in the landscape. Areas once cut regularly for reed are often still dominated by that species, and former sedge beds are still mainly characterised by fairly pure stands of *Cladium*, in which other species are poorly represented, even though they have not been managed for decades. Conversely, where areas of fen were formerly used mainly for grazing this can still be discerned by the trained botanist: saw-sedge and reed are still noticeably under-represented, while the kinds of plants encouraged by browsing – rush, and various forms of true sedge, like brown sedge (*Carex disticha*) and carnation sedge (*Carex panicea*) – remain prominent.

Many areas of open fen still remain in Broadland, especially in the valleys of the Ant and the Thurne. They form a rich and varied natural legacy, the consequence both of past and present management practices, and of a complex range of factors relating to geology, soil types and water chemistry.[211] Large areas are now in the care of such organisations as the Norfolk Naturalist's Trust and the National Trust. Commercial reed- and sedge-cutting continues on these properties, as well as on several private estates. In one or two places, as on Burgh Common in the Muck Fleet valley, areas of fen meadow are still mown or grazed. Wherever traditional forms of management have been abandoned, however, scrub and then woodland gradually encroaches. Some of the fen vegetation communities, it is true, are invaded more quickly than others: those areas formerly grazed or mown for hay and litter seem more susceptible than abandoned sedge beds which – as for example on the Brayden Marshes near Horsey Mere – sometimes display an impressive ability to resist colonisation. In the long run, however, all the open fens would become woodland unless they were managed, or unless steps are taken to clear the colonising scrub away – a regular weekend activity for numerous volunteer 'scrub-bashers' organised by the Broads Authority. Interestingly, the character of the invading woodland is itself to some extent affected by previous forms of landuse and management. In particular, carr developed over solid peat tends to contain a higher proportion of grey willow (*Salix cinera*) and downy birch (*Betula pubescens*), while that growing over former peat cuttings has a greater dominance of alder.[212]

Of course, areas of damp woodland, dominated by alder and willow, had always been a feature of the fen landscape. The slow decline in traditional management, however, has led to their steady expansion. In the Ant valley there are still around 400 hectares of open fen, but nearly 700 have tumbled to scrub or carr during the past sixty or seventy years, especially in the area around Barton Broad.[213] The situation in the Bure valley above Ant Mouth is similar. As a result, a cruise between Wroxham and Ranworth is now vaguely reminiscent of a scene from the film *The African Queen*. By a curious paradox, the wildest of Broadland's many landscapes is the most recently created.

5

The drainage windmills

The drainage windmills are perhaps the most striking, and certainly the most distinctive, feature of the Broadland landscape. They represent a unique survival, for there were once other low-lying, marshy areas of England drained by wind power, most notably the Fenlands of Cambridgeshire, Lincolnshire and west Norfolk. But from these the mills have long since almost entirely disappeared. Other methods of pumping water from the Broadland marshes were used in the past. Horse mills were sporadically employed, although none now survives; and, as we shall see, from the early nineteenth century steam pumps were used. But it is the drainage mills which make the most significant, and most characteristic, contribution to the Broadland scene.

Of the 72 drainage mills which still survive in recognisable condition, the vast majority – 62 – are brick tower mills. The others are wooden structures of various kinds, which will be discussed in due course. The brick towers come in a wide range of sizes. Some, like Swim Coots Mill, Catfield (TG 411212), are scarcely more than 6 metres high: that at Berney Arms (TG 465049), in contrast, is a huge building, towering a full 22 metres above the surrounding marshes. Slowly rendered redundant in the course of the present century, a number of mills have fallen down, or have been demolished, and those that survive do so in varying condition. A small number – such as Berney Arms, Stracey Arms or Horsey – have been restored, although none now fulfils a practical function. A number of others are undergoing restoration, and around a third have been converted to other (usually residential) uses. The majority, however, are derelict and in various states of ruination although – thanks to the valiant efforts of the Broads Authority and the Norfolk Windmills Trust – further decay has often been retarded by the installation of a temporary aluminium cap, which protects the mill and its remaining machinery from the effects of the weather.

Given their striking impact upon the landscape, and the fact that they represent the densest concentration of windmills in England, it is not surprising that the Broadland mills have received a good deal of attention from industrial archaeologists and others. The noted windmill historian Rex Wailes devoted a whole chapter to them in his seminal work *The English Windmill* in 1954, and published an important article on the subject in 1956.[214] A. J. Ward, in an unpublished typescript (since sadly destroyed in the disastrous Norwich Library fire of 1994) attempted to catalogue all known examples and made extensive use of oral history evidence.[215] Arthur Smith, while only briefly discussing the history of these structures, assessed their current condition in two exhaustive surveys, in 1971– 78 and 1985–89.[216] Yet in spite of all this work, the observation made in 1970 by Susanna Wade Martins – that a comprehensive account of the typology and historical development of Broadland's drainage mills still needs to be written – remains true.[217] What follows represents a preliminary attempt to provide such an account, an attempt based partly on documentary evidence, and partly on an analysis of the surviving structures.[218]

Such an investigation is fraught with difficulties. In archaeological terms, the surviving towers are often difficult to date. Moreover, many of the mills have been extensively rebuilt and refitted, often on more than one occasion, as technological change led to improvement and adaptation. Two of the oldest mills in Broadland, those at Oby (TG 409138: 1753) and on the Brograve Level (TG 448236: 1771), are thus both fitted with turbine pumps, a device not invented until the 1850s, and only one surviving eighteenth-century mill still contains much of its original machinery. As we shall see, many mills were heightened, or 'hained' to use the local term, in the course of the nineteenth century. In addition, mills often required extensive repairs as a consequence of gale damage or subsidence. Great pains were taken to avoid the later by erecting the towers on piles, and by only laying a limited number of courses of brick each day. Nevertheless, many mills show signs of cracking and distortion, later straightening, or are supported by wrought-iron tie bars (up to six in the case of Upton 'Black Mill': TG 405141). As a result of all this, few drainage mills survive as originally built. Another problem is that the documentary evidence relating to the mills is generally meagre, and – like that supplied by maps – is often hard to relate firmly to the surviving physical remains. This is because mills were often completely demolished, and rebuilt from scratch, on the same site: and thus a mill shown on a map, or described in a document, at a certain place may have been a completely different structure to that which we see standing on the spot today. Nevertheless, in spite of such difficulties, the broad lines of the development of the Broadland mills are now tolerably clear, and make a fascinating – and at times surprising – story (Figure 36 a and b).[219]

The earliest mills

Drainage mills were already a common feature of the Broadland landscape by the end of the eighteenth century. William Faden's map of Norfolk (and the adjacent parts of Suffolk), published in 1797 but surveyed a few years earlier, shows no less than 47 of them (Figure 37). What remains unclear is precisely when they first appeared in the region. Most authorities agree that they began to be erected here towards the end of the seventeenth century, and gradually proliferated in the course of the eighteenth, and such evidence as there is seems to

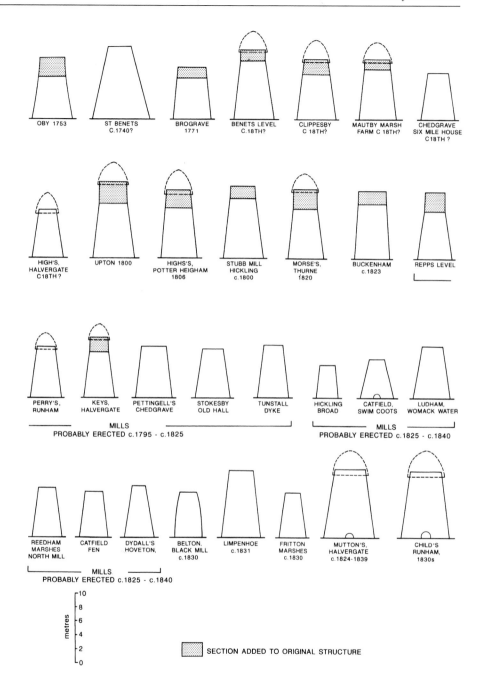

OBY 1753

ST BENETS
C.1740?

BROGRAVE
1771

BENETS LEVEL
C.18TH?

CLIPPESBY
C 18TH?

MAUTBY MARSH
FARM C 18TH?

CHEDGRAVE
SIX MILE HOUSE
C18TH ?

HIGH'S,
HALVERGATE
C18TH ?

UPTON 1800

HIGHS'S,
POTTER HEIGHAM
1806

STUBB MILL
HICKLING
c.1800

MORSE'S,
THURNE
1820

BUCKENHAM
c.1823

REPPS LEVEL

PERRY'S,
RUNHAM

KEYS,
HALVERGATE

PETTINGELL'S
CHEDGRAVE

STOKESBY
OLD HALL

TUNSTALL
DYKE

HICKLING
BROAD

CATFIELD,
SWIM COOTS

LUDHAM,
WOMACK WATER

MILLS
PROBABLY ERECTED c.1795 - c.1825

MILLS
PROBABLY ERECTED c.1825 - c.1840

REEDHAM
MARSHES
NORTH MILL

CATFIELD
FEN

DYDALL'S
HOVETON,

BELTON,
BLACK MILL
c.1830

LIMPENHOE
c.1831

FRITTON
MARSHES
c.1830

MUTTON'S,
HALVERGATE
c.1824-1839

CHILD'S
RUNHAM,
1830s

MILLS
PROBABLY ERECTED c.1825 - c.1840

metres

10
8
6
4
2
0

SECTION ADDED TO ORIGINAL STRUCTURE

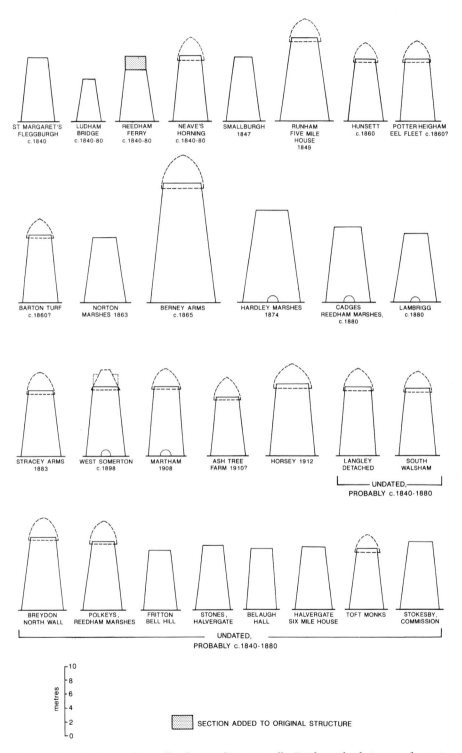

ST MARGARET'S FLEGGBURGH c.1840 · LUDHAM BRIDGE c.1840-80 · REEDHAM FERRY c.1840-80 · NEAVE'S HORNING c.1840-80 · SMALLBURGH 1847 · RUNHAM FIVE MILE HOUSE 1849 · HUNSETT c.1860 · POTTER HEIGHAM EEL FLEET c.1860?

BARTON TURF c.1860? · NORTON MARSHES 1863 · BERNEY ARMS c.1865 · HARDLEY MARSHES 1874 · CADGES REEDHAM MARSHES, c.1880 · LAMBRIGG c.1880

STRACEY ARMS 1883 · WEST SOMERTON c.1898 · MARTHAM 1908 · ASH TREE FARM 1910? · HORSEY 1912 · LANGLEY DETACHED · SOUTH WALSHAM

UNDATED, PROBABLY c.1840-1880

BREYDON NORTH WALL · POLKEYS, REEDHAM MARSHES · FRITTON BELL HILL · STONES, HALVERGATE · BELAUGH HALL · HALVERGATE SIX MILE HOUSE · TOFT MONKS · STOKESBY, COMMISSION

UNDATED, PROBABLY c.1840-1880

metres 10 8 6 4 2 0

SECTION ADDED TO ORIGINAL STRUCTURE

Comparative elevations of Broadland tower drainage mills. (Evidence for dating: see footnote 219).

Figure 36 (a) and (b)

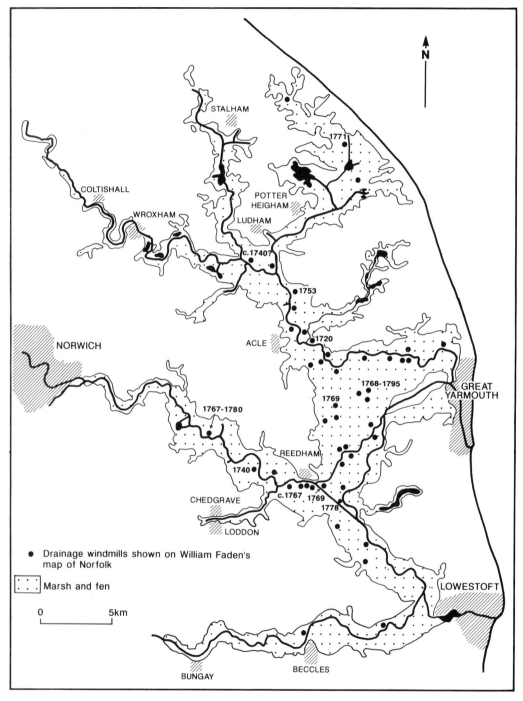

Figure 37   The distribution of drainage mills in the late eighteenth century. This map shows all the
                   drainage mills depicted on William Faden's map of the county of Norfolk, published 1797,
                   surveyed *c*.1795. Where known, their dates of origin are given.

support this view. So far as I am aware no seventeenth-century document refers to one and no map shows one (although the intriguingly named 'Mill Brigg Marsh' near Ant Mouth is recorded as early as 1617).[220] By 1702, however, a list of owners and properties in the Halvergate Marshes drawn up by the Sea Breach Commission was able to refer to 'part of Merie Marsh called the Mill Marsh' in Halvergate parish; while a map of 1702, of the Bishop of Norwich's lands at St Benet's Abbey 'with the marshes belonging to the same', shows a small drainage mill in elevation, although not the famous brick structure which now sits within the medieval gatehouse (Figure 30).[221]

Stray pieces of cartographic and documentary evidence suggest that the number of mills increased gradually during the eighteenth century. The low-lying common at Stokesby was enclosed by parliamentary Act in 1720 – the earliest parliamentary enclosure in Norfolk. A map drawn up shortly afterwards shows a mill – occupying the same position as the present Stokesby mill, although clearly not the existing building – which had presumably just been erected to drain the newly enclosed common.[222] In 1740 the accounts for the Beauchamp-Proctor estate record a payment for the construction of a mill in the Round House Marshes (in Hardley);[223] the large drainage mill built within the abbey gatehouse at St Benet's is said to have been erected as early as c.1740, and was certainly in existence by 1781;[224] while the low tower mill at Oby carries a date-stone of 1753.

More abundant evidence comes from the last third of the century, however, and it seems probable that this period saw a marked increase in the construction of mills: something perhaps related to the slow improvement in agricultural prosperity in the region in the period after c.1760 following a time of relative depression. This may explain why Marshall, writing in 1787, was under the impression that drainage mills had only appeared on the Halvergate Marshes some twenty years earlier.[225] An undated document, probably drawn up in the mid-1760s, thus refers obliquely to the construction of a drainage mill in Norton,[226] and by c.1768 another document was able to list 'The Contents of ye several Marshes [225 acres in all] lying in Norton belonging to Wm Windham Esq wch are Drain'd by ye New Engine.'[227]

William Windham of Earsham was clearly much involved in drainage work, for in August of the following year an agreement was drawn up between him, John Berney of Bracon Ash, John Fowle of Broome, and Dionissa his wife, all of whom owned substantial blocks of land in the adjacent Thurlton Marsh (60 acres, 80 acres, 230 acres respectively), to erect a drainage mill.[228] The lands in question were 'Subject to be overflowed and have been freqtly damaged by Floods and Inundations of water for want of a Mill or Engine and other proper Works Cuts Drains Dams Sluices and Outlets to carry off the same.'

The three parties resolved to erect a mill on Berney's land, paying for the work between them 'rateably and in Proportion to ye Number of Acres wch Each of them . . . have or hath in the sd parcells of Marshes'. The mill was to be fenced off from the rest of Berney's grounds and supplied with all the necessary 'Bridge Trunks Arches Dams Sluices and the Great drain leading towds the River'. Berney was to be compensated for the loss of land occupied by the mill and associated works by a regular payment made yearly by the other parties. In fact the document makes it clear that the mill had already been erected at a cost of £259. 19s. 5d.

Such joint funding of the construction and maintenance of drainage mills developed naturally out of earlier co-operation concerning sluices and embankments, and reflects both the complex intermixture of properties in many areas of marsh and the high costs of mill construction. It was to be repeated many times. Thus in September of the same year (1769) rather similar articles of agreement were drawn up between Miles Branthwaite of Gunthorpe and John Houghton of Bramerton for the erection of a mill on Scarsdale Marsh in Halvergate, close to what is now Manor Farm. These stated how Branthwaite was the owner of 'A certain Marsh lying on and being in Halvergate . . . called Scarsdale Marsh' and that Houghton, who owned the adjacent areas of marsh, had 'for the better Improvement of his said Marsh Lands . . . lately at his own Costs and Charges erected and built a Windmill or Water Engine for draining the water off his said Marshes'. This, however, had been built over the 'old way or Road there leading through his marsh to the said Marsh of the said Miles Branthwaite'. Houghton had made a new road, and in return for this, its maintenance by him, and the use of the mill to drain Scarsdale Marsh as well, Branthwaite and his heirs were to pay 10s. yearly, 'During all such time as the said Windmill or Water Engine shall continue to work and the said marsh called Scarsdale Marsh shall be drained by means thereof.' He also agreed to make 'sufficient' banks and walls against the Fleet and all other dykes and drains 'except against the marshes of the said John Houghton and others agreed to be drained by the same mill'.[229]

Sometimes much larger groups of proprietors were involved in these agreements. In 1778 proposals were drawn up for draining 'certain Marshes in Raveningham and Towns Adjoining'.[230] The document points out that for want of drainage work the marshes in question had become 'of little value', and that in consequence two of the principal owners, Jane Welham and E. Clarke, 'are come to a resolution of Erecting a Mill for Draining the same'. On this occasion, however, a further eight proprietors agreed to pay 2s. per acre every year for the next twenty years towards the costs of maintaining the mill and associated works.

Interesting though such documentary evidence is, it is unfortunately insufficient to allow us to establish the dates of origin of many of the 47 mills shown on Faden's map of 1797. In fact, only one other example can be assigned a firm date – that at Brograve level, Hickling, which until recently carried a date-stone of 1771. One or two others, however, can be ascribed broad date brackets on the basis of maps or documents. Thus the mill shown by Faden in the Buckenham Marshes must have been built between 1767, when a survey shows the site as empty, and 1780, when the Beauchamp-Proctor estates here were surveyed[231] (Figure 37).[232]

The evidence provided by a small number of surviving structures, and by early illustrations, allows us to state with confidence the essential features of eighteenth-century drainage mills (Figure 38). Most, if not all, were towers with moveable wooden caps. Like contemporary corn windmills, they were equipped with 'common' sails – that is, sails which consisted of a wooden framework over

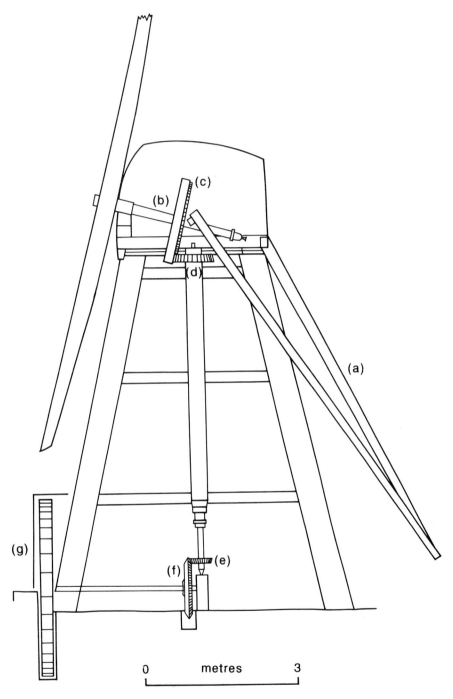

Simplified diagram of the internal workings of an eighteenth-century brick drainage mill.   Figure 38
The mill is provided with common sails and has a long tailpole by which it can be hauled
in to the wind. (a) tailpole; (b) windshaft; (c) wallower; (d) vertical axle; (e) spur wheel;
(f) pit wheel; (g) scoop wheel.

Plate 14   A scoop wheel: Pettingell's Mill, Chedgrave Detached.

which a narrow sheet of canvas was stretched. This had to be adjusted in different wind conditions – 'reeved', like the sails of a ship. The marshman responsible
for the mill had to stop it when such changes needed to be made. He also had to
winch the cap of the mill manually into the wind, whenever the latter's direction
changed, and for this reason early mills were equipped with a long 'tailpole'
extending down from the rear of the cap. Both factors served to limit the height
of the mill: the alternative, of building a balcony or stage from which the cap and
sails could be adjusted, was seldom adopted in Broadland. The sails – always four
in number – turned an axle called the *windshaft* on which was mounted a large
cog wheel, variously known as the *brakewheel* or the *headwheel*. This meshed with
another large wheel, the *wallower*, which was mounted on an upright axle running vertically through the mill from top to bottom. Mounted on this, near ground
level, was the *crown wheel* which meshed with the *pit wheel* and thus drove a
horizontal axle on which the *scoop wheel* was mounted. This resembled the wheel
of a watermill, and acted like one, but in reverse, lifting water up from the marshes
and over the low wall into a higher-level dyke or river. Early mills generally had
wheels with a diametre of around 3 metres, although later examples might drive
ones of 7 metres or more (the height a wheel could lift, so it was said, was around
$\frac{3}{8}$ its diameter). So far as the evidence goes, all eighteenth-century mills had their
scoop wheel set in a semi-circular weatherboarded housing adjoining, but outside, the structure of the mill itself (Plate 14).

A number of commentators have suggested that most early mills were wooden weatherboarded structures of 'smock' construction, rather like that which still stands at Herringfleet (although this is, in fact, of nineteenth-century date, and no earlier examples survive in Broadland) (Plate 15). Mills like this were widely used in the Cambridgeshire and Lincolnshire Fenlands in the eighteenth century, and Broadland examples are illustrated on the St Benet's map of 1702, on the Stokesby map of c.1720, on an estate map of the Buckenham Marshes of 1780, and on a number of paintings by members of the Norwich School.[233] Many of the mills shown on Faden's map, however, must have been brick tower mills, for these are also shown on a number of early nineteenth-century paintings. More-over, as early as 1787 William Marshall described the standard Broadland drain-age mill as having a body 'built of brick, about twenty feet high, with sails similar to those of a corn mill, but somewhat smaller'.[234]

Hardly any of the surviving tower mills in Broadland are of eighteenth-century date, but those which are conform, on the whole, to Marshall's descrip-tion: that is, they were originally low structures, their brick towers 7 metres or less in height. Of the 47 shown on Faden's map of 1797, only twenty still have mills on (or very near) their sites; and of these, the majority were completely rebuilt in the course of the nineteenth century. Thus, as already noted, a mill was erected on the Round House Marshes in Hardley in 1740, and a mill is clearly shown here by Faden: but the tall brick tower which now occupies the site bears a date-stone of 1874. In fact, there are only three mills in Broadland which are certainly, and five probably, structures which were in existence when Faden's map was surveyed.

As already noted, two of these can be dated by the date-stones they carry, or until recently carried: Oby (TG 409138: 1753) and Brograve Level (TG 488256: 1771). The brick tower of the latter is c.7.3 metres high, but has been raised at some point in the past by c.1.5 metres: when originally built it must have had a total height of less than 6 metres, and a very squat profile, almost as broad as high. Oby has today a rather taller tower (8.75 metres) but here, too, careful examination suggests that it has been raised, and was originally only c.6.5 metres in height, suggesting a total height, with cap, of around 8 metres: again, a rather squat structure. Clippesby Mill (TG 409128) cannot be ascribed a firm date but a number of similarities with the two towers just described suggest that it may well be the mill shown on this spot by Faden's map. Again the tower has been raised, by c.2.3 metres: and again its original height must have been slightly over 6 metres. Like Brograve and Oby, it is built very solidly in header bond and must have had a rather stumpy profile, although here the 'batter' or slope of the sides is more pronounced. Almost identical in form and dimensions is Mautby Marsh Farm Mill on the Bure (TG 489099), which has likewise been raised and altered in the nineteenth century. Similar, although lower and more squat in profile, is the mill at Six Mile House, Chedgrave Detached. Although extensively rebuilt in the 1870s, the original structure, probably of late eighteenth-century date, has not been heightened, so that the capless shell retains a height of only c.6.6 metres. Two other mills which are probably of similar vintage – High's Mill on the Fleet Dyke, Halvergate (TG 444034) (Plate 1), and St Benet's Level Mill on

Plate 15   Herringfleet Mill on the river Waveney. Although constructed in the 1820s, the mill is
                typical of the wooden smock drainage mills of the previous century. Note the common
                sails and long tailpole.

the Thurne (TG 399156) – are also rather low structures (although the latter has subsequently been 'hained'). These, however, have rather more slender profiles. High's Mill is the only one of these early mills which retains much of its original machinery. All the others have been extensively refitted at various times in the nineteenth century (both Oby and Brograve, as already noted, now have turbine pumps, rather than their original single external scoop wheels) and none retain their original caps.

St Benet's Abbey Mill on the Bure (TG 3870158), the only other drainage mill in Broadland which is unquestionably of eighteenth-century date, is in many ways an exceptional structure. Erected on firmer ground than most – on the edge of the 'island' of Cow Holme – and given additional stability, and a ready-made 'stage', through being built into the ruins of the abbey gatehouse, it is – at 10.5 metres – considerably higher than any other drainage mill built before the mid-nineteenth century (Plate 6). Some writers have cast doubt on whether in fact this mill was ever used for drainage: or if it was, whether this was its original function. It has been suggested that its main purpose was to grind cole seed and rape seed, grown on the marshes and presumably brought to the site by boat.[235] It is certainly possible that the mill was also used for this purpose, for other Broadland mills had dual functions. But there is no real doubt that it was primarily used for drainage. The low arch, through which the axle driving the external scoop wheel passed, can still be seen (though now bricked up) low down on the western side of the building; while an undated nineteenth-century engraving shows, quite clearly, the shuttered housing for the wheel itself, slightly detached from the main body of the building.[236] When the antiquary J. W. Fenn visited the site in 1788 he reported that the ruins of the gatehouse had been disfigured because 'a windmill for draining the marshes, built with brick somewhat in the form of a sugar loaf, is erected in such a manner that the west front of the gate is now enclosed within it'.[237]

Although drainage mills were a common feature of the Broadland landscape by the end of the eighteenth century, they were not uniformly distributed. To judge from Faden's map there were none in the valley of the river Ant, only four in that of the Thurne and none in the valley of the Bure upstream of St Benet's; and although it is possible that his surveyors missed some examples this pattern of distribution is probably broadly correct. Most mills – a total of twenty five – were in the main marshland 'triangle' of Halvergate. Almost all the others were in the lower reaches of the rivers Bure and Yare. They were, that is, largely associated with silt soils, with areas of long-enclosed private grazing marsh, and not with commons, although there were one or two possible exceptions.

Given that these areas had long been embanked and drained, it is not entirely clear why the eighteenth century should have seen this gradual proliferation of mills. Presumably simple drainage by flap sluices was becoming less efficient due to a continuing fall in relative land/sea levels, although other factors may also have led to problems of drainage in this period. Contemporaries certainly believed that increased tidal flows, due to better dredging of the rivers – and the increased quantities of water flowing in the lower reaches of the rivers resulting

from reclamation higher up (especially in the valley of the Thurne) – were increasing the threat of flooding within the Halvergate 'triangle'. As a consequence,
as one observer put it in 1803, 'The marshes could not be kept dry from the
water, were it not for the Engines – the water came thro' the banks every year,
little or much.'[238] It is, however, worth noting that even in the nineteenth century several portions of the Halvergate Marshes were kept dry without the assistance of wind pumps. One of the detached sections of Acle parish (Trevetts, or
Scare Gap Marsh) was never served by a mill, and in 1829 sales particulars for
a property here boasted that it was not subject to any drainage rates.[239] A sketch
map of 1799 shows what are probably simple flap sluices positioned at the points
where each boundary drain (and one of the internal drains) meets the river.[240]
In some cases, perhaps, mills were constructed not so much to preserve the
marshes from serious inundation, but rather to improve the quality of the pasture,
by ensuring that water was removed from them more quickly in winter: damper
ground produced poorer grazing, dominated by rushes and other coarse herbage.

The proliferation of mills: *c.1795–c.1825*

The late eighteenth and early nineteenth centuries saw a massive expansion in
the number of drainage mills in Broadland. Some impression of the scale of the
increase can be obtained by comparing Faden's map of 1797 with that published
by Bryant in 1824: whereas the former shows forty-seven drainage mills, the
latter has no less than seventy-three. Moreover, there are good grounds for believing that Bryant was less than complete in his representation of these structures. A more or less contemporary map, drawn up in 1825 by William Cubitt
and Richard Taylor in connection with proposed improvements to navigation on
the river Yare, shows in considerable detail the course of that river between
Norwich and Reedham, and that of the Waveney between Fritton and Lowestoft.[241] This shows at least five mills not depicted by Bryant. The unpublished
draft drawings made by the Ordnance Survey in the area in *c.1816* similarly
show some mills which appear on later maps, but not on Bryant's, such as High's
Mill in Potter Heigham. If we allow for such omissions the total number of drainage mills by 1825 was probably in excess of 80: in other words, their number
must have nearly doubled in the three decades after 1795 (Figure 39).

To judge from Bryant's map, however, this increase in numbers did not radically change the overall pattern of their distribution. Three mills had now appeared in the Ant valley, and one in the upper Bure, but otherwise they were still
largely concentrated on the silt soils and avoided the deposits of peat. It was those
areas of silt and clay which had formerly been rather sparsely supplied with mills
which saw the greatest increase: the majority of new mills were thus on the
fringes of the great Halvergate 'triangle'; in the Thurne valley (where numbers
rose from four to eleven); and on the Waveney above St Olaves. The explanation
for this structured pattern of proliferation is simple. As we saw in earlier chap-
ters, in this period extensive tracts of common land were enclosed by parliamen-

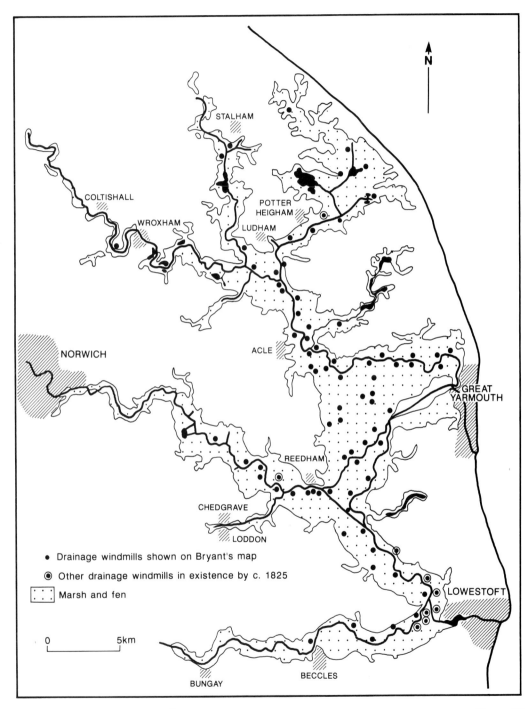

The distribution of drainage mills, *c*.1825.   Figure 39

Legend within figure:
- Drainage windmills shown on Bryant's map
- Other drainage windmills in existence by *c*. 1825
- Marsh and fen

0   5km

tary Acts. While most of the damper areas of fen ground were, at least for the time being, left in an unimproved state, those occupying areas of silt soil, which had formerly been used as common grazing marsh, were now subjected to more systematic drainage. Around two-thirds of the new mills seem to have been erected as a direct consequence of Enclosure Acts, many of which not only stipulated that a mill should be erected but also made arrangements for its maintenance (and that of other drainage works), through the establishment of Drainage Commissions, composed of the principal proprietors in a parish: hence the term 'Commissioners' Mill' used at Hickling, Stokesby and elsewhere. Even when the terms of the Act did not stipulate the construction of a mill, one was often erected soon after enclosure, by individual proprietors or by a group acting together. Not all these new mills, however, were erected following the enclosure of common land. Landowners continued to build and rebuild them in areas of long-enclosed marsh. Thus Tunstall Marshes had long been enclosed when Tunstall West Mill was erected some time between 1795 and 1816.

Of the 72 drainage mills still surviving in Broadland, less than a dozen can be ascribed, with varying degrees of confidence, to the period *c.*1795–1825 (Figure 36a). The majority of these, like those from the previous period, have subsequently been raised or 'hained'. Yet although their towers were thus originally fairly low they were, for the most part, slightly taller than the earlier structures. Most were between 7 and 8 metres high to the base of the cap, giving an overall height of 9 or 10 metres. Moreover, while some – most notably Pettingell's Mill on the Chedgrave Marshes (TG 459016) – perpetuated the rather stumpy, squat profile of early mills like Oby or Brograve, the majority were more slender structures, with a more pronounced 'batter'. As a result, where they have subsequently been heightened the change is normally obvious, for the shape of the tower changes suddenly from conical to cylindrical. This produces a distinctive profile which is most familiar, perhaps, from the picturesque Morse's Mill at Thurne (TG 401159) (Plate 16), the original lower section of which was built following the parliamentary enclosure of 1820.[242] Although almost all the mills surviving from this period are low brick towers, wooden smock mills continued to be erected: there is a contract in the Norfolk Record Office for constructing one at Neatishead in 1810 (at a cost of £226. 10*s.* – no small sum), and as already noted the surviving smock mill at Herringfleet was erected in the 1820s.

All the surviving tower mills from this period, and presumably those which have not survived, were originally equipped with a single external scoop wheel and, to judge from their height, must presumably have had 'common' sails, spread with canvas. The latter feature is of some interest, for it suggests an unwillingness on the part of Drainage Commissioners or landowners to invest in more modern structures. For in the eighteenth and early nineteenth centuries a number of key improvements had been made in mill technology, improvements which were rapidly adopted by the builders of corn mills on the uplands. As already noted, the towers of early windmills were generally low so that their caps could be hauled round to face the wind – winched round by their tailpole. They also needed to be low so that their sails could be adjusted whenever the wind speed

Morse's Mill, Thurne Dyke. Originally built in 1820, following the parliamentary enclosure of the parish of Thurne, the mill was later raised and provided with patent sails and a fantail. Later still, its scoop wheel was replaced with a turbine pump.

Plate 16

changed. A number of eighteenth- and nineteenth-century innovations, however, allowed an increase in the height of mills, in the diameter of their sails, and thus in the amount of power they could produce. Firstly, in 1745 Edmund Lee invented the fantail or fly, the now familiar small vaned wheel attached to the back of the cap, at right-angles to the sails.[243] This was connected through gears to a winding mechanism. As the wind changed direction, the fantail rotated and turned the cap, and therefore the sails, automatically into the wind. The mill could thus respond, almost instantaneously, to quite minor fluctuations in wind direction. This invention was followed by various improvements in the design of sails. In 1772 the Scottish millwright Andrew Meickle invented a totally new kind of sail, composed of a large number of parallel shutters, arranged widthways across the sail and connected by a long rod or 'shutter bar'. A spring at the windshaft end kept the shutters closed under normal conditions, but allowed them to open during gusts. Most important of all, however, was the invention in 1807 of the 'patent sail' by the engineer William Cubitt – a local man, born at Dilham, who was also responsible for the design of the New Cut and other works on the Yare Navigation in the 1820s. In this, the opening of the shutters was controlled by a rod, connected to a complicated mechanism called a 'spider' positioned at the point where the sails joined the windshaft. The windshaft itself was hollow – cast in iron, rather than made of wood – and a rod ran from the spider, through the windshaft, to a rack-and-pinion drive. This was controlled by a chain which hung down the back of the mill, attached to a light tailpole. By adjusting this, the rod controlling the shutters could be moved up and down, and thus the shutters themselves opened or closed. Weights could be hung on this chain, so that the shutters could be kept closed against wind pressure, but allowed to open if there were gusts. Changing the weights could therefore cater for changes in wind conditions without stopping the mill. These improvements meant that new mills could now be built taller, with longer sails, and could therefore be more powerful: which explains, of course, why many existing towers in Broadland were heightened in the course of the nineteenth century. What is interesting, however, is that few if any of the mills erected before 1825 seem to have adopted the new technology. In part this was because knowledge of patent sails spread too slowly to affect the rash of mills erected in the period up to *c.*1815. In addition, after this period agriculture experienced a mild recession following the boom years of the Napoleonic War period. Both private landowners, and Drainage Commissions, would have been keen to save as much money as possible, and therefore opted for the cheaper mills on the old pattern.

The development of drainage mills after *c.*1825

All this, however, changed rapidly in the middle decades of the nineteenth century, as agricultural fortunes revived. In 1840 the drainage mill at Burgh St Margaret – which had been established following the enclosure of the common here in 1804 – was blown down in a storm, and the Drainage Commissioners:

Berney Arms High Mill. This, the tallest drainage mill in Broadland, was erected around 1865. Unusually, it was also used to grind cement clinker and had its massive scoop wheel set in a separate housing several metres away (Derek Edwards, Norfolk Landscape Archaeology).

Plate 17

Resolved and agreed that a new Tower should be erected and that the same should commence from the present Foundations of the old mill at the top of the door . . . the tower shall be built on the best and most improved principal so as to carry the machinery with self acting winding tackle and patent sails.[244]

The new mill was over 9 metres high to the curb, and other mills on this new model erected in the 1830s and 1840s were of similar stature (Figure 36b). Limpenhoe Marshes Mill (TG 395019: 1832) was 9.6 metres to the curb; Mutton's Mill in Halvergate (TG 441063: 1830s) just over 10 metres; and Dilham Dyke Mill, Smallburgh (TG 344248: 1847) 9.2 metres. Some of those built from the 1840s were even taller. Runham Five Mile House (TG 478098: 1849) stands over 12 metres to the curb; Hardley Marshes Mill (TG 387024: 1874), over 13 metres; while Berney Arms Mill (1865) has a total height of 22 metres (Plate 17).

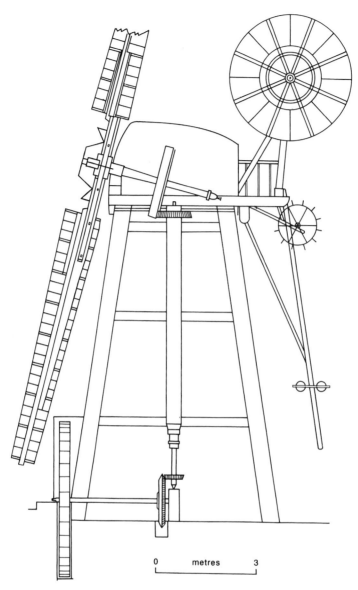

0   metres   3

Figure 40   Simplified diagram of the internal workings of a typical mid-nineteenth-century drainage
mill, with patent sails and a fantail.

Some of these tall, sophisticated structures were equipped, like previous mills,
with a single external scoop wheel (Figure 40). In some, however – such as
Mutton's Mill in Halvergate or Child's Mill in Runham (TG 470160) – the scoop
wheel was now placed *inside*, the water passing beneath the body of the mill
through a low arched opening. Others – like Hunsett Mill (TG 364237) and Turf

Fen Mill (369188) – were provided with two external scoop wheels, an indication of the extra power provided by these larger structures; while others still drove particularly large scoops – like Berney Arms Mill, where the wheel is 7.3 metres in diameter (and located in a detached housing several metres from the body of the tower) (Plate 17).

By the time these examples were being erected, however, many mills were being provided, not with scoop wheels, but with the new and more powerful turbine pump, invented by Appold in 1851 (Figure 41). This comprised sets of fans or vanes mounted in a cylindrical metal housing: low gearing allowed the vanes to rotate rapidly, and it was said that such pumps could lift half as much again as a conventional scoop wheel, at least in a steady wind. Sometimes the turbine was housed outside the mill: often, however, as at Randalls Mill in Calthorpe (*c*.1880: TG 410264), Lambrigg Mill (*c*.1880?: TG 432752), West Somerton Mill (*c*.1898: TG 464202)) (Plate 18), or Hardley Marshes Mill (1874), it was placed within the body of the tower, with the dyke again passing beneath it, through an arched opening. Turbine pumps were sometimes added to older mills, either in the nineteenth or in the early twentieth centuries. The much-visited Stracey Arms Mill, for example, powered a scoop wheel when originally built in 1883, but was later given a turbine (Plate 19). Turbines were usually placed outside the mill, often (as at Stracey Arms, or at Eel Fleet Dyke Mill, Potter Heigham (TG 449202)) in the old scoop wheel housing, although occasionally (as at Brograve Level) they were located inside the structure.

It should not be imagined, however, that these various forms of tall, sophisticated tower mill were the only kinds of drainage pump being erected in Broadland in the middle and later decades of the nineteenth century. Cheaper brick structures – low towers, lower in fact than any of the mills surviving from the period before *c*.1825, and sometimes fitted with common sails – were still being built. The diminutive Swim Coots Mill in Catfield (TG 411212), for example – a brick tower only 5.6 metres high – was probably built between *c*.1816 and 1840 (Plate 13), while the tiny mill just to the north of Ludham Bridge on the river Ant (TG 372172), 5.9 metres to the curb, was erected between 1840 and 1880. The low mills at Hickling Broad (TG 419221: 4.7 metres), Reedham Marshes ('North Mill', TG 444036: *c*.7 metres) and beside Womack Water in Ludham (TG 400175: *c*.7 metres) all probably date to the period after 1816, and probably after 1825.[245] Once built, low mills like these might subsequently be heightened: in other words, the classic 'hained' appearance typified by Morse's Mill does not necessarily indicate a very early mill which was raised in height when improved technology first became available. Reedham Ferry Mill (TG 4090170), for example, originally 7.5 metres high and later raised to *c*.9.5, was constructed in the period after 1840 (it is conspicuously absent from the Reedham Tithe Award map). Smock mills of various sizes also continued to be built throughout the century – that which still survives at Herringfleet beside the Waveney (TM 465977) was erected in the 1820s (Plate 15), while that on Tunstall Dyke (TG 423092), only the stump of which still exists, was built between 1880 and 1908.[246] There was thus no simple progression in the nineteenth century from low, archaic struc-

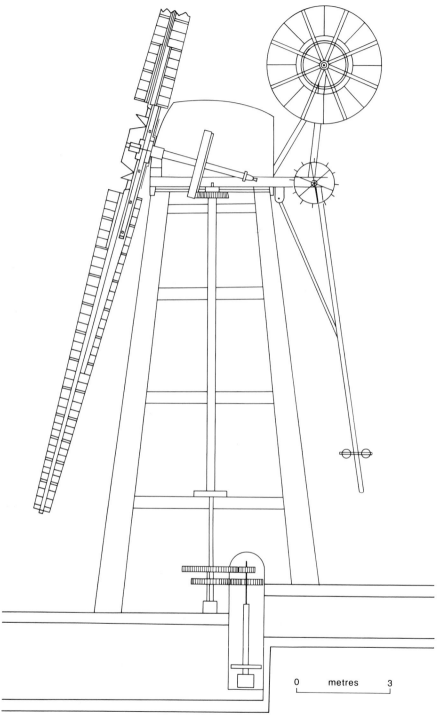

Figure 41   Simplified diagram of the internal workings of a typical late nineteenth-century drainage
             mill. Like the mill in Fig. 40, it is provided with patent sails and a fantail, but it drives a
             turbine pump rather than a scoop wheel.

West Somerton Mill. Erected shortly before 1900, the mill is equipped with an internal   Plate 18
turbine pump. Water thus flowed under the mill – the exit arch can be seen on the left of
the building.

tures to tall, sophisticated ones. Where only small areas needed to be drained, individual proprietors might choose to build low, cheap mills on the old pattern.

Indeed, what the middle and later decades of the nineteenth century witnessed was not simply an increase in the sophistication of drainage mill technology, but rather the development of different kinds and varieties of mill, suited to different circumstances and requirements. For in addition to the various forms of tower and smock mills already described, the period also saw the proliferation of two quite different kinds of wind pump: the 'skeleton' or trestle mill, and the hollow post mill. Both were comparatively cheap structures, made of wood, designed to drain relatively small areas of marsh. The first type comprised a low tower of open wooden framing, sometimes enclosed in boards, surmounted by a cap with fantail and patent sails (Plate 20). The latter consisted of a sturdy hollow upright post, held steady by diagonal wooden bracing, which contained a vertical iron driveshaft and which carried a diminutive cap and either a fantail or else vanes, rather like weather vanes, which served a similar purpose (Plate 21). Hollow post mills were usually equipped with plunger pumps, occasionally with small scoop wheels; trestle mills generally drove scoop wheels or turbines. It is not entirely clear when the two forms were invented. Bacon in 1844 implied that

Plate 19   Stracey Arms Mill. The mill was built in 1883 and extensively modified in 1912.

Boardman's Mill, How Hill. Erected in 1897, this is one of the few surviving examples of   Plate 20
a trestle mill in Broadland.

hollow post mills were then a fairly recent innovation,[247] but there are grounds
for believing that some may have been erected in the previous century (the form
was long-established in the Netherlands): either way, their numbers appear to
have increased markedly in the mid-nineteenth century. Trestle mills, in contrast, seem to have been invented by the millwright Edwin Daniel England as late
as *c*.1870.[248]

In general, less is known about these cheap structures than about tower mills,
largely because, being made of wood, relatively few have survived in the modern
landscape. Whereas brick tower mills, once abandoned, need to be deliberately
destroyed to leave no trace, these diminutive wooden structures usually deterior-
ate rapidly once redundant, leaving only the scant remains of their brick bases.
There are thus only two remaining examples of hollow post mills, both restored
to working order although not on their original sites. Palmer's Mill was moved
from its original position near Acle to the Upton Marshes (TG 403129) in 1976;
while Clayrack Windpump was moved to its present site beside the Ant at How
Hill (TG 369194) having been rescued from dereliction on the Ranworth Marshes
in 1981 (Plate 21).[249] Trestle mills have fared little better. The only surviving
examples are Boardman's Mill at How Hill (TG 370192) (Plate 20), built by

Plate 21   Clayrack Windpump. This typical hollow post mill once stood in the Ranworth Marshes,
                but was moved to How Hill when restored in 1981.

Daniel England in 1897 and equipped with a turbine pump; Hobb's Mill at
Horning (TG 347163), which powered a scoop wheel; and the somewhat idio-
syncratic St Olaves Mill at Fritton (TM 457997), which is essentially a hybrid
between a trestle and a smock mill. Trestle and hollow post mills continued to be
built into the present century, as on Barton Common, where in 1908 a trestle
mill replaced the smock mill erected by the Drainage Commissioners following
the enclosure of 1810.[250]

As well as seeing the proliferation of these new varieties of drainage mill, the
middle and later decades of the nineteenth century also saw a further increase
in the number of mills in Broadland: and by c.1890, to judge from the highly
accurate First Edition Ordnance Survey 25 inch maps, there were over 100 of
them, although this probably represents a decline from an earlier peak (Figure
42). Certainly, on the silt soils there had been some reduction in numbers since
the 1820s. In part this was probably because the more powerful mills which
came into use in the middle decades of the century could drain more extensive
areas of marsh. Indeed, the middle decades of the century saw much readjust-
ment and reorganisation of the pattern of drainage within these areas. Mutton's
Mill in Halvergate is a good example. As already noted, a mill was erected to the
south of Manor Farm in or soon after 1769 and is clearly shown here on a map

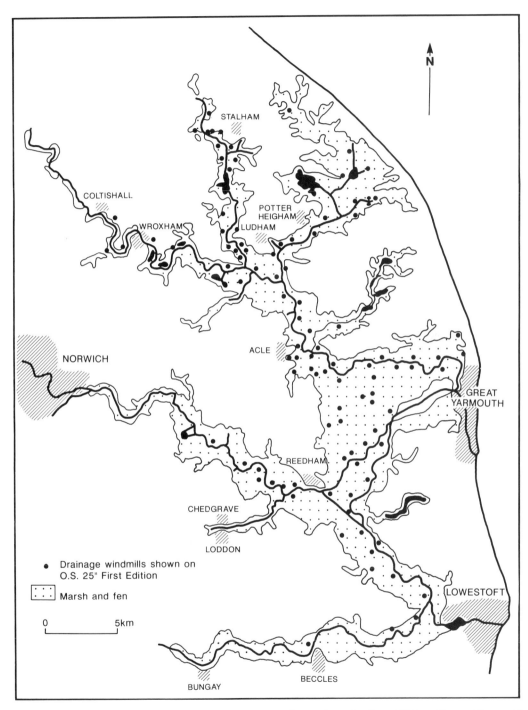

The distribution of wind drainage mills in *c*.1890, as depicted on the First Edition OS 25-inch maps.

Figure 42

of 1803, on the OS draft of *c.*1817, and on Bryant's map of 1824.[251] This, however, was demolished by 1839 and replaced by a new structure in a new position, *c.*200 metres to the south-west.[252] As in earlier periods, the erection of new mills on long-enclosed land was often a co-operative endeavour. In 1831 an agreement was drawn up between eleven owners of a level at Limpenhoe and Southwood, and a contractor, by which the latter undertook to carry out drainage work on 350 acres of marsh, erect a mill and cottage, and make sluices and drains, all for a cost of £744. As usual, the various proprietors agreed to share the cost in proportion to the numbers of acres they held. By 1843, the marshes drained by the Limpenhoe Mill comprised 100 pieces of land in the hands of twenty two proprietors, a total of 510 acres.[253]

But there was a more important reason why the number of mills declined in the course of the century on the silt soils. As we shall see, steam pumps were beginning to be employed in the middle decades of the century, leading to the abandonment and dereliction of some mills here, especially those of more primitive, wooden type erected during the eighteenth century.

This reduction in the numbers of mills on the silt soils, however, was more than compensated for by an increase on the peat deposits higher up the river valleys, especially in that of the Ant. The appearance of new mills in these locations was, in fact, one of the most striking developments of the middle decades of the nineteenth century. This was the period of Victorian 'high farming', in which landowners were investing substantial amounts of money in the improvement of marginal land: and as we have seen, several areas of peat fen were embanked and drained at this time in an attempt to turn them into good-quality grazing land. It is, however, possible that some of the mills erected here may have served a rather different purpose, for this was also a period in which extensive peat extraction resumed, and some may have been used to keep the new workings dry.

While some of the new mills on peat soils were substantial brick towers, like Hunsett Mill (TG 364239) or Turf Fen Mill (TG 369188), the majority were cheap mills of the 'trestle' and 'hollow post' varieties. This explains why the overwhelming majority of the mills shown on the 1880s OS maps in these areas have subsequently vanished: the rate of attrition has been far greater here than on the silt soils, where more durable forms of mill were generally erected. Once again the numbers of mills shown by the OS maps of the 1880s may portray a decline from an earlier peak: the retreat from these marginal grounds was perhaps already under way when the maps were made. Certainly, a map of the Woodbastwick estate, made in 1845, shows two drainage mills on the fens to the south-west of Decoy Broad, both of which had disappeared by the time the OS 25 inch map was surveyed.[254]

Not only did the middle and later decades of the nineteenth century witness a considerable increase in the number of drainage mills in Broadland. In addition, many existing mills were either completely rebuilt, or extensively modified, in this period. As a result, the vast majority of surviving mills are either entirely, or largely, of mid or late nineteenth-century date: brick tower mills surviving unaltered from before 1835 are extremely rare. The drainage mills of the Norfolk

Broads are thus, for the most part, a Victorian heritage, and it is from this period that evidence survives about the men who were responsible for their construction. The brick towers were often constructed by local builders, but the machinery was installed by various firms of millwrights, including those of Robert Barnes of Yarmouth, William Rust of Martham, Edward Stolworthy of Yarmouth, and Thomas Smithdale, whose company moved to Acle from Panxworth in 1890.[255] The most important firm, however, was Englands of Ludham. This company was closely associated with William Cubitt and pioneered the use of patent sails in the area; it probably invented the distinctive boat-shaped cap which, by the mid-nineteenth century, had become universal in the region; it was the first to adapt Appold's turbine pump for marsh drainage; and first developed the trestle mill, in the later decades of the nineteenth century.

It should be noted that not all Broadland mills were used exclusively for drainage. Because they were only regularly in use during the winter months, it made sense to adapt them to some subsidiary employment. Thus the mill at St Benet's Abbey was also used, as we have seen, to grind oil seed; that at Berney Arms ground cement clinker; the mill at Oby operated an estate saw bench; while Dilham Dyke Mill in Smallburgh and (probably) Swim Coots Mill at Catfield were used for grinding corn. A few of the mills were actually inhabited by the marshmen who tended them, such as Eastfield and Stubb Mills, Hickling (TG 437220); and many more were provided with some basic comforts to cheer their minders through the long nights. A number, including High's Mill on the Halvergate Fleet (TG 457027), and those in Catfield Fen (TG 368209) and at Six Mile House (Chedgrave Detached) (TG 452034), had internal fireplaces, while at Clippesby Mill the ceilings were rushed and plastered.

The end of wind drainage

Steam drainage began to supplement wind power in Broadland in the first half of the nineteenth century. As early as 1844 Bacon was able to describe the improvements carried out at Surlingham, and at Buckenham, where:

> Sir William Beauchamp Proctor has within the last four or five years been greatly improving the drainage of the large tract lying between that place and the New Cut, by the erection of a steam mill, that will in a very few years render them very valuable grazing grounds.[256]

Another steam mill had been erected near Yarmouth by one Mr Baker (probably Benjamin Heath Baker, who occupied Scaregap Farm at the time of the Tithe Award survey in 1838).[257] This, Bacon reported, was so effective that when a friend went to visit it on the day it began to work, he found it had stopped: not through mechanical breakdown, but because in the course of a few hours 'it had so entirely drained the tract, that the ditches were empty'.[258] According to Ward, at least 46 such pumps once existed in Broadland, although not all were necessarily in operation at the same time. Around 30 seem to have been working in 1930.[259] They were housed in sheds of brick and/or corrugated iron. Some – like those at Hardley and Langley – were beam engines, but the majority were of more conventional horizontal or vertical type.[260] Their chimneys, belching smoke out across the surrounding marshes, must once have been a familiar sight in Broadland. Remains of their sheds – in various states of ruination – can still be seen in a number of places, often beside pre-existing mills (as at Randall's Mill, Calthorpe, or Lambrigg Mill); but only at a few places – including Strumpshaw Mill, Black Mill on the Waveney near Somerleyton, and Seven Mile House on the Yare – do more or less intact examples, complete with chimneys, survive. The impact of steam drainage was not limited to large fixed engines in purpose-built sheds, however. Portable steam engines were frequently used to drive scoop wheels or turbines when drainage mills were becalmed.

It might be thought that the advent of steam pumps meant that the days of wind drainage were numbered. Certainly, in 1885 Walter Rye could describe the landscape of Halvergate as a 'Tediously winding river dragging itself along through a flat uninteresting marshy country, varied only by drainage mills in various states of dilapidation';[261] while in 1903 Dutt feared that the 'picturesque' structures would 'at no very distant date' be replaced by 'ugly brick or corrugated iron housed steam pumps'. It comes as something of a surprise, therefore, to learn that drainage mills were still being extensively refitted, and even constructed anew, right through the late nineteenth and into the early years of the twentieth century. West Somerton Mill (TG 464202), for example, was built from scratch in the late 1890s (the tenders for the contract still survive); Martham Mill (TG 442192) was constructed in 1908, and extensively altered in 1912; while Horsey Mill (TG 457221) was demolished, and entirely rebuilt, in the same year. Both drainage commissioners and private landowners often preferred to invest in the 'old' technology, rather than in the new. The reasons were largely economic. As agriculture moved into recession in the decades after 1880, both private landowners and Drainage Commissions were careful not to spend more money than was absolutely necessary. True, many of the windmills built around the turn of the century were substantial structures, sophisticated machines which did not come cheap: the surviving tenders for the new mill built at West Somerton in 1895 range from £900 to over £1,000. But steam engines in purpose-built houses were generally more expensive still – the Haddiscoe, Haddiscoe Thorpe and Aldeby Drainage Board spent £2,534 on a steam engine and its housing in 1869.[262] More importantly, their running costs were fairly high, compared with those of windmills, which required nothing in the way of fuel and were comparatively cheap to maintain.

Even before the onset of agricultural recession Drainage Commissions were often uneasy about investing in steam. In 1873 the Burgh and Billockby Drainage Commissioners met to determine 'Whether it would be expedient that Steam drainage should be carried out in connection with the existing Drainage ... inasmuch as the present drainage by means of the existing mill is inadequate.'[263]

Tenders were put out for a steam engine and turbine pump: but when the bids came in at between £878 and £1,007 the plan was dropped, and instead the millwright Daniel Rust was instructed to make an estimate of the 'cost of a new wheel of 3 feet increased diameter and to raise the laying shaft 6 inches and also to give an estimate for constructing a rigger to turn such Wheel by means of a portable engine'.[264]

There was thus no simple, steady progression from wind to steam. Indeed, on occasions the process went the other way. Tunstall West Mill was replaced by a small steam engine at some point before 1880, to judge from the 25 inch OS; but by 1908 (to judge from the next edition of this map) this too had been replaced – by a smock mill, the cut-down remains of which still stand beside the dyke here. Similar evidence of technological 'regression' is apparent elsewhere. In 1896 the millwrights Smithdales were asked by the Winterton and Somerton Drainage Commission to 'form some conclusion as to the cost of Wind Power to be applied to [the] existing steam mill at the same place'.[265]

The drainage of the Broadland marshes thus developed along rather different lines from that of the fens of west Norfolk and Cambridgeshire, where steam pumps had almost entirely replaced windmills by the end of the nineteenth century. In part the difference is due to the fact that the more fragmented nature of ownership, and of drainage responsibility, in Broadland ensured that only limited areas of marsh were drained as single units. Above all, however, it was a consequence of the fact that the Fens were an area of peat which was largely converted to arable in the course of the nineteenth century. The peat rapidly contracted and wasted, to the point where the surface of the land lay too far below that of the principal watercourses to be drained by wind power. Broadland, in contrast, was largely an area of silt soils which remained, for the most part, under pasture. Not only did less shrinkage of the surface occur, but in addition the dominant form of landuse ensured that a far higher water-table, more easily maintained by wind drainage, could be tolerated.

In fact, even internal combustion engines, which began to be used for drainage in the first decades of the twentieth century, seem mainly to have been used to supplement rather than replace wind power: located within or beside windmills they drove the scoop or turbine when the mill was becalmed.[266] It was the spread of the National Grid and the use of electric pumps which finally led to the abandonment of wind drainage: a development which went hand-in-hand with the reorganisation of drainage districts following the establishment of the East Norfolk Rivers Catchment Board, and the various Internal Drainage Boards, in the 1930s. More powerful pumps were now installed, which could effectively drain the much larger areas of marsh for which these new institutions were responsible. Nevertheless, many mills – especially those owned by private individuals – were still operating at the start of the Second World War. That at Ashtree Farm on the river Bure, four kilometres above Yarmouth, was only abandoned when its sails and part of its windshaft were blown off in February 1953.[267]

So striking and prominent in the level marshes, it is hardly surprising that generations of artists and writers have seen Broadland's drainage mills as a quintessential part of the landscape. Broadland wouldn't be Broadland without them. Yet the mills are not some timeless adornment of the scenery. They are practical industrial features with a *history*: of technical ingenuity, mediated by economic demands. That history, moreover, is in many ways a surprisingly short one. In terms of the long chronology of Broadland's landscapes, most of the mills were built the day before yesterday.

6

The industrial landscape

Today Broadland is valued as a rural backwater, and the traffic on the broads and rivers principally consists of innumerable pleasure boats. Before the late nineteenth century, however, the waterways played a more fundamental role in the wider economy of the region. They were arteries of trade, and the ease of transport which they afforded ensured that industry was a far more prominent feature of the landscape than it is today.

Cargoes, canals and improvements

The Broadland waterways would have been plied by boats in Roman times, and in the Middle Ages scattered references attest the importance of river traffic. Thus in 1343, when the *Blithesburghesbot* sank at Cantley *en route* from Yarmouth to Norwich, the cargo lost included salt, sea coal, barrels of iron, as well as 40 men and women passengers.[268] Nothing is known about the kinds of boat employed at this time, but from at least the early seventeenth century the principal craft to ply the rivers was the *wherry*: a distinctive form of sailing boat, clinker-built of oak planks, with a single black sail and a very shallow draught (suitable for sailing the shallow reaches in the upper rivers).[269] Unique to the Broads, numerous writers have considered them a quintessential aspect of the local landscape: 'Wherries are as much a part of Broadland as are reed-beds and windmills.'[270] Until the middle decades of the nineteenth century the wherry was accompanied by a more primitive form of craft called a *keel*: a ship which had the same shallow draught but which was rather smaller, and which carried a central square sail.[271] The fortunes of the keel declined as those of the wherry waxed: by the late 1790s 120 wherries were registered for use on Broadland rivers, but only 36 keels,[272] and by 1829 Stracey was able to observe that keels were 'chiefly restricted to the freightage of timber and are far less numerous than formerly'.[273]

These boats together carried a diverse range of cargoes: coal, tar, grain, bricks, tiles, iron, millstones, timber, wheat, barley, malt, and much more. The bulk of

Plate 22   Stalham staithe: early nineteenth-century buildings associated with a small inland wherry
                port.

the river traffic – and all the larger wherries – operated on the river Yare, running between Norwich and Yarmouth. Smaller craft, however, plied the upper
reaches of the rivers, and the narrow dykes leading to a host of landing places or
staithes (the term derives from the Old English *steath*, 'landing place'). As late as
1903 Dutt was able to describe how 'It is by way of these dykes that the farmers
whose lands lie along the borders of the marshes send away large quantities of
their corn, and receive cargoes of coal for their houses and oilcake for their
stock.'[274] Some staithes lay at the end of such straight artificial cuts; some, like
that at Ranworth, were on broads which were themselves connected by artificial
cuts to the river; others, like that which once existed at Buckenham,[275] lay on the
river itself. Inland ports like these, however diminutive, were often provided with
some storage facilities. Small storehouses survive at Barton Turf; at Wayford
Bridge an imposing three-storey granary and two-storey warehouse can still be
seen; while at Stalham Staithe there is an impressive commercial complex featuring a three-storey warehouse of 1805 and storehouses of 1820 and 1837 (Plate
22).[276]
       Both public and private staithes had existed in some numbers since medieval
times. The suggestion sometimes made, that most originated with the Enclosure
Acts of the early nineteenth century, is erroneous: the pre-enclosure landscape

was littered with them. Thus we learn in a document of 1678 of 'Hardley Stath' and of the 'Stath house and yards thereto belonging';[277] while at Langley in 1736 there was a 'Stathe and Statehouse with a warehouse and stables new built'.[278] Seventeenth- and eighteenth-century maps show both the staithes, and the channels leading to them, much as they are today, and their origins are lost in the distant past. Enclosure awards usually only ratified existing customary landing places, and invested their maintenance in the parish surveyors. The terms of the enclosure awards usually stipulated that the staithes were to be used 'for the laying and depositing of . . . corn, manure, and other things belonging to the landowners and proprietors': the wider public use now made by tourists was not envisaged by the enclosure commissioners! Enclosure awards also often safe-guarded existing rights of navigation. Thus the Enclosure Act for Irstead in 1807 reserved 'one piece of land covered with water containing by measure one hun-dred and eighteen acres', part of Barton Broad, 'to be forever subject to the same right of navigating vessels over the same to which it has been heretofor subject'. Sometimes, however, such rights were not clearly safeguarded, leading – as we shall see – to a number of later disputes over rights of navigation.

The waterways were thus vital transport routes and it was imperative that they were maintained in navigable condition. Before the eighteenth century there was little official regulation of navigations, although the Norfolk and Norwich Commission of Sewers – a body responsible for maintaining internal land drain-age in serviceable condition – took some interest in keeping the waterways free from obstructions, and this would have assisted the passage of traffic. Typically, actual maintenance work was devolved to local communities. Thus in 1679 the Commission observed that the Bure above Woodbastwick was in the summer months 'much hindered and obstructed in its free passage by the weeds growing in the said river . . . for want of timely and seasonably cutting the same yearly as they ought to be'. Every person with property fronting on the river, and 'the inhabitants of all and every town . . . having any common pastures adjoyning to ye said river' were to clear the banks and channel of vegetation before 1 April.[279] Local endeavours of this kind were partially superseded in 1722 when the Yar-mouth Pier and Haven Act laid down that the tolls charged on cargoes unloaded at Yarmouth could be used not only for maintaining the haven, but also for keeping the principal rivers in Broadland dredged. The Commission administer-ing this arrangement, which was composed of 12 members appointed in equal numbers by Suffolk, Norfolk, Norwich and Yarmouth, continued to oversee navi-gation until 1860 when, as a result of reorganisation, separate commissions for the Bure (including the Ant and Thurne), and the Yare and Waveney, were established.[280]

The teeming river traffic stimulated a number of related industries and activ-ities. Boat-building flourished in numerous places, often combined with farming as a dual occupation before the nineteenth century. There were, in the nine-teenth century, particularly important works at Carrow near Norwich, and at Coltishall, where the last trading wherry to be built – the *Ella* – was launched in 1912.[281] Riverside inns were ubiquitous. Sailing down the Yare in the 1880s a wherry would have passed the Yare Hotel at Brundall, the Ferry Inn at Buckenham, the Red House at Cantley, the Ferry Inn at Reedham, and the Berney Arms close to Breydon Water. As the names of two of these hostelries indicate, inns were (and still are) often located where waterways were crossed by bridge or ferry, so that the landlord might benefit from both riverine and terrestrial traffic (landlords were often responsible for operating the ferries). Some inns, however, were in more remote locations, not readily accessible by land, like the Chequers beside St Benet's Abbey, which burnt down in a fire in the 1880s, or the Berney Arms, on the Yare just south of Breydon Water, which is still trading.

It is hard to over-emphasise the importance of river transport in England, especially for bulky cargoes, in the centuries before the advent of the railways. Hardly surprising, then, that attempts were made to improve and extend the network of waterways in Broadland (Figure 43); nor that these often met with strong opposition from vested interests, not least because communities flourished at the highest navigable point of a river, and trade would decline if navigation was artificially extended inland. The earliest major attempt at improvement came in the seventeenth century. In 1656 Francis Matthew argued for the creation of a 'Mediterranean Passage', connecting Yarmouth in the east of Norfolk to Kings Lynn in the west, by improving the course of the Waveney and the Little Ouse and linking the two by cutting a canal to connect their headwaters, through the minor watershed that separates the two in the area around Lopham, Redgrave and Blo Norton.[282] This was a hopelessly ambitious plan, and could never have succeeded. Nevertheless, one element of Matthew's scheme was implemented. The Waveney between Beccles and Bungay was improved, probably in the 1670s, by works which involved the construction of three locks: one between Shipmeadow and Geldeston, the second at Ellingham, and the third at Wainford (Plate 23).

The most important extensions to the Broadland waterways, however, were in the north of the region, where three navigations were created. The first was the Aylsham Navigation, established by a parliamentary Act of 1773. This began at Coltishall, and ran along the river Bure for more than 15 kilometres as far as the market town of Aylsham. Construction commenced in 1774, and the waterway was opened in 1779.[283] For the most part it simply followed the course of the old river but there were short diversions – each supplied with a lock – to avoid the mills at Horstead, Buxton and Burgh-next-Aylsham; and also at Aylsham itself, where a lateral canal (again with a lock) was made for about a mile on the north side of the river, terminating at 'Dunkirke', a basin with granaries and warehouses (fragments of which still survive). The canal appears to have been moderately successful until the 1880s, when competition from the newly constructed Wroxham–Aylsham railway, running parallel to it, caused a decline in income from tolls.[284] Nevertheless, it continued to operate until badly damaged by the floods of 1912.

More successful, and more important, was the North Walsham and Dilham Canal.[285] This was instituted by an Act of Parliament of 1812, although local opposition from vested interests delayed work on construction until 1825. Then, however, under the direction of the engineer J. Millington, it was completed within

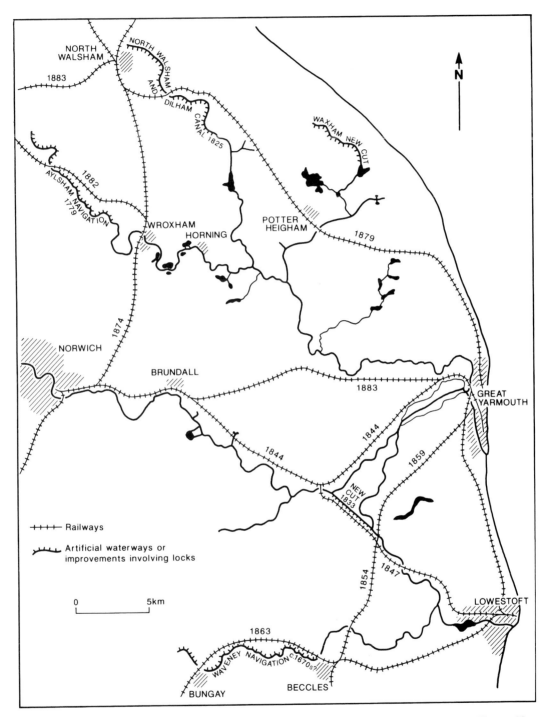

Railways and navigations in Broadland.   Figure 43

Plate 23   Wainford lock on the Waveney navigation, photographed in the early years of the twentieth
                century (courtesy of the Norfolk Local Studies Library).

twelve months. The canal was nearly 14 kilometres long, with six locks which –
like others in Broadland – were larger than those on conventional canals, 15 m
long and 3.75 m in width, in order to accommodate wherries (which were rather
bigger than normal narrow boats). The surplus water from the four lower locks
was used to power watermills constructed beside them (remains of a lock with an
attached mill can be seen at Briggate, at Honing, where there is also a substantial
warehouse associated with the canal). The canal was moderately successful until
the middle decades of the nineteenth century when, once again, competition
from railways and the improvement of local roads increased the relative costs of
water-borne transport. By 1886 trade had almost disappeared, and the canal
was sold to one Edward Press, a North Walsham miller, who hoped to develop it
for pleasure boating. But there was insufficient money available for maintenance
and the northern portion of the canal was closed in 1892. The canal changed
hands a number of times before finally closing to traffic in 1935, although it still
holds water as far as Swafield Bridge, North Walsham.[286]

    The third extension to navigation in the north of Broadland was less ambi-
tious, and less is known about its history. The Waxham New Cut ran from the
northern end of Horsey Mere for just over 6 km as far as Lound Bridge. Passing
through level marshes around the headwaters of the Thurne, it was constructed
without the need of locks. It was apparently dug in the 1820s, partly to facilitate

The New Cut. This ruler-straight artificial waterway was dug in the early 1830s as part of the ambitious scheme to make Norwich accessible to sea-going vessels. To the left is the Reedham–Lowestoft railway line, built in 1847.

Plate 24

drainage, partly to provide access to the villages around the headwaters of the Thurne, and to a number of industrial concerns, like the brickworks at Lound Bridge. It remained largely navigable until 1953 when – following changes to the drainage system on the Brograve Level – it was closed above Bridge Farm, Waxham. It is still just navigable for much of its length, with care, in a small boat.

The most ambitious scheme for improving navigation in Broadland, however – and the one that has left the most dramatic mark on the landscape – was the excavation of the New Cut, which was completed in 1832. This runs, ruler-straight, through the level drained marshland for a distance of 4 km from St Olaves to Reedham (Plate 24). It was part of a more ambitious scheme which was carried out between 1828 and 1833, with the combined aim of providing Lowestoft – then a minor fishing village – with a safe harbour, and Norwich with direct access for coastal vessels.[287] Up to this time Yarmouth had served as an entrepôt for the city, with cargoes being transshipped from ocean-going ships to smaller keels and wherries. Only the very smallest sea-going vessels could make the journey up the Yare. Such a situation was not popular with Norwich businessmen (not least because of the high tolls charged at Yarmouth) and in 1814 the Norfolk engineer William Cubitt was engaged to make a survey of the river, and to submit plans for its improvement. In 1821 he produced his ambitious proposal for making a new outlet to the sea at Lowestoft which, combined with other improvements, would make Norwich directly accessible to sea-going vessels.[288]

There was considerable and understandable opposition to these plans from the port of Yarmouth, and also from the proprietors of the North Walsham and Dilham Canal and the Aylsham Navigation. All were worried that the new navigation would divert traffic from Yarmouth to Lowestoft, that it would thus lead to a neglect of the channels through Breydon, and ultimately to the damage of navigation on the Bure and the Ant.[289] The Norwich and Lowestoft Navigation Bill was, in fact, defeated in Parliament in 1826: but a revised bill was passed in 1827, and construction work began soon afterwards.

The first part of the scheme involved the creation of a channel, some 500 metres in length, which would connect Lake Lothing – which was at this time a fresh-water lake, connected only to Oulton Broad – with the sea. Work began in 1832 and was completed within the space of six months. The channel leading out to sea was scoured by ponding back the waters behind a sea-lock at the upper end of the cut. Following the connection of the lake and the sea, Oulton Dyke – a watercourse of uncertain origin, connecting the broad with the river Waveney – was improved and widened. These alterations created the unusual circumstances of a watercourse – the new dyke – which was tidal in two directions. Tides flowed up the Waveney, and along Oulton Dyke, about an hour and a half later than those coming directly from the sea into Lake Lothing. This necessitated the construction of a lock – Mutford Lock – between the lake and Oulton Broad, of unusual form. Locks usually have pairs of lock gates that meet in the middle at a slight angle, forming a point which is directed towards the higher water level, so that they are better able to withstand the water pressure. Here, however, two sets of gates were required, in order to withstand the alternating direction of pressure.

When the water on each side of the lock was at equal height, ships passed through from the lake into the broad, and then went up the Oulton Dyke to the Waveney. At St Olaves, however, they no longer sailed down the Waveney to Breydon Water, but instead by-passed it, by passing along the New Cut. Some deepening of the Yare was also attempted as part of the improvements, principally that section of the river between Foundry Bridge and Carrow Bridge in Norwich, and the whole length of the river, down as far as Low Street near Reedham, was dredged to a depth of 12 ft (3.7 m). The resulting 50 km-long 'canal' was effectively opened in September 1833, when the first vessels to reach Norwich direct from the sea by way of the New Cut were welcomed by the mayor.[290] The navigation was never much of a financial success, however. The average size of ocean-going vessels was increasing fast during the nineteenth century and many were soon too large to pass through the New Cut (only 21 metres wide). The proposed harbour at Norwich was never built, as the costs of maintaining the improvements began to outstrip the revenue from tolls. By 1847 the navigation was bankrupt, and was purchased by the entrepreneur Sir Morton Peto of Somerleyton Hall, mainly to facilitate his plans for expanding Lowestoft harbour. The New Cut itself was badly damaged by the great floods of 1953, and very nearly closed. It is now, like the rest of the Broadland river system, used exclusively by pleasure boats.[291]

The importance of the Broadland waterways for commercial transport declined in the course of the nineteenth and twentieth centuries, largely through competition with the railways and with improved roads and road transport. This decline was, however, slow. As late as 1903 Dutt believed that were still 'in all probability, as many wherries as ever on the Broadland rivers'.[292] By 1915 some owners were attempting to make their craft more competitive by supplying them with steam engines, but to no avail.[293] The last commercial wherry ceased trading during, or shortly before, the Second World War. As river traffic declined, the peripheral parts of the waterways system (especially the northern navigations) became derelict. Already by 1903 the Waveney above Beccles, the North Walsham Navigation and the Waxham Cut were becoming impassable.[294]

By the 1930s commercial traffic had virtually disappeared from the Bure and the Waveney, although the Yare remained fairly busy. This was partly on account of the sugar-beet factory established at Cantley in 1912, partly because of the construction of Boulton and Paul's riverside steelworks in Norwich during the First World War, and partly as a result of the opening of the coal-fired power station at Thorpe in 1927.[295] Within living memory – indeed, within my own memory – foreign sea-going ships still docked at Norwich in some numbers. Since the 1960s and 1970s, however, commercial traffic has dwindled to virtually nothing.

Chalk and lime

Although the wherries carried a phenomenal range of bulk cargoes, some were of particular importance: either because they were vital to the agricultural economy of the uplands, or because they stimulated the development of new industries, close to the waterways. By the second half of the eighteenth century one of the most important of these cargoes was 'marl'. Marling was the practice of spreading a calcareous subsoil on the surface of the land, in order to neutralise acidity and thus enhance crop growth. It had been carried out in Norfolk since medieval times, but in the seventeenth and eighteenth centuries was adopted on an ever-increasing scale. In the west of Norfolk marling was a relatively straightforward practice, for chalk could be found at no great depth below a relatively thin layer of glacial sand and gravel. In the east of the county, however, the chalk was more deeply buried: here not merely beneath superficial drift deposits, but under the thick, shelly Pleistocene layers of the Norwich Crag. Some chalky material occurred in sporadic patches in the surface drift in north-east Norfolk, and these were widely exploited. But there were only two places in the area where the solid chalk could be reached with relative ease from surface pits. These

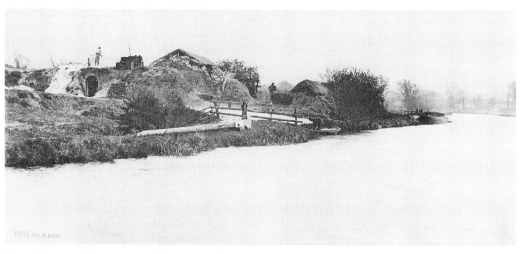

Plate 25   A late nineteenth-century photograph by P. H. Emerson showing a working riverside lime
            kiln somewhere in Broadland.

were in the valley of the Yare between Norwich and Brundall: and in the valley
of the Bure between Aylsham and Coltishall (and also in the lower reaches of
some of the tributary streams in this stretch of the river). The existence of these
exceptional and isolated exposures, coupled with the ease of transport afforded
by the adjacent rivers, ensured the development of a major industry based in
particular at Whittlingham and Thorpe-Next-Norwich in the valley of the Yare;
and at Horstead, Wroxham and Coltishall in the valley of the Bure. The produce
of these pits was, by the second half of the eighteenth century, being widely
disseminated by wherry throughout the north and east of Norfolk – a mode of
transport considerably cheaper than movement by road. William Marshall in
1787 described how the farmers at Woodbastwick obtained their marl from the
pits near Norwich by water, via Yarmouth – the distance was more than forty
miles (64 kilometres), although by road it was little more than six.[296]

The chalk was not always applied directly to the fields. It was often, and increasingly in the nineteenth century, burnt in kilns to produce lime, a substance
which was also much in demand for making mortar and plaster for building.
Because chalk was bulkier and therefore more expensive to transport than
lime, the kilns were usually located close to the pits, especially at Thorpe and
Whittlingham. The ease and cheapness of water transport in the region also
ensured, however, that some riverside kilns were constructed far from the
chalk outcrops (Plate 25). Examples of such riverside kilns, of eighteenth- or
nineteenth-century date, are known from Acle Bridge, Barton Turf, Reedham,
Ludham, Stalham, Dilham and Yarmouth, and elsewhere.[297] Most surviving
examples are dangerous or impossible to enter, but one at Coltishall, located
behind the Railway public house, has been restored and can be visited with the
permission of the landlord.

The major chalk extraction centres produced distinctive industrial landscapes. At Horstead by the end of the eighteenth century the workings were served by a network of canals, by means of which wherries could be brought right into the pits. The extensive area of quarries, spoil heaps and artificial waterways here later became known as 'Little Switzerland', and the area to the north as the 'Hills and Holes'. For a time they became something of a tourist attraction. At Whitlingham by the 1850s the chalk was taken to the river's edge via a narrow-gauge wooden railway, on trucks pulled by horses.[298]

Bricks and cement

Chalk was not the only material to be excavated on a large scale in Broadland in the eighteenth and nineteenth centuries. There are a number of deposits of clay suitable for making bricks, and once again the ease of transport afforded by the waterways encouraged their exploitation. Brickearth, a buff-coloured sandy clay, occurs sporadically amongst the varied glacial deposits in the uplands, especially on the island of Flegg: while on the lower ground there are deposits of more recent estuarine clay. The latter material produces bricks with a rather flaky structure, and which weather badly; but when mixed with the brickearth makes a very serviceable brick.[299] In the nineteenth century William Bracey had an upland pit by Hemsby Road in Martham and a marsh pit just to the east of the Martham Ferry Dyke. Carts would run from one to the other, taking brickearth one way and estuarine clay the other: the materials would be mixed and fired at both sites. The marsh pit had a wind pump to keep the water levels low, and a ramp leading up to a loading staithe on the river Thurne which, in the early years of the century, was equipped with a light railway.[300] On the other side of Martham Ferry Dyke there was another important works, Chapmans Pit (so called since the seventeenth century). The three clay pits here, now filled with water, are locally referred to as the 'Bottomless Pits': there are also remains of a kiln. By the nineteenth century the site seems to have specialised in making tiles. Brick fields were not restricted to Flegg, of course, but were widespread throughout Broadland in the eighteenth and nineteenth centuries, with large concerns at Rockland St Mary, Surlingham and elsewhere.

The largest concentration of industrial activity, however, was on the Waveney near Breydon Water, where there were three major businesses involved in the production of bricks and cement. One former brickyard, its site now occupied by boatyards, can be seen at Somerleyton. This was probably established in the early 1800s by John Green, on land which – prior to the enclosure of Somerleyton in 1803 – had been part of the parish common. His great-nephew, another John Green, sold the enterprise to Sir Morton Peto of Somerleyton Hall in 1849. The sales agreement describes 'All that brick and tile yard now or late in the occupation of Mr John Green, together with all the erections theron comprising 7 brick Sheds, 3 Tile Sheds, 2 leanto Sheds, 2 brick Kilns, 4 brick Clamps, 1 coal Shed, Blacksmiths Shop, Barn, Stable and Hovels, 4 new and substantially built

Labourers Cottages . . .'.[301] Peto used the yard's products in the 1850s, to build the estate's picturesque 'model village'. But the yard was soon leased to Lucas Brothers, building contractors of Vauxhall, and the bricks were then transported much further afield. They were even used for the construction of Liverpool Street Station in London. The yard was connected to the Waveney by a cut, known as the Brickfield Canal, which reduced to 30 metres or so the distance which bricks had to be carried to the wherries. The works finally closed in 1939.

Rather larger was the Burgh Castle Brick and Cement Company, which was founded by William Claxton in 1859, on a site which is again now occupied by a boatyard. Many of the mooring pools here were originally constructed to accommodate wherries, and the nearby single-storey cottage was once the company's office. Two types of clay were dug close to the river, to produce both red and white bricks. From 1875 the company also produced Portland cement: chalk brought by a fleet of eight wherries from the Whittlingham pits was mixed with mud dredged from the bed of Breydon Water, baked to a high temperature in kilns, and the resulting clinker ground into cement powder. The yard had settling ponds for washing and purifying the clay, a puddling pit, chalk crushers, calcining kilns for the cement, and by the end of the century a continuously burning brick kiln. Coal and clay as well as chalk were brought to the site by water, and at one time as many as 150 people were employed here.[302]

This was not the only place in the vicinity where cement was produced in the nineteenth century. As early as 1821 a five-storey drainage windmill at Berney Arms was being used to grind cement for Thomas Trench Berney's Reedham Cement Works: chalk from Whittlingham was again mixed with mud dredged from the river, baked in kilns, and then ground by the mill. The mill was replaced by the present structure, which also doubled as a drainage mill, in *c.*1865.[303] A sizeable settlement had developed alongside the river Yare here by the later nineteenth century, with kilns, cottages, a pub, and a chapel, and with a railway station a little way away. The company closed in the 1880s and the site gradually dwindled: only the Berney Arms public house, and the tall mill, still remain.[304] The station survived until the 1970s but was then demolished, although trains still stop here in what now seems a truly rural backwater.

Malting and milling

Two of the main industries in Broadland were directly related to the processing of local crops: milling and malting. The former has left comparatively few marks on the landscape. Most local windmills were on the uplands, away from the rivers, and most of these have disappeared. Among the survivors, however, is Sutton Mill, reputedly the highest windmill in Norfolk. Watermills are not a characteristic feature of Broadland. The rivers were too slow-moving, and had gradients too gentle, to supply the required head of water, unless a substantial mill pond could be created. But the valleys were too wide to dam effectively, and too prone to tidal action and flooding: while the erection of dams and sluices would have interfered with navigation. Hence the only watermills – large, industrial structures for the most part, of late eighteenth- or nineteenth-century date – occur in the upper reaches of the rivers, at or beyond the natural limits of navigation: at Horstead and Buxton on the Bure, Chedgrave on the Chet, or Ellingham and Wainford on the Waveney. As already noted the construction of the North Walsham and Dilham Canal led to the building or rebuilding of a number of large mills in the 1820s and 1830s, their mill ponds doubling as reservoirs for the canal, which also served to transport their raw material and produce. Particularly striking today are the dramatic, ivy-clad remains of Ebridge Mill near Honing.

Malting has had a more noticeable impact on the local scenery, a reflection both of the industry's importance in this prime barley-growing area, and also of the fact that it was powerfully attracted to the water's edge. Malt is produced from germinated barley, and the malting process involved soaking the barley for about three days in tanks or 'steeps' before turning it out on to a germination floor, where it was turned and moved every few days and steadily heated in order to maintain an even temperature. When the grains reached the right stage of germination to produce the particular kind of malt required, they were placed on the perforated tiles of the floor of the kiln to be 'cured', the temperature being gradually raised over a period of three or four days to around 210 degrees fahrenheit. The requirements of the process – a long germinating floor and a kiln – ensure the distinctive features of the external appearance of early maltings: longer than they are wide, with two or three floors, and a cube-shaped kiln at one end, usually with a four-sided roof that tapers to a swinging cowel on top. Such maltings were located beside the navigable waterways partly in order to facilitate the import of the raw barley, and the export of the finished product: but also because water supplies were essential for the malting process.[305] Notable examples can still be seen in Coltishall (a particularly important centre for malting and brewing); beside Malthouse Broad at Ranworth; beside Womack Water in Ludham; and on the Waveney at Wainford. The First Edition OS 25 inch maps show that in the 1880s there were many more of these structures beside Broadland's rivers.

In the late nineteenth century the small local family firms which had formerly dominated the trade were increasingly replaced by larger companies, often running two or three maltings.[306] The scale of the individual maltings also increased, and there was a major change in the distribution of the industry. As the railway network expanded, so too did the market for East Anglian malt, which could now more easily be taken to London. Much larger malting plants were now established, usually within easy reach of the railways but also – because of the need for water – still beside major watercourses. The Waveney valley, where railway and river ran close together, attracted a number of such works by the end of the nineteenth century. Particularly striking examples of massive late nineteenth-century maltings can be seen at Oulton Broad, Beccles, and Ditchingham (the latter, interestingly, originally erected as a silk mill in 1832 by Gout and Company of Norfolk, and extended and converted to its new use in the 1890s: the Waveney valley has a long history of textile manufacture).

Although now largely valued as a 'natural' landscape and a rural backwater, Broadland thus has an important *industrial* history: and we must never forget, of course, that the broads themselves are a relict industrial landscape. Nor have the signs of industry quite been banished from Broadland. The great mass (and distinctive aroma) of the Cantley sugar-beet factory, established in 1912, still dominates the scenery of the middle Yare valley; while the tall chimney of Yarmouth South Denes power station is visible throughout the Halvergate marshes.

Roads and railways

Looked at in one way, the Broadland waterways were arteries of communication through which the industrial and commercial life of eastern Norfolk (and north-eastern Suffolk) pulsed. But looked at in another way, they constituted a series of barriers, obstructing the passage of terrestrial traffic. In the early Middle Ages fords were established at key points – Ludham Bridge, Potter Heigham, Wroxham, Wey Bridge near Acle and Wayford Bridge between Smallburgh and Stalham.[307] The name of the last two crossing points – derived from the Old English *waeg*, 'road' – presumably attests the pre-Conquest origin of some at least of these crossings. The lower relative water levels of early medieval times probably meant that the rivers could be more easily forded in their upper reaches, and the location of fords was determined not so much by the existence of shallows at these particular points as by the constricted nature of the valleys, and thus the shorter distance that had to be crossed over low marshy ground. In the course of the Middle Ages bridges were erected at all these places and also – courtesy of the neighbouring Augustinian priory – at St Olaves on the Waveney. Only that at Potter Heigham, probably built in the late fourteenth century, still survives to vex the pleasure boater (Plate 26). Where the rivers were too wide or deep to be crossed by bridge or ford, ferries sometimes developed. In the nineteenth century there were examples at Surlingham, Buckenham, Reedham, and Brundall on the Yare; at Horning and Stokesby on the Bure; and at Martham on the Thurne. Only two of these still operate, both vehicle-carrying chain ferries: at Reedham (which is motorised) and at Martham.

To reach bridges or ferries, roads have to cross often fairly wide areas of marsh. In many cases their present alignments are fairly recent, older routes having been tidied up and straightened by enclosure commissioners in the early nineteenth century. The most important new road created in Broadland in the nineteenth century, however, was the 'Acle Straight' – the Norwich–Acle Turnpike, established in the 1830s. Prior to this, as we have seen, the main route across the Halvergate Marshes to Yarmouth followed the meandering course of the Halvergate Fleet. The route taken by the new road, as finally agreed after several changes of plan, could hardly have been more different: it runs across the marsh in two ruler-straight sections, one 7 km long, and one 4 km. These join near

The medieval bridge at Potter Heigham.   Plate 26

Stracey Arms Mill, and close to this point a straight branch road, leading south-
west towards Halvergate village, was laid out.

One of the most striking features of the Broadland landscape are the lines of
low, pollarded willows which border the principal roads and tracks running across
the lower ground (Plate 27). The trees seem usually to have been planted at
intervals of around 4 metres, on the edge of the verge immediately above the
flanking ditch. In some places – as on the branch road to Halvergate – the trees
are well-preserved on both sides of the road. Elsewhere, as on the Acle Straight,
the remains are more patchy, many of the trees having been removed in comparatively recent times (the RAF aerial photographs of 1946 show them as much
more continuous).

The willow rows appear to be very much a part of the 'traditional' Broadland
scene, but like so much else they are in reality a fairly recent addition to the
landscape. While individual willow pollards, and even groves of such trees (as on
Oxholmes near Beccles) had long existed in the upper reaches of the river valleys,
they were not a feature of the drained marshland where most of the rows
are now to be found. It is true that early maps of the area do sometimes show
lines of pollards. Thus a map made in 1749 of an area of marsh to the west of
Reedham church shows pollards growing beside some of the dykes: another line

Plate 27   Pollarded willows on the branch road from Stracey Arms to Halvergate village.

of trees appears on the same map, surrounding an intake from Reedham Common.[308] Similarly a map made in 1825 of the line of the proposed New Cut shows trees – again presumably willow pollards – growing on the side of a track running down to Oulton Dyke, and also bordering some of the field dykes to the north of this.[309] But the vast majority of early maps do not show trees on the marshes, even though they might depict them in the hedgerows of the neighbouring upland, and the various nineteenth-century paintings of the marshes similarly attest the landscape's open, treeless quality.

With few, if any, exceptions, the willow rows are associated with roads which were either newly created, or extensively improved, in the nineteenth century. Local tradition is unanimous regarding their purpose: the trees were planted to 'hold the shoulder of the road' – that is, to prevent the road from subsiding into the flanking ditches. The pollarding was essential to keep them low, so that they would not be brought down by the wind. It also allowed a narrow spacing, and thus a maximum amount of root structure to bind the ditch banks.[310] Once again we see how a 'traditional' feature of the Broadland landscape developed for rather mundane reasons, in comparatively recent times.

Roadside willows provide one interruption in the flat landscape of the drained marshes. Railways provide another. Often, when walking alone in the distant recesses of the marsh, you suddenly become aware of a train passing close by on a low embankment, striking and surreal in this flat and lonely landscape. Before the 1960s railways would have been an even more noticeable presence in Broadland, for many lines have been lost in successive waves of closure: in the first half of this century the area, like many in rural England, was criss-crossed with railways (Figure 43). But it was one of the last to acquire such a dense network. True, Norwich and Yarmouth were linked (via Reedham) as early as 1844, the line from Reedham to Haddiscoe was opened in 1847, that from Haddiscoe to Yarmouth followed in the 1850s and that running along the Waveney from Beccles to Bungay was opened in 1860. But the Norwich–Wroxham–Cromer line was only established in 1874, that from Yarmouth to North Walsham (via Stalham) in 1879, those running from Aylsham to Wroxham, and from Acle to Yarmouth (beside the 'Acle Straight') were not completed until 1882 and 1883 respectively, while the Breydon viaduct, carrying a line linking Yarmouth South Town with Yarmouth Beach stations, was opened as late as 1903.[311]

The direct impact of railways upon the landscape was relatively limited – in such level terrain there was little call for stupendous feats of Victorian engineering. But their indirect effects were more profound. On the one hand, as we have seen, the slow spread of rail led to the gradual demise of waterborne traffic, a key element in the 'traditional' economy of Broadland. On the other, the railways encouraged the development of a new industry which was to radically transform the landscape of the area, and the lives of its inhabitants: tourism.

7

The landscapes of tourism and conservation

The development of the tourist industry

The Broadland rivers and lakes have been used by the local inhabitants for recreation and entertainment for centuries, and by the late eighteenth century the 'water frolics' at Wroxham, Yarmouth and Thorpe St Andrew near Norwich were social events of some importance.[312] By this time, too, many landowners in the area had their own pleasure craft, kept in boat houses on the rivers and broads. But it was only gradually, in the course of the nineteenth century, that Broadland began to attract people from further afield, and that the area started its career as a major holiday centre. The industry seems to have developed very gradually at first, from the 1850s, following the construction of the main railway lines from Norwich to Yarmouth in 1844 and from London to Norwich in 1849. The earliest visitors were few in number, generally keen yachtsmen, artists or anglers, and accommodation was fairly limited.[313] But tourists began to appear in ever-increasing numbers in the last two decades of the century.

The development of a wider popular interest in Broadland is usually attributed to G. Christopher Davies, a solicitor by training who wrote a number of books, two of which were of crucial importance in attracting visitors: *The Handbook to the Rivers and Broads of Norfolk and Suffolk*, published in 1882; and the more substantial *Norfolk Broads and Rivers, or the Waterways, Lagoons, and Decoys of East Anglia* of 1885; both of which went into numerous editions.[314] But while Davies' influence should not be underestimated he was, to some extent, catering for a market which was anyway expanding. As the wealth of the upper sections of the middle classes increased in later Victorian England, and as the railway network steadily improved, holiday resorts expanded in many areas of England, especially those within easy reach of major population centres. By the 1880s Norwich could be reached from London in less than four hours.[315] Already in 1883 one railway guide included a chart displaying the best places for fishing in Broadland, and provided details of boat hire (and of the nearest railway stations).[316]

Davies was the first of many writers to extol the beauties of Broadland. Others included E. R. Suffling (whose *Land of the Broads* of 1885 was the only serious rival to Davies' *Handbook*) and John Payne Jeannings. Indeed, such was the flood of books on the Broads that one reviewer (in the magazine *Nature* in 1897), discussing the latest batch, commented wryly:

> Surely no spot in the British Isles has been so 'be-guided' as the Norfolk Broads . . . hardly a magazine exists . . . which has not opened its pages to the flood of contributions on this apparently fascinating subject; and the whole has culminated in a shower of guide-books which enlivens the railway bookstalls with their gay exteriors.[317]

No less than thirty-three books on the Broads were received by the British Museum Library between 1880 and 1900.[318]

The expansion of the holiday industry in the last two decades of the nineteenth century was dramatic. John Loynes was the only boatbuilder offering boats for hire in the first edition of Davies' *Handbook*. By the time the 1891 edition appeared, there were no less than thirty-seven companies advertising, offering boats from three to seventeen tons. Many were converted wherries: as Davies noted in 1890 'Wherries are frequently hired by private parties, the hatches are raised a plank or two higher to give greater head-room, the clean-swept hold is divided into several rooms, and a capital floating house is extemporised.'[319]

Such boats could be converted back to trading use once the holiday season was over. But already permanent conversions were being made, and even some new boats, pleasure craft built to the traditional wherry design (although with white rather than black sails), were appearing: 'There is now a fleet of permanently-fitted pleasure wherries on the rivers, which have ample accommodation for a party or a family, and are to be hired at from 8 to 15 guineas a week.'[320]

Hire boats were soon being made in a variety of forms, the impact of tourism encouraging the development of new kinds of craft. Loynes – one of the first entrepreneurs in the industry – produced a range of boats 'especially suited for the Norfolk broads', some of which were being advertised at the Sportsmen's Exhibition in London as early as 1882. Davies praised Loynes' four-ton boats, 'beamy, of light draught – to enable them to visit the shallowest of the Broads'. By 1900 steam launches were also becoming available.

Although the smaller boats might be manned by the hirer alone, most of the larger ones came supplied with 'watermen', who would sail them, and who would usually also do the cooking. In the nineteenth century a sailing holiday on the Broads was thus something which only the more affluent could afford. Further expansion of the industry in first half of the twentieth century, however, made such holidays available to a wider section of the middle class. The first motor launches, powered by internal combustion engines, were developed in the 1910s and were being hired out from the early 1920s, initially by Alfred Ward, whose boatyard was at Thorpe.[321] The number of boats for hire increased inexorably in the middle decades of the century: in 1920 there were around 165, of which only four were motor cruisers. By 1949 there were 547, of which 301 were motor cruisers. By 1979 the figures had risen to 2,257 and 2,150 respectively (they have since declined somewhat).[322] Moreover, as the industry expanded, its

organisation became more complex. Agencies devoted to finding boats for pro-
spective customers had begun as early as 1895 under Ernest Suffling: but they
really became important with the development of Blakes, still the most important hiring agency on the Broads, from 1907. Hoseasons, the other principal
agency, was established in the late 1940s.[323]

People were lamenting the deleterious effects of tourism on Broadland almost
from the beginnings of the industry. Davies complained of the unruly behaviour
of some holiday-makers as early as the 1880s, and described how he had been
woken at 7a.m. while moored on Wroxham Broad, by the occupants of a neighbouring boat loudly playing the piano.[324] Right through the first half of the
twentieth century successive writers blamed the worst excesses on the wrong
'kind' – by which they generally meant, class – of holiday-maker.[325] Miller in
1935 described how:

> Each year they had seen the crowds growing and the holiday season lengthening,
> until it seemed that the beautiful waterways would be turned into a Blackpool or a
> Brighton . . . great fleets of tripper-boats . . . hired yachts, floating ice-cream vendors,
> bum-boats and craft of every description, largely in the hands of people who had not
> the slightest knowledge of how to manage them.[326]

Writers like Dutt insisted that only in the winter could the primeval beauty of
the Broads still be enjoyed: there were, in effect, two parallel worlds, that of the
visitor on the one hand, that of nature and the indigenous inhabitants on the
other. By October, he wrote:

> The cruising yachts which have lingered late on the rivers disappear as if by magic,
> and at Oulton, Wroxham and Potter Heigham the fleets of white-winged craft are
> rapidly dismantled, drawn up on to the 'hard' or hauled in to the boat sheds . . . For
> the next eight months the wherrymen, reed-cutters, and eel-catchers will have the
> rivers and Broads to themselves.[327]

Many writers in the early years of the century posited such a contrast, but in so
doing they perhaps exaggerated the slow and unchanging pace of life of the
natives. Several repeated the unlikely claim that the inhabitants of the area dis-
played clear evidence of their supposed Viking ancestry: Dutt described the 'typical marsh farmer' as 'a tall, fair-haired, blue-eyed, ruddy-cheeked giant, who
might have stepped out of the pages of the *Saga of Burnt Njal*'.[328] In reality, the
locals were already a fairly cosmopolitan bunch: Arthur Patterson describes one
African or Afro-Caribbean waterman, and one of his Breydon punt-gunners was
a German.[329] In a similar way, P. H. Emerson's striking photographs of Broadland
labourers seldom show any machinery (Plate 28): all these middle-class commentators (and visitors) were in search of an archaic, untouched, 'natural' world,
which they feared was on the point of being destroyed by the influx of outsiders.[330]
The easy conflation, apparent in so much contemporary writing, of the inhabitants of the area and its natural environment, masks of course a more complex
reality. In particular, the need to protect wildlife (in part to reserve it for upper-
class consumption, through flight-shooting and angling) ensured a spate of

The Reed-Cutters. A typical P. H. Emerson photograph from the 1890s, showing an idealised   Plate 28
(and somewhat posed!) view of Broadland labourers.

legislation in the last decades of the century which was intended to limit the
depredations of local people using traditional methods of procurement. The Game
Laws of 1862, the Norfolk and Suffolk Fisheries Act of 1879, and the Acts for the
Protection of Wild Birds (1872, 1876 and 1880) meant that many traditional
methods of shooting and fishing practised in Broadland were effectively declared
illegal.

The increasing use of the Broads by holiday-makers brought a number of
conflicts, as the rights and privacy of local landowners were increasingly threatened by tourism. The main disputes were over fishing and navigation rights. A
number of landowners claimed that various broads were private property, and
that the fishing was private and access by boat limited to channels leading to
parish staithes. As Davies noted regretfully in 1890, 'The old times when one
could come and go upon the Broads as a matter of apparent right are now past.'[331]
There were a number of celebrated disputes. In 1901, for example, the riparian
owner of Ranworth inner broad denied that there was any public right of access
to the staithe there: a major argument broke out on the staithe, and a houseboat
was placed so as to block the channel leading from the outer to the inner broad.
The owner subsequently proved his claim in law.[332] More celebrated was the

dispute over Wroxham, where the High Court ruled that the broad itself was private property (although the victorious owner only levied a charge for fishing, and allowed continued access for sailing, although not for mooring).[333] The chalk-workings at Horstead, with their access dyke, had been abandoned in the 1870s: grown up with secondary woodland, they became something of a local attraction and were given the fanciful name 'Little Switzerland'. By 1890, however, it was reported that the owner was discouraging entry along the dyke; by 1903 the dyke was chained off, and entry impossible.[334]

The development of the tourist industry from the late nineteenth century had many beneficial effects, of course, and these should not be forgotten (although they generaly were by middle-class writers like Dutt). The new industry provided alternative sources of employment at a time when the local agricultural economy was in a state of recession, and when the river transport trade – and the boat-building yards and riverside public houses which depended upon it – was under increasing threat from the railways. Marsh farms thus began to provide accommodation for visitors; wherrymen were increasingly employed on pleasure craft.

Tourism and the leisure industry also had a profound effect on the landscape, in three main ways: in the expansion of existing settlements; in the erection of boatyard complexes; and, in a few areas, in the construction of riverside chalets. Such developments were, and still are, often seen as a 'threat' to the 'traditional' landscape of the Broads. But they too are a part of Broadland's history.

The landscape of tourism

The early development of the holiday industry was intimately bound up with the railways. The Great Eastern Railway and the Eastern and Midland both wished to encourage visitors to the region: the GER sponsored some editions of John Payne Jennings' *Sun Pictures of the Norfolk Broads*, and in 1893 published its own *Summer Holidays in the Land of the Broads*. In the nineteenth century, and in the early twentieth, rail was the only practical means of reaching the Broads. It is not surprising, therefore, that the greatest impact of toursim upon the landscape occurred where railway stations existed in close proximity to rivers. But this is not the only factor which explains the great expansion of Wroxham, Horning, Hoveton, Brundall and – to a lesser extent – Potter Heigham; for Acle, Reedham or Haddiscoe, all of which had railway stations by 1890, did not experience any similar degree of development. Another factor was the aesthetic preferences of most early visitors. The majority shared the view that while the more wooded and undulating scenery in the upper reaches of the rivers, around Coltishall and Wroxham on the Bure and around Thorpe and Brundall on the Yare – where many of the broads could also be found – had real picturesque beauty, the more level areas of marshes and fen ground, and in particular the drained marshland of the Halvergate 'triangle', were much less attractive. Davies thus praised the upper valleys, 'bordered by pleasant woodlands, whose fresh green in early summer and glorious hues in autumn made them as lovely as many of the leafy backwaters of the upper Thames'. True, he also believed that some parts of the lower reaches of the rivers were 'not without their elements of picturesque beauty': but the Halvergate 'triangle' did not score at all well, the twelve miles of river between Acle and Yarmouth being summarily dismissed as 'very uninteresting'.[335]

From the start, then, pleasure traffic was not evenly distributed throughout Broadland, but was concentrated on the upper Bure and its tributaries, and in the upper reaches of the Yare. It was this combination – of aesthetic preferences, and the location of the principal railway stations – which determined the location of the main holiday centres. The one exception to this general rule was Oulton Broad, which grew rapidly in the last decades of the nineteenth century. Early tourists generally avoided the river Waveney (to some extent they still do), largely because of the absence of broads. But Oulton Broad not only possessed a fine, extensive area of water. It also had a railway station, and was only a short distance from the flourishing seaside resort of Lowestoft.

At many places development was occurring on a significant scale by the 1890s. As early as 1903 Dutt bemoaned the transformation of Oulton Broad: 'for the red-brick villas and castellated houses which have sprung up on this side of the Broad have ... robbed Oulton of what little beauty it once possessed'; while Wroxham had already been spoilt 'by the erection of unsightly modern houses for the accommodation of visitors'.[336] Late nineteenth-century development, as Dutt implies, largely took the form of red-brick houses little different from those which could be found in most of England's expanding suburbs. But in the twentieth century, and especially in the inter-war years, small chalet bungalows in a range of distinctive pseudo-vernacular styles were erected in large numbers, usually in riverside locations. Most were typical of inter-war 'plotland' development: small in size, with low pitched roofs, ornamental finials and, as often as not, verandas facing the river. They were constructed of light wood or iron framing, covered with weatherboarding or painted corrugated iron, and provided with roofs of wooden shingle tiles or corrugated iron. Some are thatched, and this, combined with the effect of false timber framing, gives them a classic, inter-war 'Tudoresque' feel. The particular range of styles adopted was the consequence of several factors. In part, it simply reflected the fact that developers sought a cheap form of construction: these were holiday homes, so insulation against the winter weather and extensive provision of rooms were unnecessary. The choice of materials was determined by the fact that many of the sites on which these properties were erected were inaccessible by road, and occupied areas of unstable peat or silt soils. Many in fact were erected on the marshy ronds between the wall and river itself, on plots leased from the parish Drainage Commissioners. In addition, however, their design echoed not only the 'Tudoresque' homes being erected in innumerable suburbs during this period, but more specifically the loose interpretations of Norfolk's own vernacular architecture adapted for some large houses in the region around the turn of the century – most notably for the rambling mansion of How Hill, designed by the architect Edward Boardman for his family in 1904.

Many of these distinctive chalets were built by the Norwich firm of Boulton and Paul, but smaller local firms were also involved, like Donald Curson of

Plate 29   Inter-war holiday chalets, Potter Heigham.

Wroxham.[337] Many examples were provided with a diminutive boat dyke and often a small boat house, with low thatched roof, on their narrow plot. Examples of riverside chalets can be seen in a number of places, but the most striking development was along the Thurne, above Potter Heigham Bridge (Plate 29). Here, mainly along the northern bank of the river, but to a lesser extent on the southern, a line of chalets runs for nearly 1 km up to, and beyond, High's Mill. After a short gap, another concentration occurs, this time along the south bank, between Martham Mill and Martham Ferry.

More intrusive in the flat Broadland landscape are the extensive boatyards with their vast corrugated sheds, which cluster in particular around Wroxham, Brundall, Potter Heigham and Horning, although minor yards can be found near many small village staithes. Most of the features at such sites are of comparatively recent date, but older inter-war timber boat houses, quays and headings still survive at a number of places – as at Eastick's yacht station, Acle.

The threat to the Broads

The threat posed by tourism to the Broads came not only from the fixed structures in the landscape – from boatyards, garish public houses, chalets or (a

The landscape of tourism: a quiet day at Wroxham.   Plate 30

development of the 1960s, particularly prominent at Wayford Bridge) fixed house-boats – but also from the effects of mobile pleasure boats. As the quantity of traffic escalated through the 1950s and 1960s, the waterways – for a large part of the year – became increasingly congested, and lost much of their rural tranquillity (Plate 30). In addition, the wakes from speeding craft damaged reed beds on the edges of rivers and broads, leading in many places to severe erosion of their banks. This in turn necessitated the erection of unsightly metal piling. Tourism and pleasure boats were not, however, the only threats to Broadland in the post-war period.[338] The broads themselves, once so clear that their bottoms could easily be seen, became increasingly cloudy as a result of the 'bloom' of tiny algae or phytoplankton: the numbers of submerged water plants, and those of aquatic animals which fed on them, declined dramatically. This change – which in some cases culminated in a final phase of blue-green algal 'bloom' – was caused by the build-up of nutrients (nitrogen and especially phosphorous) in the sediments on the floor of the lakes.[339] The precise causes of this development are complex and are still a subject for debate and research, but were related ultimately to the nature of the water entering Broadland's waterways, the quality of which had declined dramatically due to changes in farming practices, and in methods of sewage disposal, on the adjacent uplands.

The intensity of farming during the Victorian 'high farming' era, together with the growth of local populations (especially in Norwich) and the increasing quantities of sewage consequently discharged into the rivers had already, before the turn of the century, led to an increase in the amount of nutrients in the waterways, which had in turn produced some changes in the character of the vegetation in the broads: specifically, low-growing plants in open water began to be replaced by taller, faster-growing weeds. But it was only in the 1950s that the problem became really serious. This was mainly as a consequence of the spread of mains drainage on the surrounding uplands, which considerably increased the amount of phosphorous entering the rivers; but it was also, in part, a result of the increasing application of fertilisers on adjacent farmland, which significantly raised the levels of nitrogen in the local waterways. As well as contributing to algal bloom, the latter form of pollution also contributed to the damage being caused by river traffic to reed beds, for it encouraged the plants to grow tall and brittle and thus rendered them more susceptible to the impact of the wakes of passing pleasure craft. The age-old tendency for the broads to become invaded by marginal reed-swamp was thus reversed, although more general contraction through silting has continued.

Yet a third threat to the landscape and ecology of Broadland materialised in the 1970s. The pricing structure of the European Economic Community's Common Agricultural Policy ensured that farmers could make more money from growing cereals than they could from raising cattle. At the same time, the Ministry of Agriculture, Food and Fisheries' farm improvement grants scheme offered farmers loans – partly directed through the Internal Drainage Boards, following the Land Drainage Act of 1976 – to deep-drain and plough marshland.[340] These policies had calamitous effects on the drained marshland landscape, both within the Halvergate 'triangle' and also in the upper valleys, especially around the headwaters of the Thurne. The wide expanses of open marsh turf began to be replaced by a dreary arable landscape, reminiscent of the Fenlands of Lincolnshire and Cambridgeshire. Dykes were deepened and their profiles altered, causing severe damage to the dyke vegetation. This was a particularly serious development given that the dykes were the only home for a number of species of floating and submerged water plant which had by now been eradicated from the broads themselves.[341] In addition, some of the marsh soils put to the plough, especially in the upper Thurne area, contain quantities of pyrites (FeS_2), formed long ago by bacterial reduction of the sulphates present in the sea water which had affected such areas in the past, during ancient transgressions or flooding incidents. Once deep-drained for arable use the pyrites oxidised, creating sulphuric acid and soluble iron, which caused damage to water life and extreme discoloration of the local watercourses.

Arable conversion was the most severe threat to Broadland's landscape and ecology, and produced a commensurate response. A major public row erupted in 1980, involving conservation groups and various government bodies. Long and complex negotiations culminated, in 1985, in the government's instigation of an experimental livestock support scheme, the Broads Grazing Marshes Conservation Scheme. Broadland thus became the first Environmental Sensitive Area (ESA) in England: that is, an area within which landscape and wildlife are protected by a complex funding scheme which rewards farmers for following a range of 'traditional' forms of landuse and management: a scheme later extended to the whole of Broadland, and indeed, far up the river valleys.

The Halvergate controversy was the first major problem faced by the Broads Authority. This originated in 1978 as a Joint Local Authority Committee, established under the terms of the 1972 Local Government Act, following extensive discussions between a range of bodies, anxious about the mounting threats to Broadland: the region, unlike many others of comparable environmental or landscape importance in Britain, had never been made a National Park (although this had, in fact, been recommended by the Addison Committee in the 1940s).[342] The new Authority, principally funded by the Countryside Commission, was reconstituted in 1989 with more extensive powers, including control over navigation in the area. Broadland was now, in effect, given the status of a National Park, covering an area of $c.287$ sq km (largely, however, restricted to the fens and marshes of the river flood-plains, and thus excluding the neighbouring uplands). The Authority's remit, under the terms of the government-sponsored Act as finally amended by parliamentary committee, was to manage the area for the purposes of: (a) conserving and enhancing the natural beauty of the broads; (b) promoting the enjoyment of the broads by the public; and (c) protecting the interests of navigation.

The Authority has an awesome responsibility, balancing the many conflicting interests in Broadland. Of course, even before its establishment planning constraints had been exercised, by the County and District Councils, under the terms of the 1947 Town and Country Planning Act: although even in the 1950s, 1960s and 1970s some exceedingly intrusive developments had been allowed, especially at Brundall. Much tighter controls have been in operation since 1989, and the Broads Authority is now the most important influence on the development of the region's landscape, although other bodies (like the National Trust, the Norfolk Naturalists Trust, and English Nature), along with wider government policy, also play a significant role.

The landscape of conservation

Looked at in one way, these bodies are involved in protecting an unspoilt, 'traditional' landscape against the pressures of tourism and agribusiness. In other words, they are busy defending a range of distinctive landscapes, created by a specific set of social, economic and technological circumstances which no longer exist, against a whole range of other economic activities which have very different effects upon the environment. In areas of grazing marsh, the activities of farmers are thus now influenced not only by the need to provide food, but also by the requirements of conservation. Here, at least, the landscape is protected, more or less, through the activities by which, and for which, it was created. More problematical is the maintenance of some other Broadland landscapes through very untraditional methods, and for very untraditional ends. As we have seen, the regular mowing, grazing and peat-cutting which created the distinctive environments of the valley fens are no longer, in most places, carried out as practical economic activities. Instead the encroaching scrub is cleared away simply to keep the fens open, and in places – as on the Woodbastwick reserve – areas of mature woodland are systematically felled, in order to re-establish vanished areas of fen. More bizarrely, a scheme for recreating new turf ponds is now under way: no one needs the peat but a number of uncommon plant species need these vital, if unstable, niches. And sometimes entirely new landscape features are established, which have little or no historical precedent. Thus an extensive network of lagoons has been created near Barton Broad, to store nutrient-rich silt from the broad and thus improve its water quality, something which has had a major impact on the landscape; while on the RSPB reserve near Berney Arms areas of marsh are regularly flooded with shallow water for parts of the year, in a way which would have been strenuously avoided in the past, for the benefit of wading birds.

Such practices, however 'untraditional', are perfectly reasonable. Old landscapes must be adapted to new needs. One of the main roles of Broadland is now wildlife conservation, and its environmental richness should be maintained and enhanced by whatever methods are required. Another vital role is tourism, and the visitors who flock to Broadland do not expect to be confronted with developments which are clearly at odds with what they perceive to be the region's character. New additions to the landscape must therefore be modified and controlled accordingly, in order to avoid developments which 'are incongruous with riverside settlements and intrude on the landscape rather than being a harmonious part of its character'.[343] Yet, while perfectly reasonable, these activities should be recognised for what they are. The bodies responsible for managing Broadland are, in reality, as much in the business of creating a *new* landscape, geared to the needs of conservation and recreation, as they are in that of protecting an old one – although this obvious reality is everywhere suppressed.

This emerging landscape is, of necessity, carefully clothed in the garbs of the past. If the 'traditional' landscape is to be preserved from significant change, then all new contributions must be cast in its image. Yet therein lies a paradox: for to freeze a landscape at a single point in its development, for the benefit of posterity, can only be justified by constructing an image of an unchanging, ancient, 'traditional' landscape. In reality there never was an unchanging, stable world of nature and 'tradition'. The landscape had always been changing, responding to a complex interaction of social, economic and environmental influences, and the Broadland which we enjoy today is not some timeless entity but an amalgam of numerous phases of development, many of no great antiquity. Once the complexity of history is thus denied, 'tradition' becomes a guiding principal in landscape management but, unquestioned and undefined, this term is rapidly emptied of whatever meaning it once possessed, and the real world of life and labour is forced to masquerade as historical pastiche. Farmers are encouraged to erect farm buildings of appropriate form to 'fit into and be in keeping with the Broadland setting': 'Asymmetrical or lopsided building forms should be avoided because they look odd'; 'Gutters . . . look better if kinks and bends are avoided'.[344] Ultimately, 'traditional' comes to mean little more than 'as things were before we were born'. We even learn of something called 'traditional' Broadland chalets:[345] presumably the same as the wooden structures which, when first erected during the inter-war years, were castigated as a 'disgusting spoliation of Broadland scenery'.[346]

Indeed, many things in the Broadland landscape would, when first created, have filled modern observers with horror and revulsion: they are relics of industry, once new, ghastly and intrusive in the rural landscape. The broads themselves must, when originally dug, have been about as aesthetically appealing as a modern gravel pit. Many cherished features of the Broadland scene are nothing like as old as this. In 1788 the antiquary J. W. Fenn was clearly appalled at the way the ancient gatehouse of St Benet's Abbey had been disfigured by the modern drainage mill built on top of it. The resultant ensemble is now an icon of Broadland. William Dutt in 1903 lamented the intrusion of the 'huge and ugly' modern malthouses in the scenery of Oulton Broad. They are now converted and carefully conserved. Even a short space of time thus serves to hallow mundane and practical features of the landscape. If the sprawling cement works at Berney Arms in the heart of Halvergate had survived longer, would it too have become part of the 'traditional' landscape, perhaps utilised as a heritage centre? Many of the drainage mills in Broadland are little older: some are much more recent, and all are pieces of practical industrial plant. Current proposals to restore, almost to working order, vast numbers of these redundant structures are more than faintly bizarre. Mills like Martham or Horsey are younger than my grandmother.

Of course development must be controlled, and the beauty and environmental richness of Broadland maintained through careful management. Few who have walked alone across the Halvergate Marshes on a wild spring day, or lingered among the reed beds of Catfield on a heavy summer afternoon, could think otherwise. Naturalists, ecologists, anglers, sailors, artists, landscape historians – all fall under Broadland's spell, however much they might disagree over specific issues of management. But future management will involve new additions to the landscape, and these may not all be in what we today define as 'traditional' form.

Precisely how Broadland will develop in the future is not, however, the concern of this book. Historians study the past and are thus perhaps the worst people to ask about the *future*: others have written with knowledge and authority on these matters.[347] All we can be sure about is that conflicts of interest will continue, as they have always done, in Broadland: and that local human struggles, concerns and endeavours, while of crucial importance in moulding the landscape, will always take second place to the wider, grander sweeps of environmental change. After all, if global warming proceeds, much of Broadland will become once more a network of estuaries and saltings. Perhaps within the lifetime of some alive today, the tides may flow freely once more across Halvergate, and waves lap the walls of the drainage mills.

Notes

1 W. Marshall, *The Rural Economy of Norfolk*, 2 vols (London 1787), vol. II, p. 276.
2 M. George, *The Land Use, Ecology and Conservation of Broadland* (Chichester 1992), pp. 277–312.
3 H. Cook and H. Moorby, 'English Marshlands Reclaimed for Grazing: a Review of the Physical Environment', *Journal of Environmental Management*, 38 (1993): 55–72.
4 J. E. Mosby, *Norfolk* (Land Utilisation Survey of Britain No. 70) (London 1938), pp. 195–6.
5 Mosby, *Norfolk*, p. 195; W. A. Dutt, *The Norfolk Broads* (1903), pp. 200–3.
6 J. M. Lambert and J. N. Jennings, 'Appendix A, Section II: Special Features and Overgrowth of Individual broads', in E. A. Ellis (ed.), *The Broads* (London 1965), pp. 275–311.
7 George, *Broadland*, pp. 51–5.
8 G. Larwood and B. Funnell, *The Geology of Norfolk* (Norwich 1970).
9 W. Tatler and W. M. Corbett, *Soils in Norfolk III: Sheet TG 31 (Horning)* (Harpenden 1977).
10 Tatler and Corbett, *Soils*, pp. 1–10.
11 Tatler and Corbett, *Soils*, pp. 10–16; J. A. Catt, W. M. Corbett, C. A. Hodge, P. A. Madgett, W. Tatler and A. H. Weir, 'Loess in the Soils of North Norfolk', *Journal of Soil Science* 22 (1971): 444–52.
12 A. Young, *General View of the Agriculture of Norfolk* (London 1804), p. 12.
13 The following account is based on: J. M. Lambert and J. N. Jennings, 'Alluvial Stratigraphy and Vegetational Succession in the Region of the Bure Valley Broads: Detailed Vegetational and Stratigraphical Relationships', *Journal of Ecology*, 39 (1951): 120–48; B. P. Coles and B. M. Funnell, 'Holocene Palaeoenvironments of Broadland, England', *Special Publications of the International Association of Sedimentology*, 5 (1981): 123–31; B. M. Funnell, 'History and Prognosis of Subsidence and Sea-Level Change in the Lower Yare Valley, Norfolk', *Bulletin of the Geological Society of Norfolk*, 31 (1979): 35–44; M. Godwin, *Microbionization and Microbiofacies of the Holocene Deposits of East Norfolk and Suffolk*, unpublished Ph.D. thesis, School of Environmental Studies, University of East Anglia 1993.
14 Environmental Resource Management Ltd and Trans Econ Ltd, *Acid Sulphate Soils in Broadland* (Broads Authority, Norwich, 1981).
15 A. Rogerson, 'Excavations on Fuller's Hill, Great Yarmouth', *East Anglian Archaeology*, 2 (1976): 131–246.
16 George, *Broadland*, pp. 35–7.
17 Norfolk Record Office (hereafter NRO) MSC 6/6; NRO NRS 4193 M9E.

18 NRO EAW 2/118.

19 NRO EAW/2/119–36.

20 A. Davison, *The Evolution of Settlement in Three Parishes in South-east Norfolk. East Anglian Archaeology, 49* (Dereham 1990), p. 73.

21 T. Williamson, 'Early Co-axial Field Systems on the East Anglian Boulder Clays', *Proceedings of the Prehistoric Society*, 53 (1987): 419–31.

22 Davison, *Evolution of Settlement*, pp. 15–16.

23 A. Lawson, *The Archaeology of Witton, near North Walsham, Norfolk. East Anglian Archaeology, 18* (Dereham 1983).

24 A. Knowles, 'The Roman Settlement at Brampton, Norfolk: interim report', *Britannia*, 8 (1987): 209–21.

25 D. Gurney, 'The Saxon Shore', in S. Margeson, B. Ayers and S. Heywood (eds), *A Festival of Norfolk Archaeology* (Norwich 1996), pp. 30–9; S. Johnson, *The Roman Forts of the Saxon Shore* (London 1976). For a rather different view of the role of these defences, however, see J. Cotterill, 'Saxon Raiding and the Role of the Late Roman Coastal Forts of Britain', *Britannia*, 24 (1993): 227–40.

26 Gurney, 'Saxon Shore', p. 32; S. Johnson, *Burgh Castle: Excavations by Charles Green 1958–1961. East Anglian Archaeology, 20* (Dereham 1953).

27 T. Williamson, *The Origins of Norfolk* (London 1993), p. 64.

28 Davison, *Evolution of Settlement*, p. 66.

29 K. Wade, 'The Early Anglo-Saxon Period', in Lawson, *Witton*, pp. 50–69.

30 Williamson, *Origins*, p. 91.

31 Williamson, *Origins*, pp. 119–21.

32 G. Garmondsway (ed.), *The Anglo-Saxon Chronicle* (London 1953), p. 76.

33 Karle Inge Sandred, 'The Vikings in Norfolk: Some Observations on the Place-Names in -*by*', in *Proceedings of the Tenth Viking Conference* (Oslo 1987): 309–24. For the most recent discussion of Scandinavian settlement in Norfolk, see S. Margeson, 'Viking Settlement in Norfolk: a Study of New Evidence', in Margeson, Ayers and Heywood (eds), *Festival of Norfolk Archaeology*, pp. 47–57.

34 Sandred, 'Vikings in Norfolk', p. 320.

35 H. C. Darby, *The Domesday Geography of Eastern England* (Cambridge 1957), pp. 111–18; T. Williamson and K. Skipper, 'Late Saxon Population Density', in P. Wade Martins (ed.), *An Historical Atlas of Norfolk* (Norwich 1993), pp. 42–3.

36 Williamson, *Origins*, pp. 167–71; Peter Wade Martins, *Village Sites in the Launditch Hundred. East Anglian Archaeology, 10* (Dereham 1980). A. Rogerson, *Fransham: an Archaeological and Historical Study of a Parish on the East Anglian Boulder Clay*, unpublished Ph.D. thesis, University of East Anglia, 1995.

37 S. Heywood, 'Round-Towered Churches', in Wade Martins, *Historical Atlas*, pp. 56–7.

38 W. Goode, *East Anglian Round Towers and their Churches* (Lowestoft 1982).

39 S. Heywood, 'The Round Towered Churches of East Anglia', in J. Blair (ed.), *Ministers and Parish Churches: the Local Church in Transition 950–1200* (Oxford 1988).

40 B. Campbell, 'Population Change and the Genesis of Common-Fields on a Norfolk Manor', *Economic History Review*, 33 (1980): 174–92.

41 D. Hall, *Medieval Fields* (Aylesbury 1980).

42 B. Campbell, 'Commonfield Origins: the Regional Dimension', in T. Rowley (ed.), *The Origins of Open Field Agriculture* (London 1980), pp. 112–29.

43 B. Campbell, 'Agricultural Progress in Medieval England: Some Evidence from Eastern Norfolk', *Economic History Review*, 36 (1983): 26–46.

44 N. Evans, 'Worstead and Linen Weavers', in Wade Martins, *Historical Atlas*, pp. 150–1.

45 The brief account that follows is principally based on: E. P. Loftus Brock, 'The Abbey of St Benets at Holme', *Journal of the British Archaeological Society*, 36 (1880): 15–21; J. Snelling and W. F. Edwards, *St Benets Abbey, Norfolk* (Norwich 1971); F. M. Stenton,

'St Benets of Holme and the Norman Conquest', *English Historical Review*, 37 (1922): 225–35. The fieldwork was carried out by undergraduate students of the University of East Anglia in 1993 and 1994.

46 A. Gransden, *Legends, Traditions and History in Medieval England* (Hambledon 1992), pp. 98, 104.

47 Williamson, *Origins*, pp. 144–5.

48 K. Penn, 'The Early Church in Norfolk', in Margeson, Ayers and Heywood, *Festival of Norfolk Archaeology*, pp. 40–7.

49 NRO Snelling 11/12/73 P 150 B5.

50 Public Record Office (hereafter PRO), E 178/1667.

51 NRO DN HAR 3/3, p. 204.

52 G. C. Davies, *The Handbook to the Rivers and Broads of Norfolk and Suffolk* (London, 1890 edn), p. 53.

53 S. Wade Martins, *Historic Farm Buildings* (London 1991), pp. 138–58.

54 B. A. Holderness, 'East Anglia and the Fens', in J. Thirsk (ed.), *The Agrarian History of England and Wales, vol. V, 1: Regional Farming Systems 1640–1750* (Cambridge 1985), pp. 197–238.

55 K. P. Bacon, *Enclosure in East Norfolk: Particularly Non-Parliamentary Enclosure and Consolidation in the Hundreds of Happing and Flegg*, unpublished MA thesis, Centre of East Anglian Studies, University of East Anglia, 1993.

56 Bacon, *Enclosure*, pp. 38–9.

57 NRO C/Sca2/331.

58 PRO, Tithe Files, 6153.

59 NRO BR90/8/3.

60 Bacon, *Enclosure*, pp. 58–9.

61 A. Young, *General View of the Agriculture*, pp. 12–14.

62 This argument was first advanced by Keith Bacon, *Enclosure*.

63 Marshall, *Rural Economy*, vol. II, pp. 276–7.

64 D. Defoe, *A Tour through the Whole Island of Great Britain* (1722), (Harmondsworth 1976), p. 88.

65 Quoted in S. Wade Martins, 'The Study of the Drainage Mills of the Norfolk Broadlands', *Norfolk Archaeology*, 35 (1970): 152–3.

66 Marshall, *Rural Economy*, vol. II, p. 281.

67 Mosby, *Norfolk*, p. 198.

68 NRO C/Scf 6/1.

69 NRO EAW 1/8; EAW 1/3, MC 2.

70 The sixteenth-century 'Hutch Map' from Yarmouth, which purports to show the Halvergate estuary as still largely extant in early medieval times, is an early but erroneous exercise in landscape history.

71 Godwin, *Microbionisation and Microbiofacies*.

72 J. Field, *English Field Names* (London 1972), p. 106.

73 B. Cornford, 'Past Water Levels in Broadland', *Norfolk Research Committee Bulletin*, 28 (1982): 14–18; p. 16.

74 A. Lark, 'Havens and Marshes of Yarmouth', *Yarmouth Archaeology*, 1990: 18.

75 J. R. West (ed.), *St Benet of Holme 1020–1210: the Eleventh and Twelfth Century Sections of Cott. Ms Galba E ii, the Register of the Abbey of St Benet of Holme*, Norwich Record Society, vol. II (Norwich 1932), p. 84.

76 West (ed.), *St Benet of Holme*, pp. 54, 87, 135.

77 Cornford, 'Past Water Levels', p. 18.

78 B. Campbell, 'Agricultural Progress in Medieval England', p. 35.

79 Norfolk Research Committee Bulletin 1, 1948, p. 1. C. Green, 'Archaeological Evidence', in J. M. Lambert, J. N. Jennings, C. T. Smith, C. Green and J. N. Hutchinson, *The Making of the Broads: a Reconsideration of their Origin in the Light of New Evidence* (London 1960), p. 131.

80 Norfolk Archaeological Unit, Gressenhall, Sites and Monuments Record, site no. 21103.
81 The survey work was carried out the winter of 1995/6, partly with the assistance of Jo Parmenter.
82 S. Rippon, 'Medieval Wetland Reclamation in Somerset', in M. Aston and C. Lewis (eds), *The Medieval Landscape of Wessex* (Oxford 1994); M. Bailey, ' "Per Imperetum Maris": Natural Disaster and Economic Decline in Eastern England, 1275–1350', in B. Campbell (ed.), *Before the Black Death: the Crisis of the Early Fourteenth Century* (Manchester 1991), pp. 184–209.
83 Sir H. Ellis (ed.), *Chronica Johannes de Oxenedes* (1859).
84 NRO College of Arms 326/73 (M19/61).
85 NRO DCN 49/57.
86 NRO DN HAR 3/1.
87 NRO DCN 49/66B/304.
88 H. Manship, *The History of Great Yarmouth* (ed. C. J. Palmer, Yarmouth 1854), p. 65.
89 Cornford, 'Past Water Levels'.
90 NRO DN/HAR 3/3.
91 Quoted in Cornford, 'Past Water Levels', p. 19.
92 George, *Broadland*, p. 240.
93 NRO DCN 49/66B.
94 NRO DCN 52/1, p. 127.
95 NRO EAW 1/1.
96 NRO KNY 27.
97 NRO KNY 27.
98 NRO EAW 1/2.
99 NRO WKC 1/370 392 X 9.
100 NRO Clayton Mss 3329 4B2.
101 NRO Clayton Mss 3329 4B2.
102 NRO Clayton MSS MS 3354.
103 Young, *General View of the Agriculture*, p. 373.
104 N. Bacon, *The Report on the Agriculture of Norfolk* (London 1844), p. 294.
105 Marshall, *Rural Economy*, vol. II, p. 278.
106 NRO C/Scf 6/1.
107 NRO PD 66/32
108 NRO MC 214 667 X 8.
109 Cornford, 'Past Water Levels'; Campbell, 'Agricultural Progress', p. 37.
110 NRO 9/96 Inv 5/131; Inv 9/197.
111 H. E. Hallam, *Settlement and Society: a Study of the Early Agrarian History of South Lincolnshire* (Cambridge 1965), pp. 174–96; Rippon, 'Medieval Wetland Reclamation'.
112 Defoe, *Tour through the Whole Island*, p. 88.
113 Marshall, *Rural Economy*, vol. II, pp. 279–80; Bacon, *Agriculture*, p. 26.
114 Mosby, *Norfolk*, p. 198.
115 George, *Broadland*, pp. 244–5.
116 Marshall, *Rural Economy*, vol. II, pp. 228.
117 NRO FEL 387.
118 NRO DCN 59/15.
119 NRO MS 21509/29, 368 X 5.
120 NRO DCN 49/663.
121 NRO Hansell 12/1/71, R 187 B No. 2.
122 Marshall, *Rural Economy*, vol. II, p. 280.
123 Mosby, *Norfolk*, pp. 198–9.
124 NRO BEA 5196 D.
125 Dutt, *The Norfolk Broads*, p. 86.

126 *Yarmouth Mercury*, 17 Feb. 1950.

127 Peter Allard, *pers. comm.*

128 *Eastern Evening News*, 30 Dec., 1971.

129 M. J. Armstrong, *History and Antiquities of the County of Norfolk* (London 1781), p. 93.

130 NRO EAW 2/118.

131 NRO C/Sca 2/235.

132 NRO DCN 52/2.

133 NRO FEL 387.

134 Bacon, *Agriculture*, p. 294.

135 Mosby, *Norfolk*, p. 198.

136 Runham Enclosure 1802, NRO C/Sca 2/235; Acle Enclosure 1799, NRO C/Sca 2/1; Stokesby estate map 1659, NRO Mc 359/1, M 10; Tunstall, n.d. early nineteenth century NRO NRS 4192; ibid. NRS 4049; 'Estate of John Houghton lying in Halvergate' 1733 (copied 1812), NRO FEL 1068; 'Certain Marshes in Acle' (Scaregap), 1799, NRO MC214/3 667 X 8; Map of Dean and Chapter lands in Fowlholme and Sketeholme, 1733, NRO DCN 127/19 U2; Estate of John Arden in South Walsham, NRO MS 4553; Marshes in Acle, n.d., NRO AG 86; Halvergate *c.*1803, NRO BR 90/7/11.

137 NRO DCN 59/15/6.

138 NRO MS 4553.

139 NRO C/Sca2 /273.

140 NRO Accn Foster, Calvert and Morris per NRS.

141 NRO Snelling 11/12/73 (P150 B5); NRO DN HAR 3/3.

142 George, *Broadland*, p. 39.

143 L. Dudley Stamp and W. G. Hoskins, *The Common Lands of England and Wales* (London 1963); P. Clayden, *Our Common Land: the Law and History of Commons and Village Greens* (London 1985).

144 Roger Sweet, *Beccles to Burgh St Peter: a Landscape History of the Marshes*, unpublished MA dissertation, Centre of East Anglian Studies, University of East Anglia, 1989; Beccles Town Hall, Archive, 'Laws, Ordynances and Constitutions', 1613.

145 Marshall, *Rural Economy*, vol. I, pp. 319, 320.

146 Sweet, *Beccles to Burgh St Peter*, p. 27.

147 Lowestoft Record Office, Beccles Fen Reeves' Account 1552: transcript by the Beccles branch of the Workers Educational Association, 1977.

148 B. Cornford, 'The Commons of Flegg in the Middle Ages and Early Modern Periods', in M. Manning (ed.), *Commons in Norfolk* (Norwich 1988), pp. 14–20; p. 20.

149 NRO MC 76/1.

150 Beccles Town Hall Archive, Order Book E; Sweet, *Beccles to Burgh St Peter*, p. 15.

151 Beccles Town Hall Archive, Order Book E.

152 H. C. Darby, *The Domesday Geography of Eastern England* (Cambridge 1957), p. 129.

153 Sweet, *Beccles to Burgh St Peter*, p. 7.

154 M. C. H. Bird, 'The Rural Economy, Sport and Natural History of East Ruston Common', *Transactions of the Norfolk and Norwich Naturalists Society*, 8, 5 (1909): 631–66.

155 NRO Ms 19424 103 X 4.

156 R. Malster, *The Broads* (Chichester 1993), pp. 28–9.

157 Malster, *Broads*, p. 29.

158 Cornford, 'Commons of Flegg', pp. 18–19.

159 NRO MC 36/123.

160 NRO MC 121/238.

161 NRO Case 16e/108.

162 B. D. Wheeler, 'Observations on the Plant Ecology of Upton Fen, Norfolk, with Special Reference to the Doles', *Transactions of the Norfolk and Norwich Naturalists Society*, 27, 1 (1985): 9–32.

163 J. M. Lambert, J. N. Jennings and C. Green, 'The Origins of the Broads', in Ellis (ed.), *The Broads*, pp. 37–68; J. M. Lambert, J. N. Jennings, C. T. Smith, C. Green and J. N. Hutchinson, *The Origins of the Broads* (Royal Geographical Society London Research Series 2 (1952); George, *Broadland*, pp. 79–98.
164 Lambert *et al.*, *Origins of the Broads*.
165 Lambert, Jennings and Green, 'Origins', pp. 43–6.
166 George, *Broadland*, p. 79; H. B. Woodward, 'The Scenery of Norfolk', *Transactions of the Norfolk and Norwich Naturalists Society*, 3, 4 (1883): 439–66.
167 George, *Broadland*, p. 87.
168 NRO MF/RO 265/4.
169 NRO MF/RO 389/17.
170 Lambert *et al.*, *Origins of the Broads*, p. 56.
171 NRO CUL/1/44.
172 NRO BEA (S 196 D).
173 East Suffolk Record Office 295.
174 R. Payne-Gallway, *The Book of Duck Decoys* (London 1886).
175 A. H. Patterson, *Man and Nature on Tidal Waters* (London 1909), pp. 11–18.
176 R. E. Baker, 'Norfolk Duck Decoys', *Transactions of the Norfolk and Norwich Naturalists Society*, 27, 1 (1985): 1–8; T. Southwell, 'Norfolk Decoys', *Transactions of the Norfolk and Norwich Naturalists Society*, 2 (1879): 538–55.
177 OS 25 inch First Edition Map, 1880.
178 Payne-Gallway, *Decoys*, p. 2.
179 Baker, 'Norfolk Duck Decoys', p. 1.
180 NRO BEA 9/7 433 X 5.
181 A. H. Patterson, *Nature in Eastern Norfolk* (London 1905), p. 56.
182 NRO Snelling 11/12/73 (P150 B5).
183 East Suffolk Record Office 295.
184 NRO DN/HAR 3/3.
185 Cornford, 'Commons of Flegg', p. 16.
186 NRO MS 7458, 736; NRO MS 19913 123 X 1.
187 NRO BEA 72–4, 435 X 6.
188 NRO BEA 76/1.
189 Cornford, 'Commons of Flegg', p. 16.
190 W. E. Tate and M. E. Turner, *A Domesday of English Enclosure Acts and Awards* (Reading 1978), pp. 178–90.
191 George, *Broadland*, p. 240.
192 NRO C/Sca 2/294.
193 NRO PC 18/1 & 2.
194 Bacon, *Agriculture*, pp. 293–4.
195 George, *Broadland*, p. 193.
196 Bird, 'The Rural Economy, Sport and Natural History of East Ruston Common'.
197 NRO P/CH1/51.
198 NRO P/CH1/19.
199 K. E. Giller and B. D. Wheeler, 'Past Peat Cutting and Present Vegetation Patterns in an Undrained Fen in the Norfolk Broadland', *Journal of Ecology*, 74 (1985): 219–47.
200 B. D. Wheeler, *Turf Ponds in Broadland* (Norwich 1983).
201 Jo Parmenter, *Report of the 1991–94 Broadland Fen Resources Survey* (11 vols, Broads Authority 1995), vol. I.
202 NRO 834.
203 NRO PD 89/160 C1.
204 NRO Case 16e/108.
205 G. Lohoar and S. Bullard, *Turf Digging at Wicken Fen*, n.d., p. 5.
206 Dutt, *The Norfolk Broads*, p. 85.
207 C. F. Carrodus, *Life in a Norfolk Village* (Norwich 1949), p. 19.

208 Giller and Wheeler, 'Past Peat Cutting'. Parmenter, *Broadland Fen Resources Survey*, vol. I, pp. 27–30.

209 Parmenter, *Broadland Fen Resources Survey*, vol. I, pp. 27–30: much of this section is based on Parmenter's published work. See also B. Wheeler and K. Giller, 'Species Richness of Herbaceous Fen Vegetation in Broadland, Norfolk, in Relationship to the Above-Ground Plant Material', *Journal of Ecology*, 70 (1982): 179–200.

210 Dutt, *The Norfolk Broads*, pp. 161, 140.

211 Parmenter, *Broadland Fen Resources Survey*, vol. I, *passim*; B. D. Wheeler, 'The Wetland Plant Communities of the River Ant Valley, Norfolk', *Transactions of the Norfolk and Norwich Naturalists Society*, 24, 4 (1978):153–87; p. 153.

212 A. Burrows and G. Kennison, *Woodland Resource Survey of the Bure Broads and Marshes SSSI* (Report for English Nature/Broads Authority, n.d.).

213 R. Fuller, *Vegetation Mapping of Broadland Using Aerial Photographs*, unpublished report for the Broads Authority (Institute of Terrestrial Ecology, 1984); quoted in George, *Broadland*, p. 229.

214 R. Wailes, *The English Windmill* (London 1954); R. Wailes, 'Norfolk Windmills Part II: Drainage and Pumping Mills, including those in Suffolk', *Newcomen Society Transactions*, 30 (1956): 157–77.

215 A. J. Ward, *Drainage Pumps*, unpublished ms., *c*.1968, Norwich Library: now destroyed by fire.

216 A. C. Smith, *Drainage Windmills of the Norfolk Marshes: a Contemporary Survey* (Stevenage 1979; 2nd edn, 1990).

217 S. Wade Martins, 'The Study of the Drainage Mills of the Norfolk Broadlands', *Norfolk Archaeology*, 35 (1970): 152–3.

218 Much of the fieldwork on which this chapter is based was carried out with the assistance of Jo Parmenter.

219 The probable dates of surviving windmills are given in Figure 36. They are based on the following evidence or arguments:

(i) *Eighteen-century mills*. Oby and Brograve are dated by external date-stones. For St Benet's, both Wade Martins and Apling suggest a date of *c*.1740. The mill was certainly in existence by 1781, when it was referred to by M. J. Armstrong in his *History and Antiquities of the County of Norfolk*. The other mills (Benet's Level, Clippesby, Mautby Marsh Farm, Chedgrave Detached, High's Mill in Halvergate) are tentatively dated on the basis of map evidence – mills are shown at these places on Faden's map of 1797 – and on typological grounds.

(ii) *Mills erected between c.1795 and 1825*. Upton Black Mill has an external date-stone. Morse's Mill, Stubb Mill and High's Mill (Potter Heigham) are all dated by references in Enclosure Awards. The construction of Buckenham Mill is referred to in the Beauchamp-Proctor estate accounts (NRO BEA 5196 D). The others (Repps Level, Perry's, Key's, Pettingell's, Stokesby Old Hall and Tunstall Dyke) are again dated on the basis of map evidence – no mills are shown on these sites on Faden's map, but appear on the OS draft drawings of 1816, and/or on Bryant's map of 1824 – and on stylistic/typological similarities with dated examples.

(iii) *Mid nineteenth-century and later mills*. Reedham North Mill, Catfield Fen, Catfield Swim Coots, Ludham Womack Water and Hickling Broad are all absent from the draft OS 1816 and Bryant 1824, but appear on the relevant Tithe Award maps of *c*.1839/40. It is possible that some of the smaller examples may have been omitted by the surveyors of these earlier maps, although most are in contexts – wet peat fens – in which a relatively late date might be expected. Mutton's Mill in Halvergate replaced a mill *c*.200 to the NE between 1824 (Bryant) and 1839 (Tithe Award), and Runham Child's Mill is so similar in size and form, particularly in its use of an internal scoop, that it was almost certainly built around the same time. Repps level and Ludham Bridge North are both absent from the Tithe Awards but are shown on

the First Edition 25 inch OS of 1880. Smallburgh, Runham Five Mile House, Hardley
Marshes and Martham are all dated by internal or external date-stones or inscrip-
tions. Lambrigg and Cadges are so similar to the last two mills that a date in the
1880s/90s seems highly probable.

Norton Marshes, Berney Arms, Ashtree Farm, Stracey Arms, Belton and Hunsett
are all dated from information in Wailes, 'Drainage Windmills': dates based in most
cases on the lost papers and drawings of the millwrights Englands of Ludham. Barton
Turf Mill is almost identical to Hunsett, and a similar date seems likely. Eel Fleet
Dyke, although only equipped with a single rather than double scoop, is also very
similar in a number of ways and probably roughly contemporary.

The following mills are dated by primary documentary evidence: St Margaret's,
Fleggburgh: NRO MC 554, 16–19, 774 X 9; Limpenhoe, NRO PD 164/16 CM; West
Somerton, NRO DB 2/16. A newspaper advertisement in the *Norwich Mercury*,
August 1832, implies that the mill in Fritton Marshes had then just been erected.

The other mills – all 8 metres or more in height and with single external scoop
wheels – must presumably be of mid-late nineteenth-century date, mainly *c*.1840–
80.

220 NRO DN HAR 3/3.
221 NRO Snelling 11/12/73 (P150 B5); NRO EAW 1/8.
222 NRO MC 351/2, 711 X 1.
223 NRO BEA 337/1–6, 438 X 7.
224 H. Apling, *Norfolk Corn Windmills* (Norwich 1984), pp. 276–7.
225 Marshall, *Rural Economy*, vol. II, p. 277.
226 NRO MEA 2/53, 651 X 8.
227 NRO MEA 2/53, 651 X 8.
228 NRO MEA 3/578, 659 X 2.
229 NRO FEL 154 549 X 8.
230 NRO KNY 27.
231 NRO BEA 346.
232 NRO Case 16e/108; NRO BEA 346.
233 NRO Snelling 11/12/73 (P150 B5); NRO MC 351 103 X 4; NRO BEA 346.
234 Marshall, *Rural Economy*, vol. II, pp. 282–3.
235 Smith, *Drainage Windmills*, p. 8; Wade Martins, 'Drainage Mills', p. 152.
236 In the Norwich Local Studies Library: now destroyed by fire.
237 Castle Museum, Norwich, Archaeology Department: Horning file.
238 NRO EAW 2/118.
239 NRO MC 241/9.
240 NRO MC 214/3, 667 X 8.
241 NRO, Norwich City Sectional Lists, Case 15, Shelf E, Bundle VI/83.
242 NRO C/Sca 2.
243 Wailes, *English Windmill*, p. 106.
244 NRO MC 554 16–19, 774 X 9.
245 They do not appear on the OS draft of 1816, nor on Bryant's map of 1824.
246 See below, pp. 00.
247 Bacon, *Agriculture*, p. 203.
248 Norfolk Industrial Archaeology Society, 'A Survey of Ludham', *Journal of the Norfolk
    Industrial Archaeology Society*, 3, 1 (1981): 34–51.
249 Smith, *Drainage Windmills*, p. 61.
250 Ward, *Drainage Pumps*.
251 NRO BR 90/7/11.
252 NRO: Halvergate Tithe Award map: PD 354/27 CH.
253 NRO BR 90/47/19.
254 George, *Broadland*, p. 192.

255 Wailes, 'Norfolk Windmills'; M. Fewster, 'Thomas Smithdale and Sons; a Study of a Victorian Ironfounder', *Journal of the Norfolk Industrial Archaeology Society*, 3, 1 (1981): 25–33.

256 Bacon, *Agriculture*, p. 294.

257 NRO PD 164/16 CM.

258 Bacon, *Agriculture*, p. 294.

259 Ward, *Drainage Pumps*.

260 Ibid.

261 W. Rye, *Tourists Guide to the County of Norfolk* (1885), p. 257.

262 NRO PD 208/83.

263 NRO MC 554 19, 774 X 9.

264 NRO MC 554 19, 774 X 9.

265 NRO DB2/16.

266 George, *Broadland*, p. 253.

267 Wailes, *English Windmill*, p. 72.

268 R. Malster, *The Broads* (Chichester 1993), p. 40.

269 R. Clarke, *Black Sailed Traders* (London 1972).

270 Dutt, *The Norfolk Broads*, p. 80.

271 Malster, *Broads*, p. 41; Dutt, *The Norfolk Broads*, p. 22.

272 NRO Y/C 38.

273 George, *Broadland*, p. 347.

274 Dutt, *The Norfolk Broads*, p. 102.

275 NRO BEA 346.

276 David Alderton, *The Batsford Guide to the Industrial Archaeology of East Anglia* (London 1980), pp. 107, 136.

277 NRO BEA 76/1.

278 NRO BEA 9/7, 433 X 5.

279 NRO TRAF 348.

280 George, *Broadland*.

281 Malster, *Broads*, p. 53.

282 F. Matthew, *To His Highness Oliver, Lord Protector . . . is Humbly Presented a Mediterranean Passage by Water Between . . . Lynn and Yarmouth* (1656).

283 J. Boyes and R. Russell, *The Canals of Eastern England* (Newton Abbot 1977), p. 123.

284 Boyes and Russell, *Canals*, p. 123.

285 NRO C/Scf/667.

286 Ronald Russel, *The Lost Canals of England* (Newton Abbot 1971), pp. 249–51.

287 Boyes and Russell, *Canals*, pp. 111–19.

288 W. Cubitt, *The Second Report of Mr William Cubitt to the Committee Appointed for Taking into Consideration the Best Means of making Norwich a Port* (1821).

289 H. Barrett, *A Warning Voice to the Projectors, Subscribers and Supporters of the Plan for Making Norwich a Port* (1823); Anon., *Remarks on the Report of Captain George Nicholls, Addressed to the Proprietors of Lands on the Level with the Rivers Yare, Waveney, and Bure, and to the Other Persons whose Interests and Safety May be Endangered by the Proposal* (1825).

290 Malster, *Broads*, p. 53.

291 Boyes and Russell, *Canals*, pp. 111–19.

292 Dutt, *The Norfolk Broads*, p. 24.

293 George, *Broadland*, pp. 359–61.

294 Dutt, *The Norfolk Broads*, pp. 124, 162, 183.

295 George, *Broadland*, pp. 359–61.

296 Marshall, *Rural Economy*, vol. II, p. 99.

297 Norfolk Industrial Archaeology Society, 'A Survey of Ludham', *Journal of the Norfolk Industrial Archaeology Society* 3, 1 (1981): 34–51; p. 41; J. Jones and M. Manning, 'Limeburning and Extractive Industries', in Wade Martins (ed.), *Historical Atlas of*

Norfolk, pp. 162–3; J. Jones, 'Limeburning in Norfolk', *Journal of the Norfolk Industrial Archaeology Society*, 2, 2 (1977).

298 C. Fisher, 'Early Chalk Tramways at Whitlingham', *Journal of the Norfolk Industrial Archaeology Society*, 3, 2 (1982): 89–91.

299 B. Cornford, 'Brickmaking in Flegg', *Journal of the Norfolk Industrial Archaeology Society*, 1, 1 (1971): 6–9.

300 Ibid., p. 8.

301 A. and A. Butler, *The Story of Somerleyton Brickfields*, n.d.

302 Mary and Derek Manning, 'Industrial Archaeology in Norfolk', in Margeson, Ayers and Heywood (eds), *Festival of Norfolk Archaeology*, pp. 154–8; J. Milligan, 'Brick Making at Burgh Castle', *Yarmouth Archaeology*, 1981.

303 H. Apling, *Norfolk Corn Windmills* (Norwich 1984), pp. 42–50; Malster, *Broads*, pp. 63–7.

304 Malster, *Broads*, pp. 63–7.

305 J. Brown, *Steeped in Tradition: the Malting Industry in England Since the Industrial Revolution* (Reading 1983).

306 R. Brigden, 'Norfolk Maltings', *Journal of the Norfolk Industrial Archaeology Society*, 1, 8 (1975): 6–13. Andrew Davison, 'Malting and Brewing', in Wade Martins (ed.), *Historical Atlas of Norfolk*, pp. 156–7.

307 C. Green, 'Broadland Fords and Causeways', *Norfolk Archaeology*, 32 (1961): 316–31.

308 NRO MC 27/1, 501 X 4.

309 G. Barnes and K. Skipper, 'Pollarded Willows in the Norfolk Broads', *Quarterly Journal of Forestry*, 89, 3 (1995): 196–200; p. 198.

310 Ibid., p. 200.

311 R. Joby, 'Railways', in Wade Martin (ed.), *Historical Atlas of Norfolk*, pp. 148–9; R. Joby, *Regional Railway Handbook 2* (Newton Abbot 1987); D. Gordon, *Regional History of the Railways of Great Britain, Vol. V, Eastern England* (Newton Abbot 1977).

312 Andrew Hemmingway, *Landscape Imagery and Urban Culture in Early Nineteenth-Century Britain* (Cambridge 1992), pp. 278–90; T. Fawcett, 'Thorpe Water Frolic', *Norfolk Archaeology*, 36 (1977): 393–8.

313 Dutt, *The Norfolk Broads*, p. 25.

314 Malster, *Broads*, p. 75; Dutt, *The Norfolk Broads*, p. 26.

315 G. C. Davies, *The Handbook to the Rivers and Broads of Norfolk and Suffolk* (London 1890 edn), p. 138.

316 D. Cleveland, 'Some Writers on the Norfolk Broads', in N. McWilliam and V. Sekules (eds), *Life and Landscape. P. H. Emerson: Art and Photography in East Anglia 1885–1900* (Norwich 1986), pp. 86–7.

317 Quoted in Malster, *Broads*, p. 79.

318 J. Taylor, 'Landscape and Leisure', in McWilliam and Sekules (eds), *Life and Landscape*, pp. 73–82; p. 77.

319 Davies, *Handbook*, p. 167.

320 Ibid.

321 Malster, *Broads*, pp. 90–1.

322 George, *Broadland*, pp. 366–7.

323 Malster, *Broads*, pp. 92–100.

324 Davies, *Handbook*, p. 68.

325 D. Matless, 'Moral Geography in Broadland', *Ecumene*, 1, 2 (1994): 127–56.

326 D. Miller, *Seen From a Windmill: a Norfolk Broads Revue* (London, 1935), pp. 12–13.

327 Dutt, *The Norfolk Broads*, p. 56.

328 Ibid., p. 85.

329 A. Patterson, *Man and Nature on Tidal Waters* (London 1909), p. 41.

330 S. Knights, 'Change and Decay: Emerson's Social Order', in McWilliam and Sekules (eds), *Life and Landscape*, pp. 12–20.

331 Davies, *Handbook*, p. 65.
332 Dutt, *The Norfolk Broads*, p. 139.
333 Ibid., p. 147; Davies, *Handbook*, p. 70.
334 Davies, *Handbook*, p. 78; Dutt, *The Norfolk Broads*, p. 150.
335 Davies, *Handbook*, p. 52.
336 Dutt, *The Norfolk Broads*, pp. 120, 121, 151.
337 Malster, *Broads*, p. 108.
338 M. Ewans, *The Battle for the Broads: a History of Environmental Degradation and Renewal* (Lavenham 1992).
339 For a full discussion of nutrient enrichment, see George, *Broadland*, pp. 99–154; Broads Authority, *No Easy Answers; the Draft Broads Plan* (Norwich 1993), pp. 26–39.
340 Ewans, *Battle for the Broads*; George, *Broadland*, pp. 277–312.
341 C. Doarks, *A Study of the Marsh Dykes in Broadland* (1984); R. J. Driscoll, 'Broadland Dykes: the Loss of an Important Wildlife Habitat', *Transactions of the Norfolk and Norwich Naturalists Society*, 26, 3 (1983): 170–2.
342 Again, for a full discussion see George, *Broadland*, pp. 405–48.
343 Broads Authority, *No Easy Answers*, p. 108.
344 Broads Authority, *Broads Design Guides 2: Agricultural Buildings* (1985).
345 Broads Authority, *No Easy Answers*, p. 97.
346 Editors comments, 'Preservation of Broadland', *East Anglian Magazine*, 2, 3 (1936): 97; quoted in Matless, 'Moral Geography', p. 133.
347 Most notably, of course, George, *Broadland*.

Index

Note: numbers in **bold** refer to figures and plates.